Postmodern Texts and Emotional Audiences

Comparative Cultural Studies
Steven Tötösy de Zepetnek, Series Editor

Comparative Cultural Studies is a contextual approach in the study of culture in all of its products and processes. The framework of comparative cultural studies is built on tenets of the disciplines of comparative literature and cultural studies and on notions borrowed from a range of thought including literary and culture theories, (radical) constructivism, communication theories, and systems theories. In comparative cultural studies focus is on theory and method as well as application and attention is on the how rather than on the what. Colleagues interested in publishing in the series are invited to contact the editor, Steven Tötösy de Zepetnek, at <clcweb@purdue.edu>.

Volumes in the series include:

Comparative Central European Culture. Ed. Steven Tötösy de Zepetnek.

Comparative Literature and Comparative Cultural Studies. Ed. Steven Tötösy de Zepetnek.

Sophia A. McClennen, *The Dialectics of Exile.*

Comparative Cultural Studies and Latin America. Ed. Sophia A. McClennen and Earl E. Fitz.

Jin Feng, *The New Woman in Early Twentieth-century Chinese Fiction.*

Comparative Cultural Studies and Michael Ondaatje's Writing. Ed. Steven Tötösy de Zepetnek.

Camilla Fojas, *Cosmopolitanism in the Americas.*

Imre Kertész and Holocaust Literature. Ed. Louise O. Vasvári and Steven Tötösy de Zepetnek.

Deborah Streifford Reisinger, *Crime and Media in Contemporary France.*

Philippe Codde, *The Jewish American Novel.*

Kimberly Chabot Davis, *Postmodern Texts and Emotional Audiences.*

Kimberly Chabot Davis

Postmodern Texts and Emotional Audiences

Purdue University Press
West Lafayette, Indiana

Printed in the United States of America.

Library of Congress Cataloging-in-Publication Data

Davis, Kimberly Chabot, 1968-
Postmodern texts and emotional audiences / Kimberly Chabot Davis.
p. cm. -- (Comparative cultural studies)
Includes bibliographical references and index.
ISBN 978-1-55753-479-8 (alk. paper)
1. Piano (Motion picture) 2. Kiss of the spider woman (Motion picture) 3. Puig, Manuel. Beso de la mujer araña. 4. Northern exposure (Television program) 5. Postmodernism. I. Title.
PN1997.P474D38 2007
791.43'75--dc22

2007015165

Contents

Acknowledgments

Since I first became interested in the "trickling down" of postmodern aesthetic sensibilities to popular media, this book has taken me on a long intellectual journey and clarified both the rewards and difficulties of doing interdisciplinary work. Because the research and writing took nearly ten years, I have many people to thank for help along the way. The project might never have been conceived had I not taken Patricia Gill's graduate seminar in Cultural Studies at the University of Virginia, a course that first prompted me to question the textual determinism of the hermeneutic tradition in literary criticism. I owe a great debt to Rita Felski, my dissertation advisor and mentor, for shaping my thinking about cultural studies and gender theory in innumerable ways. She encouraged me to seek other disciplinary frameworks—in sociology, communication and media studies, philosophy, and psychology—for understanding my focal topics of emotion, identification, cross-group empathy, and social and political identity formation. When I worried about the risks of doing interdisciplinary work, such as the increased difficulty of finding an institutional home, she helped me to focus on the intellectual benefits of seeing a problem through multiple lenses and of forging a rigorously synthetic methodology. I am grateful for her incisive comments on multiple drafts and for her unflinching honesty and unwavering support. Thanks are owed to Sara Blair for encouraging me to focus and contextualize my argument, to Eric Lott for inspiring me with the example of his own work, and to Krishan Kumar for alleviating concerns about how my work might be received by sociologists. Sociologist Sarah Corse offered excellent methodological advice as I constructed my interview questions. For helping me to locate the kernel of my argument within early drafts, I am grateful to Dorri Beam, Candace Caraco, Tricia Pitton, Karen Sosnoski, and Virginia Zimmerman. One of the earliest memories of my friendship with Virginia Zimmerman was talking animatedly into the wee hours of the morning after we saw *The Piano* for the first time. Thanks are also due to my students at the University of Virginia, especially Matt Chayt, for first drawing my attention to the powerful emotional impact of *Kiss of the Spider Woman*.

A Mellon postdoctoral fellowship at Cornell University was instrumental in helping me to revise the manuscript for publication. At Cornell, I benefited from the advice and intellectual comradeship of Shirley Samuels, Jonathan Culler, Paul Sawyer, Marla Segol, Nancy Wadsworth, Jaime Cardenas, Finis Dunaway, Tim Murray, Andy Galloway, Liz DeLoughrey, and Biodun Jeyifo. More recently, my vibrant colleagues in the History and Literature Program at Harvard University have helped to nurture and sustain my commitment to interdisciplinarity. I am particularly indebted to the members of my writing group, Lori Harrison-Kahan and Shilpa Davé, for their insightful suggestions about this book and other manuscripts in progress. Lynne Layton drew my attention to useful articles about identification as I revised parts of chapter two for publication in the *Journal for the Psychoanalysis of Culture and Society*. Many thanks to the editor of the Purdue series of Books in Comparative Cultural Studies, Steven Tötösy de Zepetnek, for his passionate endeavor to mark out the intellectual trajectory of comparative cultural studies, and for recognizing my work's contribution to that project. His excellent suggestions for revision, as well as those of the anonymous reviewers of the manuscript, helped me enormously in addressing my book to a wider readership.

For helping to keep me sane throughout the research and writing process, I am most grateful to my husband Jon, whose nurturance of my career goals has never wavered despite the ridiculous disparity in our wages. I knew he was "the one" when he graciously allowed me to interrupt his beloved Red Sox games to tape 100 syndicated episodes of *Northern Exposure* for my research. Finally, this study would not have been possible without the generous participation of the many viewers and readers who took the time to share their interpretations, emotional responses, and personal narratives with me. Those conversations have greatly enriched my understanding of how people inhabit their multiple identities and use culture to enrich and make sense of their lives. And now, whenever anyone asks me to fill out a questionnaire or participate in a study, I always say yes.

Chapter One

Sentimental Postmodernism, Identification, and the Feeling Audience

Postmodern literature and film have often been characterized by a thematic obsession with the disintegration of families, communities, and larger socio-political ties. Rather than painting such dark themes with the brush of tragedy, postmodern texts often adopt a tone of mocking irony or disaffected nihilism. Kathy Acker's parodic avant-garde fiction, for example, is a complex meditation on contemporary nihilism, on the "nothingness everybody now seems to want" (*In Memoriam to Identity* 263). The hipness of postmodern disaffection was cemented with the popularity of Quentin Tarantino's film *Pulp Fiction* (1994), which turns an absence of morality into fodder for black comedy. As Norman Denzin argues, apocalypse has been a key preoccupation of postmodern popular culture (e.g., *Blade Runner* and *Mad Max*), exemplified more recently by Octavia Butler's post-apocalyptic science fiction. This pessimistic view of postmodernism as a poetics of negation characterizes the theories of Fredric Jameson and Jean Baudrillard. Jameson laments the "waning of affect" (*Postmodernism* 16) that he sees in postmodern culture, while both theorists conclude that deconstructive cynicism often results in "a fundamental disgust for everything political" (Baudrillard, *The Transparency of Evil* 73). Along the same lines, cultural critic bell hooks condemns *Pulp Fiction*'s postmodern nihilism: "Tarantino's work lets us know, it's a sick, mother-fucking world and we may as well get used to that fact, laugh at it, and go on our way, 'cause ain't nothing changing. . . . It's deconstruction at its finest—all dressed up with no place to go" (hooks, "Cool Cynicism" 50).

This book questions the critical assumption that postmodern culture is emotionally destitute and politically apathetic. Toward that end, I examine late-twentieth-century texts that wed postmodern aesthetics and theoretical concerns with the affective narrative strategies of melodrama and sentimental fiction. Because Jameson and others view the ironic postmodern sensibility as antithetical to emotional engagement in social and political concerns, they might find "sentimental postmodernism"—a hybrid genre on which this study is focused—to be an oxymoron or an impossibility. German literary scholar Winfried Herget similarly argues that "irony, above all, is alien to the sentimental purpose" (7). How, then, can something be postmodern and sentimental simultaneously? As opposed to self-reflexive postmodern texts that create critical distance by calling attention to their own aesthetic and narrative construction, sentimental and melodramatic texts aim for total immersion by engaging readers emotionally rather than intellectually. One could easily employ Roland Barthes's distinctions between "writerly" and "readerly" texts to view postmodernism and sentimentality as dichotomous cultural categories. Barthes argues that avant-garde and postmodern "writerly" fiction challenges readers to construct meaning, while "readerly" popular culture invites passive reading and leaves traditional assumptions unchallenged (see *S/Z* and *The Pleasure of the Text*). Sentimental fiction and film melodrama often rest on the very foundations—rigid notions of identity, in particular—that postmodernism aims to attack. The postmodern critique of foundational beliefs in universal truth and moral order strikes at the heart of melodrama's worldview (Gledhill, "Melodramatic Field" 33). Through the use of excessive symbolism and linear narrative progression, melodrama's insistence on legibility and closure (Brooks 22) stands in contrast to a postmodern emphasis on the instability of meaning and the impossibility of order. While the emotional rhetoric of sentimental culture has often been associated with women, postmodern stoic nihilism could be called a masculine stylistic posture. The utopian humanism of many sentimental and melodramatic texts seems incompatible with the cynical vision often ascribed to postmodernism.

Although the sentimental and the postmodern may appear to be at odds with one another, many texts have embraced these competing worldviews simultaneously, particularly in the 1990s. This book argues that the generic and aesthetic mixture of sentimental postmodernism creates a productive tension that accomplishes important socio-political work. While one can see this tension at work in diverse cultural products from the novels of Toni Morrison to the television program *Buffy the Vampire Slayer*, my analysis of the political significance of sentimental postmodernism focuses on three central texts: *The Piano* (1993), a film by New Zealander Jane Campion; the American television series *Northern Exposure* (1990–95); and multiple media versions of *Kiss of the Spider Woman*, a novel by Argentinean Manuel Puig that was subsequently adapted into an English-language film (1985) and a Broadway musical (1993). These mixed-code texts work both within and against postmodernism to offer an antidote to the nihilism, emotional disconnection, antipopular spirit, and masculinist values evident in some strains of postmodern culture and theory. While postmodern irony, parody, and deconstruction have been charged with fostering political apathy and abandoning the project of social justice, sentimental postmodernist texts insist that identities, feelings, and personal relationships matter. These texts locate hope for change in the micropolitical sphere of self/other relations, in the way that we construct our identities and interact with people different from ourselves, perhaps even to the point of identifying with them. I have chosen these three texts as representative because they crystallize public debates about identity politics and diversity at the moment of their production and consumption in the late 1980s and 1990s. The utopian political interventions of these sentimental postmodernist texts are thus historically specific responses to the advent of queerness, multiculturalism, and "third-wave" feminism that sought to complicate understandings of sexual, gender, racial, and ethnic identity.

In highlighting a strain of contemporary culture that fosters sympathetic emotions and utopian political desires, this book might seem to be participating in a hermeneutic tradition that locates a politics in the texts themselves. Indeed, most critical work on the politics of postmodernism is rooted in a model of textual determinacy. In contrast, this study locates the political significance of sentimental postmodernism in the interface between text and audience, representation and reception. My methods attend both to the ideologies signified within a text, and to how a text's potential meanings are politicized at the moment of consumption. My formulation is akin to Antonio Gramsci's concept of articulation, which treats texts and reading practices as complex negotiations whose ideological significance is contingent upon social forces in a historical moment. While most critics of postmodern culture offer only textual analysis and merely speculate about how such texts are consumed, I base my claims about the cultural significance of sentimental postmodernism upon interviews and surveys that I conducted with viewers and readers. Whereas formalist critics ignore the importance of readers in the construction of meaning, analyses of audience response in cultural studies and communications often underestimate the role of the text in shaping or putting limits on interpretation. It is my contention that the mixture of generic and aesthetic codes in sentimental postmodernist texts has a significant impact upon audience response. Thus my methodology offers a symbiotic analysis of both textuality and reception within a specific historical moment, as few studies have done.

The political gestures of these hybrid texts can be linked to their strategic combination of the critical distance enabled by high art and the emotional engagement and identification fostered by popular genres. Reception scholars in the "empirical study of literature" tradition have established that the characteristics of a text—and genre in particular—strongly influence audience interpretation and emotional response (Tan and van den Boom; Nardocchio; Miall and Kuiken; Höijer; Halász). The particular generic mixture of sentimentality and postmodernism engages readers and viewers both emotionally and intellectually, intensifying both "aesthetic" and "narrative" feelings (Miall and Kuiken 223). While these texts provoke narrative identification with their characters and investment in humanistic values, the postmodern aesthetic elements of "defamiliarization" invite a "search for alternative interpretations" (Miall and Kuiken 229) and a cognitive questioning of identity formation that is usually taken for granted in popular texts. Many film melodramas and sentimental novels, such as Susan Warner's novel *Wide, Wide World* and the film weepie *Now, Voyager* (1942), show a strong allegiance to conventional typologies and narrative formulas, but these hybrid texts use postmodern strategies to challenge the audience's schemas for understanding the world and the self. By engaging audiences both affectively and intellectually, these mixed-code texts encourage people to rethink old paradigms while still acknowledging their emotional power. Thus, one could argue that sentimental postmodernism occupies a middle ground between resistance and containment. While some leftists may disdain such modes of limited subversion as ineffectual, I argue that these texts offer a powerful alternative both to radical revolt, a stance that postmodernism has rendered suspect, and to the apathetic nihilism engendered by feelings of powerlessness. In response to the postmodern "crisis of the very possibility of politics" ("Postmodernity" 290), Lawrence Grossberg calls for an "impure" politics "for people who are never innocent and whose hopes are always partly defined by the very powers and inequalities they oppose. A modest politics that struggles to effect real change, that enters into the often boring challenges of strategy and compromise" (*We Gotta* 396). His vision aptly describes the tactics of sentimental postmodernism, and helps us to locate it within the historical context of late-twentieth-century postindustrial societies suffering from political *ennui*. Rather than criticizing ambivalence as a sign of paralysis or confusion, these texts embrace it as a potent political strategy.

This strategy of ambivalence plays a key role in how postmodern melodramas treat the subject of identity. Because the texts under discussion borrow from two distinct narrative logics, they represent subjectivity in conflicting ways, invoking melodrama's essentialist stereotypes while also engaging in a postmodern questioning of gender, race, and sexual identity. Essentialism—a belief that identity is deep-rooted or even biologically determined—is juxtaposed in these texts with a poststructuralist, "anti-essentialist" notion of identity as a socially constructed and fluid surface. Sentimental postmodernism illuminates late-twentieth-century debates about identity politics by speaking to viewers and readers caught between these competing conceptions of subjectivity. While these debates began in academic circles, the critique of essentialism went mainstream in the 1990s, as popular media began to address third-wave anti-essentialist feminism and the challenge that "queer" identity posed to 1970s notions of innate gay selfhood. A politics rooted in identity had been central to the gay, feminist, and black liberation movements of the 1960s and 1970s, but the essentialist tenets of such movements were increasingly coming under fire in the 1990s, as multiculturalists and groups like Queer Nation encouraged cross-group affiliations and progressive coalitions. *Kiss of the Spider Woman*, for example, directly addresses these identity debates through the dramatic conflict established between its two main characters Valentin and Molina. *Kiss* explores the fluidity of Valentin's sexual identity from a proto-queer, anti-essentialist perspective, but also treats with respect Molina's essentialist belief that he is innately different, a gender "invert." The strong bond forged between these men with very different self-conceptions offers hope to those invested in the utopian possibilities of coalition politics. Thus sentimental postmodernist works resonated in this historical moment by offering audiences a means of negotiating their own ambivalence about the relationship between identity and political solidarity.

In order to study the effects of these textual strategies upon viewers and readers, I chose audience samples relevant to each text's thematic focus on particular identities and political positions. While all of the texts have been considered left-leaning, they each emphasize a particular identity category or group of categories as the locus for their political interventions. Because *The Piano* ruminates on gender identity and was reviewed as a feminist film, I chose to interview thirty-one students and faculty members at the University of Virginia, all of whom are self-identified feminists. For my analysis of *Northern Exposure*, I studied a pre-existing audience group—an active Internet fanclub whose members enact the program's multicultural utopian ideals in their own on-line community. *Kiss of the Spider Woman*'s exploration of the shifting and multiple meanings of sexual and gender identity led me to interview thirty homosexual, bisexual, and heterosexual men and women residing in the Washington, D.C. area.

Ethnographic research allowed me to investigate how audiences negotiate and make sense of this textual bricolage of generic codes and sensibilities, and to discover what these hybrid texts offer people in terms of political strategies for coping with the changes brought about by postmodernity. In particular, I set out to explore how audiences respond to the co-existence in these texts of both essentialist and anti-essentialist perspectives on the meaning of identity. Because identities such as gender, race, ethnicity, and sexuality are contested subjects in these narratives, the process of audience identification with characters is complicated. Many scholars, particularly those influenced by sociology, Freudian psychoanalysis, and "apparatus" film theory, have defined identification as an unconscious process of self-recognition, of connecting with a character who shares one's group identity or subject position. Such a definition is immediately put into question by sentimental postmodernism. A theory that equates identification with simple self-recognition cannot explain how audiences identify with texts in which identities are ambiguous rather than fixed, and overtly contested rather than assumed. My ethnographic work contributes to the efforts of scholars such as Kaja Silverman and Judith Butler, who re-theorize identification by taking into account a postmodern understanding of identity as mutable, ambivalent, and multiple rather than static and unitary. What distinguishes my project from theirs, however, is my attempt to bridge a methodological gap between two fields that have often been defined as antipathetic—psychoanalytic identification theory and empirical audience studies. Many psychoanalytic critics view empirical audience research as irrelevant or even inimical to their speculative textual analyses, while audience researchers tend to rely on essentialist notions of group difference, ignoring newer psychoanalytic theories of subjectivity informed by an anti-essentialist model. In contrast, the following audience studies are a form of theoretical engagement, a means of corroborating and refining current formulations and opening up new ground for a more nuanced understanding of identification.

While psychoanalysis treats identification as unconscious, sentimental postmodernism underscores that constructing an identity and identifying with others are fundamentally *political* processes. As Diana Fuss notes, "there can be no politics without identification" since politics involves the formation of cohesive social groups (*Identification* 10). Rather than encouraging an unconscious identification on the basis of shared identity, these postmodern melodramas stimulate audiences to think critically about the political implications of their own self-construction and their relationship with others. Departing from the psychoanalytical emphasis on the unconscious mind, I treat identification as a form of social and political articulation that can involve a conscious negotiation between self and other. For example, many of these audience members identified with characters on the basis of ideological affinity, such as a particular feminist viewpoint, rather than the mere fact of shared gender, race, or sexual identity. These identificatory moments highlight that identity is an ideological and political construct rather than an ontological given derived from the body or buried in the psyche. Because these texts question unitary and rigid forms of identity, many viewers and readers were encouraged to identify with characters across the boundaries of gender, sexuality, or ethnicity. Numerous film theorists, influenced by Althusserian Marxism and psychoanalysis, have argued that mass culture fosters identification in order to seduce viewers into accepting conservative ideologies and socially prescribed identities. Contrary to this expectation, postmodern melodramas encourage identifications that break open rather than solidify the boundary lines between selves. My interviews revealed that emotional connections were forged between men and women, gays and straights, ethnic/religious minorities and members of the white Protestant mainstream. Such cross-over identifications in cultural space may help to form the precondition necessary for a more public form of alliance or participation in coalition politics, or they may provide crucial affective nourishment to help strengthen the commitment to pluralism among left-leaning, politically active people. These cross-group identifications did not result in a facile solidarity that erases otherness, as some skeptics argue, because these texts also teach audiences to respect difference. By fostering ambivalent forms of cross-group identification, involving a recognition of difference as well as sameness, these texts promote possible coalitions without dismissing the gains made by identity politics.

In short, the particular kinds of identifications that sentimental postmodernism enables are the source of its emotional impact upon audiences, and therefore of its cultural power. If feeling is crucial to political engagement, then identification is the means by which these texts get audiences invested in their meanings. *The Piano, Kiss of the Spider Woman,* and *Northern Exposure* each recognize that identification is "the source of considerable emotional turmoil, capable of unsettling or unmooring the precarious groundings of our everyday identities" (Fuss, *Identification* 2) and opening up the possibility of connection across races, sexualities, and genders. These examples of sentimental postmodernism are "moving" texts in every sense of the word, offering not only an emotional experience, but one that disrupts stasis and leads a reader or viewer to new ground, to consider change in his or her own attitudes, relationships, politics, and self-constructions. These texts expand the range of postmodern affective modes beyond that of ironic detachment by fostering a sentimental faith in the emotional connections between people and a hope that inter-subjective communication can effect social change.

I contend that postmodern melodramas deserve critical attention because they help to articulate tensions peculiar to our historical moment—tensions between sentimentality and ironic cynicism, between a faith in stable identities as a means of political empowerment and a new postmodern awareness of how such identities limit our selves and social relationships. Rather than wholly embracing the sea-change in cultural sensibilities brought about by postmodernity, these texts register ambivalence and turn that ambivalence into a political stance. In the face of public apathy concerning politics, these powerfully emotive texts aim to get audiences reinvested in the political stakes of identity construction. While sentimental postmodernism does not offer pure or total resistance to hegemonic values, we should not overlook the power of these texts to encourage left-leaning political engagement and sympathy for subordinate groups. By fostering utopian coalitions, postmodern melodramas offered a compelling alternative to the political disenchantment and social balkanization of the late twentieth century.

Comparative Cultural Studies

In his endeavor to define the field of "comparative cultural studies," Steven Tötösy de Zepetnek calls for scholarship that creates dialogue between cultures and disciplines, takes a comparative approach to literature and popular media, and prioritizes methodological concerns ("From Comparative Literature" 259–60; see also *Comparative Literature*). He argues that cultural studies scholarship, which often operates within a single-culture and single-language model, could benefit from embracing the comparativist spirit of the comparative literature framework in order to avoid "entrapment in the national paradigm" ("From Comparative Literature" 243). Such a relaxation of national boundaries is particularly relevant to my study of contemporary cultural production and reception, given the international development of postmodern culture and the increasingly global dissemination of texts consumed far from their locus of production. The cross-national case studies in this book draw parallels between a film written and directed by a New Zealander (Jane Campion), an American television show (*Northern Exposure*), Manuel Puig's Argentinean novel *Kiss of the Spider Woman*, its adaptation by a Brazilian director into an English-language film, and its subsequent rebirth as an American Broadway musical. Although these texts were produced in disparate locations, they were all influenced by international movements in postmodern culture and the poststructuralist moment in Western philosophy. These case studies are unified not only by my explication of the thematic and aesthetic similarities of these works, but by my focus on their consumption by American middle-class audiences in the mid-to-late 1990s. My chapter on *Kiss of the Spider Woman*, in particular, draws attention to the problematics of studying reception across cultures, a subject which has garnered increasing scholarly attention in the age of cultural globalization (see Crane, Kawashima, and Kawasaki; László and Larsen; Liebes and Katz; Pells).

In addition to its transnational emphasis, my book takes an interdisciplinary and comparative approach in analyzing films, fiction, television, and theater.

Although my study highlights features of identification and empathy common to all narrative media—whether in print, on screen, or on stage—I contextualize each media form in relation to its particular conditions of production, distribution, and consumption, while emphasizing the differing aesthetic possibilities and cultural histories of each medium. Finding a publisher for my cross-national and cross-media study was complicated by the fact that many academic presses persist in organizing their lists and series according to national culture, media, and discipline. This compartmentalization reflects the recalcitrance of disciplinary frameworks even within an academic culture that touts the intellectual benefits of interdisciplinarity. While Tötösy laments that "all too many scholars concentrate on 'home-grown' sources" ("From Comparative Literature" 243) in both a national and disciplinary sense, my study draws upon and synthesizes U.S. and European scholarship and methods in cultural and media studies, literary criticism and theory, sociology, philosophy, cognitive psychology, communications, gender and sexuality studies, and the empirical study of the arts.

My book's methodological attention to both text and reception also places it at the center of a longstanding rift between the hermeneutic and empirical traditions in cultural and literary studies. By focusing on audience interviews and the diversity of meanings produced by different readers and viewers, this study implicitly questions the hermeneutic model of traditional literary and cultural criticism. A similar goal typifies the work of "reader response" or reception scholars (see edited collections by Nardocchio; Tompkins; Machor and Goldstein). Yet this book diverges from reception studies in cognitive psychology, communications, and sociology by placing textual interpretation at the center of the inquiry. Unlike some empirical reception studies which aim to establish general truths about reading comprehension, this study emphasizes the historical and cultural contexts influencing the reception of this specific group of texts. My training in literary studies also leads me to question the positivism of some forms of empirical research. In this methodological hybrid space, my approach borrows from the insights of Siegfried J. Schmidt and Donna Haraway, both of whom admit the contingency of all knowledge claims and reject the notion of scientific objectivity (Schmidt 144, 146; Haraway, "Situated Knowledges" 184). As Dieter Freundlieb argues in the journal *Empirical Studies of the Arts*, "an empirical study of literature . . . can't be purely empirical, no matter how hard it might try. Even at the level of choice of a domain of objects it is guided by normative considerations" (118), such as a belief in the social value of literature or a desire for progressive social change. An elaboration of my methodological choices and their consequences can be found in the following chapter.

Defining Contested Terms

Since several of the categorical concepts employed in my study—postmodernism, melodrama, and sentimentality—have been the subject of scholarly contestation, it is necessary to position my work within critical debates about their meaning. Since these meanings vary across disciplines and media contexts, the interdisciplinary nature of the study makes it even more important to clarify my definitions of these key terms. In addition to this brief key word glossary, chapter two further details my intervention in critical debates about these categories of cultural analysis.

Postmodernism

The subject of scores of scholarly books and theoretical treatises, postmodernism has been variously described as a "social condition and a cultural movement" (Jencks, "The Postmodern Agenda" 10), a historical period in the development of capitalism (see Jameson; David Harvey), an avant-garde artistic style, or a branch of poststructuralist philosophy. The relationship between postmodernism and modernist culture and systems of thought has been understood as either a radical break (see Baudrillard; Kroker and Cook) or a continuation and intensification (see Habermas). Given my book's emphasis on literature and film, critical discussions of postmodernism as an aesthetic style, rather than a historical period or stage of capitalism, will be privileged in the analysis. Yet even when comparing related narrative media like literature, film, and television, characteristics of postmodern style vary depending on the distinct formal properties and cultural histories of each medium. While each of the book's chapters explores the media-specific meanings of postmodern style and thematics, I treat all of the texts as reflections of a larger cultural sensibility that has distanced itself from the modernist worldview.

The postmodern sensibility has been strongly influenced by the insights of poststructuralism, a philosophical critique of the systems of modern thought since the Enlightenment. French poststructuralist theorists Jacques Derrida, Michel Foucault, Roland Barthes, and Jean-François Lyotard ushered in a critique of the epistemic certainty of totalizing "master narratives" (typified by classic Marxism) and a skeptical deconstruction of modern beliefs in universal truth, rationality, and progress. Derrida's critique of structuralism, which used the tools of linguistics to synthesize knowledge in the human sciences, was rooted in his complex theory of language. One of the main principles of Derridean deconstruction is that there is always a slippage ("free play") between the word or sign and the concept it aims to signify, and thus language is based on an endless deferral of signifiers, on the absence rather than the presence of meaning. Derrida argues that there is no absolute meaning outside of the "surfaces" of discourse—in other words, everything is a text to be unraveled. This tenet leads to a rejection of all concepts rooted in notions of a central truth, origin, or presence, such as metaphysical beliefs in God, Marxist views of the economic base of all culture and historical progress, or essentialist ideas of the human self (e.g., natural womanhood). In its resistance to systems, poststructuralism attacks the falseness of the structuring dichotomies of Western culture (e.g., nature and culture, woman and man). In his treatise *The Postmodern Condition*, Lyotard aligns the postmodern with poststructuralism for their shared "incredulity toward metanarratives" (xxiv) of human knowledge and progress, in light of the perceived failure of Marxism and the horrors of Nazi fascism.

Informed by the poststructuralist critique of the modernist principles of order, norm, wholeness, fixity, and universal truth, postmodern philosophers embrace anarchy, heterogeneity, fragmentation, fluidity, and pluralism. In his introduction to Deleuze and Guattari's book *Anti-Oedipus*, Foucault instructs postmodern subjects "to prefer what is positive and multiple, difference over uniformity, flows over unities, mobile arrangements over systems" (Foucault, "Preface" xiii). One of the focal points of this book is the postmodern reconceptualization of human identities enabled by poststructuralism. In his revision of Freudian psychoanalysis, Jacques Lacan influenced many intellectuals to consider the self as decentered, fluid, and fractured rather than whole and bounded. For example, anti-essentialist Lacanian theorist Judith Butler applies poststructuralist principles to gender formation, arguing that "the insistence upon the coherence and unity of the category of women has effectively refused the multiplicity of cultural, social, and political intersections in which the concrete array of 'women' are constructed" (*Gender Trouble* 19–20). If modernism has often been construed as a discourse of the center, postmodernism has often reveled in an exploration of heterogeneous difference, privileging what Linda Hutcheon calls "ex-centric" or marginalized voices (Hutcheon, *Politics* 5). For political theorists Ernesto Laclau and Chantal Mouffe, a postmodern critique of "essentialist universalism" (Laclau 2) is at the root of their vision of a radical, plural democracy that embraces multiplicitous viewpoints. An exploration of human difference and the multiplicity of the self are focal themes of the three central postmodern texts in this study.

Poststructuralist versions of postmodernism, therefore, can be seen as an oppositional attack on modern systems of thought. On the other hand, literary critics tend to view postmodernism as an intensification or extension of modernist aesthetics rather than as a radical rupture. As Hutcheon suggests, postmodernism "paradoxically uses and abuses the conventions of . . . modernism" (*Poetics* 53). Literary critics have often dubbed "postmodern" many techniques commonly associated with modernist writers and movements: fragmentation, irony, non-linear narrative structures (employed by Virginia Woolf and William Faulkner), multiple narrative voices (as in Faulkner's *The Sound and the Fury*), montage (a technique developed by silent filmmaker Sergei Eisenstein), a flouting of realism (pursued by surrealist artists in the early twentieth century), extended word play (as in Gertrude Stein's *Tender Buttons* or James Joyce's *Finnegan's Wake*), the "defamiliarization" technique of disrupting audience immersion in the fictional world (made famous by the plays of Bertolt Brecht), self-reflexivity (explored by modernist poets such as Marianne Moore and Wallace Stevens), and intertextual allusions (a chief characteristic of T. S. Eliot's *The Wasteland*). Yet Ihab Hassan, Hutcheon, and others have also drawn attention to salient differences in modern and postmodern aesthetic philosophy and tone. While modernists such as Eliot strove to wrest order and transcendent meaning out of the fragments and disturbances of modern life, postmodernism "swims, even wallows, in the fragmentary and the chaotic currents of change" (David Harvey 44), and thus postmodern texts are typified by a refusal of closure. The parodic and ludic playfulness of many postmodern texts is largely absent in works of high modernism dominated by themes of alienation and loss. Poststructuralist ideas about signification and discourse—Derrida's emphasis on the instability of meaning and Foucault's treatment of "reality" as a function of discourse—have led postmodern writers to take modernist self-reflexivity to another level, as a vehicle for exploring the limits of storytelling itself. Hutcheon has described postmodern fiction as intensely "metafictional" and "ever aware of its status as discourse, as a human construct" (*Poetics* 53). Postmodern writers could be said to rework modernist themes and aesthetic techniques with a new tone, purpose, and attitude.

One of the most dramatic shifts between the two cultural sensibilities has been a postmodern relaxation of what Andreas Huyssen calls the modernist "great divide" between art and mass culture. Modernist intellectuals such as Theodor Adorno valued art as a pure space of "transcendent critique" untainted by capitalist commodification. Rejecting this "artistically and politically sterile" vision of the elite and alienated artist (McGowan 25), postmodern cultural producers often aim for a wider audience and embrace the task of creating art within, rather than outside of, the world of commerce. The modernist hostility to mass culture, exemplified by Adorno and Clement Greenberg, has been replaced by a postmodern cultural bricolage, where intertextual references are more likely to include *The Simpsons* or rock music than Greek and Roman mythology. In identifying postmodern forms within the commodified medium of television (such as *The Simpsons* and *Twin Peaks*), Jim Collins underscores the obsolescence of the modernist artistic framework (see Collins, "Television and Postmodernism"). Yet the question remains—is postmodernism complicitous with the capitalist culture industries or a powerful form of social critique? Since my book aligns sentimental postmodernism with a politics of "limited subversion," or what Hutcheon similarly calls "complicitous critique" (*Politics* 2), it engages in an ongoing and contentious debate about the political implications of postmodern theory and culture. Many Marxists and other leftists see postmodernism and poststructuralism as apolitical or conservative, on the grounds that postmodern writers and philosophers celebrate anarchic textuality and language play while dismissing principles that have been crucial to political movements—concepts such as teleological master-narratives, faith in progress, emotional commitment to a cause, and solidarity rooted in group identity. Leftists complain that a postmodern overemphasis on formalist experimentation alienates all but elite audiences and results in the neglect of social and political critique that had once been a powerful motivator for the production of art. Steven Best and Douglas Kellner lament that postmodern theory "lacks positive notions of the social" (283), wallows in nihilism and disintegration, and prematurely jettisons metanarratives that are necessary for "social theory, critique, and politics" (281). Baudrillard paints a particularly dystopic vision of postmodern culture as a world of simulacrum, in which depth has been replaced by surface, and the real has been erased by simulations of the real.

In opposition to these pessimistic treatments of postmodernism, many literary theorists (Hutcheon), media and cultural studies scholars (Grossberg, McRobbie,

Collins), and political philosophers (Laclau, Mouffe) have celebrated resistant or subversive elements of postmodern theory and culture. Many argue that the postmodern breakdown of the high art/mass culture dichotomy has democratizing effects, which they locate in the development of oppositional postmodern popular music, television, film, and youth fashion. Marginalized and disempowered groups—including feminists—have found powerful tools in the postmodern critique of essentialist understandings of identity, in the deconstruction of universalist and normalizing notions of truth, and in the postmodern preference for heterogeneity and difference over uniformity. While my work participates in the project to uncover what Hal Foster calls a "postmodernism of resistance" (xii), it also echoes the concerns of leftist critics about pessimistic and apolitical strains of postmodern culture and theory. In identifying sentimental postmodernist texts, this book highlights a critique of social disaffection and political apathy emerging *from within* postmodern popular culture itself. By studying postmodern texts that invoke the "feminine" strategies of sentimentality, I present a feminist critique and reappraisal of postmodern criticism and theory, which will be elaborated in chapter 2.

Melodrama and Sentimentality

The following case studies will explore how the affective rhetorics of melodrama and sentimentality are being deployed within the new cultural context of postmodernism. First, however, it is important to understand the history of these related genres. Although these two cultural categories have slightly different histories, they denote a similar cluster of affective strategies and narrative structures that justifies the syncretism of my usage of these terms. In his classic work *The Melodramatic Imagination*, Peter Brooks notes that melodrama (which literally means "music drama") was coined to refer to a genre of French theater that sought to reestablish moral certainty and order in the face of the destabilization engendered by the French Revolution. The melodramatic aesthetic was pervasive in nineteenth-century European and U.S. popular culture and strongly influenced literary artists such as Charles Dickens. In the twentieth century, melodrama has remained a dominant form of both television and Hollywood film. Elements of melodrama include exaggerated emotions, stereotypical stock characters, interpersonal conflicts, Manichean oppositions between good and evil, excessive and obvious symbolism in the *mise en scène*, an emphasis on plot over character development, and an endorsement of traditional justice and moral order via an ending where evil is punished (see Brooks; Elsaesser; Gledhill, "Melodramatic Field"). Many of these very same qualities have been dubbed central features of the sentimental aesthetic exemplified by nineteenth-century fiction, and texts such as Harriet Beecher Stowe's *Uncle Tom's Cabin* or Susan Warner's *Wide, Wide World* have been described as both sentimental fiction and melodrama. As Jane Tompkins argues in *Sensational Designs*, nineteenth-century popular sentimental fiction can be recognized by its emphasis on emotionality, Christian moralism, domestic values, flat characters as in typological Christian narratives, an assertion of women's moral superiority, and an evangelical faith in the redemptive powers of suffering. Key similarities between sentimental literature and melodrama are their use of typed characters, Manichean oppositions, moral absolutes, and the attempt to induce strong emotional reactions in the service of a social agenda.

This book treats sentimentality and melodrama as two related generic and aesthetic categories, but their differences are also salient. While melodrama usually refers to a genre of stage and screen texts, sentimentality is less likely to be invoked as a textual genre except when referring to nineteenth-century women's "domestic" fiction. In many cases, the sentimental is used more broadly to signify an emotional register or a tear-jerking, reductive rhetorical mode, witnessed in texts as widely divergent as political speeches and Hallmark greeting cards. It is also worth noting that melodramas may be sentimental, but they are not always so. Gothic melodramas, in particular, contain lurid elements absent in most Christian sentimental works, which tend to focus on pathos, domestic situations, and comforting resolutions. Sentimental fiction, with its plethora of victimized female protagonists, has long been associated with feminized culture (see Suzanne Clark; Douglas), while the generic category of melodrama encompasses not only soap operas and women's weepies but also male-oriented war films, westerns, and sports tear-jerkers like *Rocky* or *The Champ* (Neale 69–71). To preserve the historical trajectories of these two terms, the term melodrama will be employed hereafter in reference to film and television texts, while sentimentality will be used for discussing literary texts. Throughout the book, I oscillate between "postmodern melodrama" and "sentimental postmodernism" depending on the particular medium under discussion, although they are intended to be equivalent terms.

As in critical discussions of postmodernism, much of the debate about sentimental fiction and melodrama concerns whether these genres support or subvert the status quo. Skeptics argue that these emotional forms trivialize epistemic social problems by reducing them to the level of interpersonal conflict and by providing oversimplified resolutions. The common critique is that they provoke an emotional catharsis that does nothing to foster real social change. On the other hand, some feminist critics contend that sentimental and melodramatic texts have the radical potential to encourage audiences to identify with victimized others and to question the status quo. My analysis foregrounds the potentially subversive power of cross-group identification and empathy, an experience that is often induced by these related affective forms.

Since this book combines textual analysis and a contextual-empirical reception study of audiences in order to analyze a hybrid cultural genre, the following chapter offers a justification for the dialectical nature of my methodology. The first part of chapter two explains the feminist intervention that this study makes in critical debates in the humanities concerning seemingly opposed categories of cultural analysis—postmodernism and sentimentality/melodrama. Drawing upon a wide array of disciplinary rubrics for thinking about textuality and reception, the latter half of the chapter argues for the importance of investigating the interface between texts and the audiences who use these cultural products to reflect on their identities and political investments. With this methodological and theoretical grounding in place, I turn to a chapter examining feminist audiences of the postmodern melodrama *The Piano* in the context of heated debates about gender and feminism in the mid-1990s. Analyzing the varied, ambivalent, and politicized readings and identifications that this film makes possible, I question psychoanalytic film critics who imply that viewers are subconsciously positioned by filmic codes into accepting static gender identities. In chapter four, I investigate how the television series *Northern Exposure* encourages its Internet fanclub members to think critically about race, ethnic, and gender difference and to envision a pluralist democratic utopia. In addition to examining the multicultural utopianism of this text and audience group, I argue that this "high-pop" television hybrid requires a rethinking of class-stratified and gender-essentialist ideas of taste communities. My final case study analyzes the three media forms (novel, film, musical) of *Kiss of the Spider Woman* as a queer and "campy" defense of the emotional politics of melodramatic mass culture. The affective strategies of *Kiss* moved my urban audience group to identify with characters across the boundaries of gender and sexual identity, and thus reinforced the pluralist, anti-essentialist ethic of queer coalition politics. Each chapter thus situates sentimental postmodernism in a historically specific reception context while also using these texts to question and revise existing cultural theory.

Chapter Two

Critical Hybridity and the Building of Methodological Bridges

The theory and method informing this study can best be described as a dialectical mediation between dissimilar cultural genres and between antagonistic scholarly traditions. The critical dialectic of sentimental postmodernism allows me to illuminate theoretical biases and blind spots in scholarship concerning both postmodernism and popular affective genres. While many theorists of postmodern culture pay lip service to the idea that postmodernism breaks down the division between high and popular culture, most of their exemplary texts are nonetheless high art or avant-garde works. Focusing on irony, self-reflexivity, avant-garde aesthetics, and poststructuralist ideas about language, many of these critics draw a picture of postmodernism that differs little from high modernism. In contrast, this book explores postmodern texts that thoroughly mix high and low cultural codes, in order to question the equation of postmodernism with the avant-garde and with poststructuralism. By analyzing a neglected subset of postmodernism—hybrid texts employing the affective strategies of popular sentimental novels and film melodrama, genres stigmatized by their association with women—this book offers an alternative to the predominant view of postmodernism as a cultural sensibility imbued with masculine values and tastes.

By investigating affect as a source of sentimental postmodernism's political power, I take my lead from feminist critics who have re-evaluated sentimental fiction and melodrama as rich forms of social and political commentary. My study builds on the work of cultural studies scholars, literary critics, political theorists, and cognitive psychologists who argue that emotion plays a crucial role in the formation of ideologies and political investments. Of course, affective rhetoric has been mobilized throughout history in the service of both hegemonic and resistant political forces. In this chapter I address critical debates about the politics of sympathy—a key strategy of affective genres—and question the move to posit a fixed political significance to the deployment of this particular rhetoric of feeling. Those critics who criticize sympathy and sentimentality for merely perpetuating the status quo often imply that the private sphere of feeling can have little effect on radical political efforts to effect change in the public sphere. Engaging this debate about the politics of sentimentality allows me to address larger questions about the connection between the public and the private—about the nature of "the political" and its relationship to culture. While I argue here for the political significance of sentimental postmodernism, I also aim to promote critical reflection about the common cultural studies practice of attributing a politics to cultural texts. In addition to its intervention in debates about cultural genres, my study presents a multi-layered analysis of both representation and consumption. In the second half of this chapter, I argue that politics is not textually determined, but is produced in the negotiation between the text and the viewer or reader. Rooting my claims in an ethnographic study of audience response, this book challenges the elitism of textual critics and theorists who dismiss audiences as unreliable sources of information concerning the supposedly unconscious process of identification. Drawing upon work in cultural studies and the school of the "empirical approach to literature and culture," this book treats the narratives of audiences as rich sources of information concerning reception, despite or even because of the contradiction and incoherence common to these response narratives. Empirical analysis allows me to question textual criticism that dismisses cross-group empathy as an inherently colonizing form of incorporation and erasure of otherness. Yet my study also uses psychoanalytic and poststructuralist theories about the fluid and multiple self to critique audience studies that rely on essentialist ideas of group difference. In my work, empirical audience research and textualist theories of identification are dialectically engaged with one another rather than at odds.

Postmodernist Theory and the Great Divide

Problematic assumptions about the relationship between politics and aesthetics have plagued the body of criticism and theory concerning postmodern culture. While theorists of postmodernism identify differences between contemporary and modernist culture, many of them continue to show an allegiance to the aesthetic and political values of high modernism. As Huyssen has argued in *After the Great Divide*, many postmodern theorists are still perpetuating the ruling ideology of the "modernist" Frankfurt School critics, whose insistence on the distinction between high art and mass culture revealed an elitist hostility toward an implicitly feminized mass audience. In contrast, this study fully explores Huyssen's major claim that postmodernism has relaxed the "great divide" between high and low.

Lyotard's *The Postmodern Condition* is the most frequently cited of all postmodern theoretical texts, but it remains profoundly modernist in its disdain for mass culture. In his appendix, "Answering the Question: What Is Postmodernism?" Lyotard presents a negative characterization of contemporary culture as a "period of slackening" (71). In his view, this confusion of boundaries threatens to "liquidate the heritage of the avant-gardes" (73) by extinguishing experimentation and abstract, rigorous philosophical thought. Equating the postmodern with an *avant-garde* striving for the unrepresentable, Lyotard argues that a postmodern sensibility stands against the illusions of realism, easy pleasure, and "the solace of good forms" (81). For Lyotard, sentimental popular culture could not possibly be subversive, for he associates mass culture with fascism as did postwar theorists Theodor Adorno and Max Horkheimer of the Frankfurt School. Lyotard writes: "under the general demand for slackening and for appeasement, we can hear the mutterings of the desire for a return of terror [and totalitarianism]" (82). I aim to refute Lyotard's central contentions—that postmodernism and popular culture are fundamentally opposed, and that mass cultural forms always support fascist values. Now that avant-garde or postmodern sensibilities have infiltrated rock music (e.g., Talking Heads, the B52's, and Beck), and television commercials occasionally look like Fellini films, the terms "popular" and "avant-garde" no longer function as an absolute dichotomy. Lyotard's modernist fear of the taste of the masses leads him to ignore the advent of mass culture's adoption of high art or avant-garde aesthetic strategies, an emerging phenomenon explored in Jim Collins's recent collection *High-Pop: Making Culture into Popular Entertainment.* In addition to the emergence of "high-pop," an equally important development is that popular cultural forms have taken on an increasingly central role in the work of serious postmodern writers such as Thomas Pynchon and Don DeLillo. For example, Manuel Puig's *Kiss of the Spider Woman* immerses readers in B movies (including Nazi melodramas) while simultaneously disrupting realist narrative technique. High and low culture are inextricably mixed in Puig's anti-fascist novel, challenging Lyotard's central dualism and his attitudes about the politics of mass culture.

I also question the position of Baudrillard, who views the hybridity and loss of boundaries in contemporary culture as a sign of cultural degradation. Although Lyotard sees postmodernism as a positive condition—the last bastion of the *avant-garde* in our decaying culture—Baudrillard sees postmodern societies as abhorrently commodified. In his viewpoint, this rampant "Disneyfication" results in a "hyperreal" environment in which every event is merely a false simulation of reality, and culture equals commodity (see *Simulacra and Simulations*). In *The Transparency of Evil*, he writes: "When everything is political, nothing is political anymore, the word itself is meaningless. . . . When everything is aesthetic, nothing is beautiful or ugly anymore, and art itself disappears" (9). Now that everyday life has been aestheticized through advertising, he laments that art has been obliterated and replaced by "a pure circulation of images, a transaesthetics of banality" (11). Popular postmodernism poses a challenge to Baudrillard's reiteration of the modernist belief that art and commerce are diametrically opposed. With the world-wide dominance of transnational capitalism, art rarely escapes the influence of the market. The film *auteur*, for example, is now a commercial marketing "strategy for organizing audience reception" rather than a mark of artistic enunciation (Corrigan 103). But this commodification does not mean that art has ceased to exist; rather, art has accepted complicity with capitalism. Despite the capitalist control of the culture industries, moments of transgression are still possible due to the power of language and images to signify in multiple ways. Critics who cling to Adorno's idealized notion of "transcendent" or pure critique underestimate the power of impure subversion from within capitalism. Furthermore, a positive effect of this ubiquitous commercialization is an increase in public access to thought-provoking culture. Postmodernism's breakdown of the high/low divide can also be viewed as a democratizing phenomenon, spreading intellectual ideas and cultural capital to a wider audience. For example, poststructuralist ideas about the fluidity of identity have surfaced in television texts such as *Northern Exposure* and *Buffy the Vampire Slayer*, a development that could contribute to a popular reconceptualizing of identity formation.

The modernist artistic hierarchies perpetuated by these philosophers can also be seen in postmodern literary criticism, which has established a high cultural canon. Ihab Hassan heralds postmodern literature for its anarchic formal experimentation and resistance to the status quo (44–45), and his postmodern "canon" is decidedly highbrow, dominated by literary figures such as Beckett, Borges, Nabokov, Pinter, Marquez, Cortazar, Robbe-Grillet, Barth, Pynchon, Barthelme, and Ashbery (85). Because these writers employ irony, parody, and self-reflexivity, many of them have also been called high modernist. It strikes me as ironic that Hassan refers to this list of high cultural (and white male) postmodernists as "heterogeneous." Because critics like Hassan locate postmodernist aesthetics only in serious literary texts written for the educated elite, Grossberg underscores an urgent need for more attention to popular culture in the debates about postmodernism (Grossberg, "Putting the Pop Back"). My study of postmodernism in film melodrama, television, and musical theater contributes to work begun by Grossberg's *We Gotta Get Out of This Place*, a study of postmodern rock music, and by Angela McRobbie's *Postmodernism and Popular Culture*, a study of the postmodern aesthetics of youth fashion and culture. Hassan attempted to address the concerns voiced by Grossberg and others by acknowledging the "Pop" side of postmodernism, but Hassan's facile embrace of the popular does not lead to an interrogation of institutionalized taste hierarchies. In an article on *Finnegan's Wake* in his essay collection *The Postmodern Turn,* Hassan argues that Joyce's postmodern text makes it necessary to revise the categories of high art and popular culture because the text "abounds in wit and sentimentality, in folklore, ribaldry, and song; the sounds of music hall, the pub, and the street" (103). He calls *Finnegan's Wake* a mixture of Pop and poesy, of the "sublime and the ridiculous" (103). While Joyce's text may reference popular culture, Hassan wrongly assumes that *Wake* "could win the common as well as the uncommon reader" (103). The text's extreme difficulty and obscure references to many languages and cultures alienate all but the most erudite of the reading public. Such quoting of street ballads did not change the status of *Finnegan's Wake* as an inaccessible high-art text, nor did it break down barriers between elite and popular reading publics.

Postmodern melodramas differ from *Finnegan's Wake* in that they mix high and popular cultural elements without hierarchizing them, and thus problematize the simplistic consumption categories of "taste" (i.e., highbrow and lowbrow) that postmodern criticism reifies. The belief that taste cultures are rigidly distinct has been perpetuated by the influential work of Pierre Bourdieu in his book *Distinction: A Social Critique of the Judgement of Taste*. Although Bourdieu attempts to denaturalize taste and connect it to social class stratification, he suggests that these categories are largely impermeable because of the entrenched social and economic order in France. He neglects to consider that either texts or readers could exhibit both a "high aesthetic" taste for critical detachment *and* a popular taste for emotional investment. Bourdieu's theory of class-stratified taste cannot explain postmodern melodramas that promote both distance and engagement, thereby appealing to people who enjoy both high art and mass culture. In contrast to Bourdieu and those postmodern critics who remain invested in taste hierarchies, Charles Jencks offers an insightful discussion of the "fragmentation of taste cultures" within postmodernism (Jencks, *What Is Post-Modernism?* 49). Jencks attributes this fragmentation and hybridity to an explosion of choices in multiple media; this wide variety of choices allows people to develop a "taste for pluralism itself, and for the juxtapositions it entails" (*What Is Post-Modernism?* 55). In his book *Uncommon Cultures*, Collins argues similarly that the bricolage of genres and aesthetic styles that characterizes postmodern textuality is a reaction to the "semiotic glut" of choices on television (78). The hybrid texts of sentimental postmodernism simulate the experience of channel-surfing between a made-for-TV women's melodrama on the Lifetime Channel and a David Lynch film on the Independent Film Channel. This hybrid cultural formation puts into question the persistent reification of the "great divide" between high and low culture.

Affect and the Anti-feminine Sensibility of Postmodern Criticism

One of the most troubling legacies of the high/low dichotomy is the gendering of this hierarchy. Huyssen has argued that modernism was partly a "reaction formation" against the threatening technologies of mass culture, which were often equated with a passive femininity (*After the Great Divide* 53). Feminist scholars and critics have long argued that this critical equation of the feminine with frivolous popular culture has kept serious works by female writers from being considered in discussions of high art. Unfortunately, postmodern theorists such as Baudrillard continue to invoke gender as if it were intrinsically related to artistic hierarchies. In *The Transparency of Evil*, Baudrillard connects the transaesthetic (textual hybridity) with the transsexual (gender-bending) and he sees both as mutations rather than positive developments. His longing for a world of hierarchical artistic value is implicitly connected to a rubric of gender difference. As Tania Modleski has pointed out, Baudrillard feminizes the masses as elusive subjects who refuse meaning and interpretation. By "equating the masses and mass culture with the feminine" (Modleski, "Femininity" 51), Baudrillard implies that a female artist is an oxymoron. These deep-rooted associations help to explain the under-representation of women writers and artists, and of genres that appeal primarily to female audiences, in discussions of postmodernism.

Gender biases are particularly apparent in postmodern film criticism, where many of the critical favorites are films aimed at male viewers and focused on male protagonists whose identities are threatened by a "fading of . . . patriarchal authority" (Sharrett 4). Postmodern film critics have written copiously about *Blue Velvet*, *Repo Man*, *Pulp Fiction*, *Videodrome*, and the work of Peter Greenaway—films that embrace the masculine sensibilities of violence, nihilism, emotional detachment, and misogyny. Many of these critics see postmodernism as a descendant of avant-garde film, a genre with roots in such misogynist surrealist endeavors as *Un Chien Andalou.* Norman Denzin describes postmodern film as a regressive "masculinized culture . . . [in which] the oppressive structures of racism and sexism are still firmly in place" (149). In a critique of the sexual violence of *Blue Velvet*, Jane Shattuc reads postmodern film as a "patriarchal form" (86) hostile to the "conventions of affect, romance, melodrama, and romantic symbolism, all forms associated with women" (84). Although a good deal of film critics, unlike literary critics, have focused on the postmodern mixture of high and popular film genres (see Corrigan; Degli-Esposti; Collins), many still conceive of postmodern film as an avant-garde critique of melodrama's feminine emotional sensibilities.

These un-interrogated gender biases have led postmodern critics and theorists to routinely neglect the complex functioning of affect in literature and art. Even Huyssen, who convincingly argues that postmodernism mixes high and low culture, does not consider the effect of this hybridization upon the emotional content of these works. As Ann Cvetkovich astutely argues, "the association of femininity with affect has led to the simultaneous devalorization of both" (1). Although nineteenth-century male sentimental novelists such as Dickens were critically celebrated, aestheticism and modernism established a divide between intellectual high culture and affective genres that continues to influence contemporary criticism. This dichotomy between affect and high art is of course specious, since modernist literature depicts complex emotional states and occasionally veers into sentimentality, as Suzanne Clark reveals in *Sentimental Modernism*. In *The Gender of Modernity*, Rita Felski contends that modernism and melodrama share an emotional sensibility in their romantic yearning for utopia (120). Modernist intellectuals, however, were often reluctant to discuss emotion explicitly unless it could be intellectualized, as in the Marxist concept of "alienation."

Despite the arguments of feminist scholars, the specious dichotomy between feminine affective genres and high art persists in contemporary criticism. Many postmodern theorists follow in the footsteps of New Criticism by celebrating art that is disaffected, cerebral, and coolly ironic. Two attitudes toward affect are prevalent among postmodern thinkers: 1) a preference for modernist and/or masculine kinds of affect; and 2) a disdain for affect of any kind because it is associated with the tyranny of the body (associated with femininity) over the rational mind (associated with masculinity). Examples of the first attitude abound in postmodern film criticism. Although many film critics study postmodernism's "contamination of genres" (Degli-Esposti 6), their choices of hybrid texts reveal a bias against feminine popular culture and the kinds of emotions it elicits. The only popular genres discussed are those that appeal to masculine tastes, such as the thriller, film noir, sci-fi, and action picture (see Sharrett; Degli-Esposti). While these texts certainly engage viewers on an affective level, their emotional palette is dominated by alienation, malaise, titillation, rage, and the catharsis afforded by violence. Although women may also feel these emotions, our culture has deemed these feelings "masculine" because they are acceptable for men to express. Popular texts aimed at women, which often induce feelings of comfort, security, empathy, hope, love, and pathos, are absent from the postmodern film "canon."

Fredric Jameson exhibits both of these attitudes towards affect in *Postmodernism, Or, The Cultural Logic of Late Capitalism.* Like Baudrillard, Jameson views postmodern literature and art as less subversive than modernism, in part because of the depthlessness and "waning of affect" (16) that he finds in contemporary culture. Before the advent of poststructuralism, Jameson argues, art was invested in the depth-model principle of expression, an outward projection of inner feeling that rests on a belief that words (signifiers) can capture the essence of things and ideas (signifieds) (*Postmodernism* 12). Poststructuralist theory discredited depth models as illusions and replaced the belief in inner depth and essences with a fragmentation of the subject and a play of surfaces. Jameson wrongly concludes, however, that a postmodernist fragmented subjectivity precludes the expression of real emotion, which he finds crucial to the development of a progressive political stance (15). Whereas Jameson lauds modernist art for depicting and attempting to elicit alienation, angst, and despair in the service of political resistance, he reasons that postmodern art is often apolitical because of its lack of depth and affect. While affect is undoubtedly crucial to political consciousness, Jameson simply ignores that affective depth-models—sentimentality and melodrama—can still be found in postmodern culture. Overestimating the impact of poststructuralism upon postmodernism, Jameson implies that the existence of surface-model concepts (such as fragmented subjectivity) in a text completely nullifies any depth-model strategies. The argument that a co-existence of surface and depth models is impossible would seem to contradict Jameson's stated belief that postmodernism thoroughly effaces "the frontier between high culture and so-called mass or commercial culture" (2). Since he argues that postmodernism has incorporated popular culture into its "very substance" (3), it would be logical to assume that the affective structures of popular culture are also present in postmodernism. By discussing the hybrid politics enabled by the conjunction of surface and depth models in sentimental postmodernism, I question the presumption that poststructuralism trumps all other sensibilities. While Jameson dismisses depth-model cultural products as merely "residual" impulses dominated by the larger "force field" of postmodernism (6), these "residual" affective forms may alternatively be understood as crucial elements of popular postmodernist texts that expand postmodernism's range of attitudes beyond that of ironic detachment.

Jameson's concern about a waning of affect reveals his preference for intellectualized emotions over feminized forms of affect. He argues that only one emotion is prevalent in postmodern culture: a sublime awe or euphoria provoked by technology and the "whole new decentered global network of the third stage of capital itself" (38). Lyotard also focuses on the sublime as a transcendental experience of recognizing the unrepresentable. By isolating the sublime as the only postmodern "emotion" worth theorizing about, Jameson and Lyotard perpetuate a hierarchy of emotions that began in the eighteenth century, when Edmund Burke and Immanuel Kant established a distinction between the sublime and the beautiful. The sublime originally signified an emotion, a feeling of awe most common among women, but it was quickly turned into an aesthetic and then "elevated" to an association with the masculine by Kant (Suzanne Clark 28). Sublimity is often conceived of as an experience of transcending the body, which has long been equated with Woman. This gendered dichotomy lingers today, as popular culture continues to be denigrated for its association with the "beautiful," which originally signified pleasing, calm, comforting, and therefore lesser forms of art. Jameson is merely one of many postmodern critics who retain the Enlightenment concept of the mind/body dualism, in which emotions—particularly of the feminized "beautiful" sphere—are relegated to the realm of the body and thus denigrated.

Even more problematic than the critics' lack of attention to the affective strategies of postmodernism, however, is their blindness to the fact that emotion is a form of cognition. To counter the view that emotions are wholly instinctive, anthropologists have argued that feeling is culturally specific, each culture granting specific meanings to different feelings or not recognizing some emotions at all. Social scientists and reception scholars such as Birgitta Höijer, Ed Tan, Reinhold Viehoff, and David Miall agree that "we can hardly think of cognitive processes isolated from emotional reactions" (Höijer 285). Miall elaborates that "emotion does not interrupt cognition," but may rather "precede and then direct cognitive functioning" ("Response to Poetry" 155). Postmodern theorists' reluctance to discuss affect suggests that they still adhere to a depth-model view of emotion as a welling-up from the body, and therefore unrelated to reason. Jameson, for example, believes that a unified "deep" self is necessary for emotional expression, because he conceives of emotion as an outward expression of the inner psyche and body (*Postmodernism* 11–14). As Cvetkovich has argued, Jameson's ideas about affect as pre-discursive "raw material" are based on the depth-model "repressive hypothesis" (29–30). In contrast to Jameson, feminist philosopher Alison Jaggar underscores the culturally constructed nature of emotions, arguing that they may be "necessary rather than inimical to the construction of knowledge" about our world (146). Similarly, this book will treat emotions as cognitive constructions, as active engagements in the development of social understanding. Thus emotions may have either conservative or progressive politics or some combination thereof. As Jaggar argues, "critical reflection on emotion is not a self-indulgent substitute for political analysis and political action. It is itself a kind of political theory and political practice, indispensable for an adequate social theory and social transformation" (164). This emphasis on emotion as active political engagement characterizes the postmodern hybrids of my study, many of which aim to foster empathy for people on the social margins.

Reevaluating the Politics of Sympathy

When critics have discussed the politics of postmodernism, they either ignore the role of affect by locating politics in formalist innovation, or they deem postmodernism apolitical or conservative because of its nihilistic evacuation of feeling. Others view the ironic detachment of postmodernism as a subversive political strategy. As an alternative to these schools of thought, I study postmodern forms that use "beautiful" emotions to further left-leaning political goals. My analysis of the politics of affect is informed by feminist criticism concerning sentimental fiction, film melodrama, and sympathy as a structure of feeling. The debate about postmodernism's evacuation of feeling and lack of political commitment may sound familiar to scholars of post-World War II anti-fascist European literature. Thus, sentimental postmodernism must also be situated in relation to the work of such authors and thinkers as George Orwell and Jean-Paul Sartre, who waged earlier attacks on the ethical disaffection of modernism and the avant-garde.

This study offers a corrective to critical analyses of postmodern aesthetics that ignore affect, but it also speaks to a debate concerning the politics of sentimentality and sympathy. Despite a celebratory moment in the 1980s sparked by Jane Tompkins's reevaluation of nineteenth-century sentimental fiction as feminist and subversive, recent critics in literary and cultural studies have tended to treat both sentimentality and sympathy as forms of cultural imperialism. Postcolonial and critical race theory has made critics in the past decade much more attentive to the colonizing desires lurking beneath facile calls for sisterhood or brotherhood. This renewed zeal to police instances of imperialism, however, has led to a neglect of potentially subversive moments of sympathetic cross-group identification, on which my study focuses. I see my work as participating in a recent trend in the field of American studies focusing on the nineteenth-century U.S.—the new call for an end to the "separate spheres" paradigm that divided public from private, masculine from feminine, the world of political action from the world of feeling. A 1998 special issue of *American Literature* entitled "No More Separate Spheres!" suggested that the line between the public and the private is a blurry one, and that these two "spheres" are in fact largely imbricated. My work on the politics of sentimental postmodernism contends that emotions experienced in the "private" sphere of reading and viewing may not be so far removed from political praxis in a more traditional sense, and that the former may in fact provide fuel for the latter. Since the term "politics" has been defined so variously in literary and cultural studies, this chapter will clarify both the distinctions and the connections to be drawn between a politics of textuality, a politics of consumption or "use," a politics of affect, a politics of identity, and the more traditionally "public" arena of political activity.

Literary critics have tended to locate the politics of postmodernism in its aesthetic innovation rather than in a text's ability to elicit particular emotional responses. In *The Politics of Postmodernism*, Hutcheon argues that the parodic self-reflexivity of postmodernism offers a political "site of de-naturalizing critique" (3). Her formalist study of representational strategies does not mention the impact of a text upon audiences, thereby implying that consumption has nothing to do with politics. Similarly, Hassan reads postmodernism as subversive for its anarchic rebellion against structure. A rebellion at the level of the aesthetic, however, is not likely to move readers to view the world differently or fight to change existing power structures. We must look at how representational strategies have impacted audiences at a given historical juncture in order to evaluate their full political significance. As cultural studies scholars have argued, the politics of a text does not reside solely in aesthetics, but also in the way it is interpreted and integrated into the lives of audience members. Emotional responses are often key to understanding a text's impact upon a reader or viewer's knowledge of the world.

Those critics who understand affect's connection to the political have located the politics of postmodernism in its irony, nihilistic indifference, and cynicism. These affective sensibilities, or the sensibility of disaffection itself, have been variously interpreted to be progressive, conservative, or apolitical in nature. Baudrillard's concepts of simulacrum and the "death of the social" lead him to conclude that our postmodern era renders politics null and void. Because one cannot tell the real from the image, Baudrillard argues that meaning, emotional engagement, and political resistance are impossible in this post-Enlightenment culture of simulacra. In his essay "The Masses: The Implosion of the Social in the Media," Baudrillard revised his belief that postmodernism is apolitical to suggest that a nihilistic, passive, ironic detachment could offer a possible political strategy for the masses. Those critics who view postmodernism as subversive—such as Alan Wilde, Richard Rorty, and Hutcheon—often cite irony as the source of its politics. Although irony can certainly have subversive effects, I share Gianni Vattimo's concern that post-apocalyptic irony can be inimical to the concept of progress essential to political change (84). In the essay collection *Crisis Cinema: The Apocalyptic Idea in Postmodern Narrative Film,* Christopher Sharrett similarly deems postmodernism "reactionary" (9) for its "unbridled negativity" (4) and cynicism. While postmodern film need not be dismissed as reactionary, we ought to consider the possibility that the ironic nihilism of postmodern culture has contributed to a political disenchantment and passivity that threatens the functioning of democracy.

Critiques of postmodern nihilism and ethical disaffection bear a remarkable similarity to pre- and post-World War II reactions against politically impotent modernist "art for art's sake." Sartre's *littérature engagée* and Orwell's anti-fascist humanist fiction can be seen as forerunners of sentimental postmodernism, although the differences are also salient. In his 1947 treatise "What Is Literature?" Sartre denounces the pre-war surrealist literature of "negation" (120) and deems it an apolitical, formalist "rebellion without effect" (122). As a more potent weapon against fascism, Sartre urges "committed writing" (*littérature engagée*) to "take sides against all injustices" (229) and thus to foster the moral goals of freedom and social change. A similar rhetoric of engagement and rejection of post-war disaffection characterizes André Malraux's 1933 social realist work *La Condition humaine* (Wilkinson 20–25) and Orwell's *1984*. The character of Winston Smith in Orwell's novel offers a powerful argument for the importance of emotion in resisting totalitarianism. Literary critic Frédéric Regard contends that by "recentering the literary on feeling" (8), Orwell protests against modernism's indifference to ethics (7). One could argue further that

Orwell reappropriates affect as a leftist strategy, wresting it back from the Nazis, who had expertly used it as a tool of fascist manipulation in such propaganda films as *Jew Suss* and Leni Riefenstahl's *Triumph of the Will*. The "resistance humanism" of the 1930–55 period renewed faith in the Enlightenment principles of liberty, equality, and democracy and fostered a humanist "respect for the individual" (Wilkinson 266). This mid-century critique of the moral and political disengagement of modernist aesthetics resonates with the contemporary criticisms of apolitical postmodernism.

In contrast to an apocalyptic postmodernism of shattered communities, dehumanizing violence, and ironic disaffection, sentimental postmodernist culture offers an alternative emotional and political sensibility that merges Sartre's *littérature engagée* with Orwell's ethics of emotion. The emotionally charged world of sentimental postmodernism is marked by a resurgence in optimism, democratic political values, and a humanist faith in the individual. The postmodern texts in my study offer "empowerment in the face of, and to a certain extent the reality of, nihilism" (Grossberg, "Postmodernity and Affect" 290). Yet these texts differ from mid-twentieth-century resistance humanism in several key ways: they operate in a decidedly post-Marxist political universe, they embrace rather than eschew formalist innovation, and they are far more invested in the popular pleasures of consumption, which Sartre deems escapist. Whereas Sartre hopes that his utilitarian texts will "irritate and disturb" (192), sentimental postmodernism combines provocation with the soothing emotions of popular feminized genres.

While Grossberg does not focus on sentimental emotional registers, he describes postmodern popular culture as an affective site of political empowerment. Emotive genres are politically powerful because they provoke identification, belonging, and investment, providing audiences with "mattering maps" which reveal "the places at which people can anchor themselves into the world, the locations of the things that matter" (*We Gotta* 82). As Grossberg argues persuasively, "affective relations are, at least potentially, the condition of possibility for the optimism, invigoration, and passion which are necessary for any struggle to change the world" (*We Gotta* 86). Grossberg's concept of mattering maps implicitly rejects the notion that global capitalism has severed our connection to reality. Despite the disorienting effects of late-capitalist societies, people have never stopped "mapping out" the politics of their social relations in local settings such as the family, and they are often guided in this process by their emotions and by popular culture. Thus, my focus on the relationship between affect and politics is informed by feminist reevaluations of the political significance of sentimental fiction and film melodrama. Throughout most of the twentieth century, these two related genres were dismissed as apolitical, escapist, and reactionary for oversimplifying complex social issues and for turning systemic problems into conflicts that can be overcome by individual action. In particular, twentieth-century sentimentalism has received overwhelmingly negative critical response due to the association of sentimentality and melodrama with fascist kitsch (Suzanne Clark 4). Anthony Savile voices the typical rationalist attack on sentimentality, which he calls an idealized "false-colouring of the world" (225) that insulates people from reality and truth and inhibits them from taking action to change their world. Ann Douglas's *The Feminization of American Culture* similarly argues that sentimental rhetoric was an anti-intellectual force that limited the possibilities for reform. This anti-sentimentalism was halted in its tracks by the ground-breaking work of Jane Tompkins, who argued that nineteenth-century sentimental fiction posed a radical challenge to the social order by discussing public social issues within a new context—the private, personal, *feminine* sphere. In *Uncle Tom's Cabin,* for example, "the very possibility of social action [for the abolition of slavery] is made dependent on the action taking place in individual hearts" (128). Stowe's sentimental melodrama places political power, therefore, in the hands of women urging Christian compassion, and the text even goes so far as to promote a matriarchal society. Tompkins's *Sensational Designs* usefully reevaluated the genre as a "political enterprise, halfway between sermon and social theory, that both codifies and attempts to mold the values of its time" (126).

More recent work on nineteenth-century sentimentality has taken a decidedly skeptical turn, using the insights of postcolonial and critical race theory to position sentimentality as an imperialist and often racist rhetoric that masks a desire for social control over its objects of sympathy. In an essay on the imperialist designs of domestic fiction and prose, Amy Kaplan argues that "the extension of female sympathy across social divides could violently reinforce the very racial and class hierarchies that sentimentality claims to dissolve" (581). Karen Sanchez-Eppler's insightful book on abolitionist white women's writing uncovers the "exploitation inherent in this also empowering political alliance" (10) between free women and slave women. Aiming to "tell a happier story about the insight and strength to be found in strategies of coalition," Sanchez-Eppler instead found incontrovertible evidence of "exploitation, appropriation, and displacement" (13). These useful critiques of the dangers of sympathy, however, should not lead us to a categorical dismissal of sentimentality and sympathy as necessarily colonizing and hypocritical. We should be wary of a return to the mid-twentieth-century disdain for sentimentality, which James Baldwin believed was "*always*, therefore, the signal of secret and violent inhumanity, the mask of cruelty" (1654; italics mine). My study of the left-leaning politics of one articulation of contemporary sentimentalism provides a counterpoint to totalizing or transhistorical denunciations of sentimental feeling. Laura Hinton's *The Perverse Gaze of Sympathy: Sadomasochistic Sentiments from Clarissa to Rescue 911* figures sentimentality and sympathy as voyeuristic strategies of "control based on an excessive need for another's objectification" (11). Her generalizing, transhistorical model spans three centuries, locating the "common features of the sentimental subject" (4) in sadomasochistic desires. Denying the progressive claims critics have made for sympathy and sentimentality, she argues that these rhetorics "invariably generate sadistic voyeuristic pleasure" (28). Locating sympathy's politics in formalist analysis, she neglects to consider how each text is articulated in local moments of production and reception, and she stridently asserts as a general principle of sympathy what may only be one effect, however persistent, of its deployment. Critics of sentimentality and melodrama need to recognize the mixed legacy of these forms and genres, given the protean ability of affective discourses to work in the direction of both social control and radical reform.

By looking at the articulation of the affective strategies of sentimentality and melodrama in a particular reception context in the 1990s, this book refuses to assign a fixed ideological significance to these multivalent rhetorical forms. Criticism of film melodrama has been particularly plagued by ahistoricism, given the formalist nature of much film theory. In the 1970s, Marxist-influenced critics began to celebrate Douglas Sirk's 1950s family melodramas for their use of irony and a parodic form of excessive *mise en scène*; these "distanciation" techniques were said to undermine the bourgeois ideology of the surface narrative (see Willemen; Halliday). Christine Gledhill argues that "there occurred a slippage of the 'subversion' argument from its attachment to Sirk as 'author' to melodrama itself" ("Melodramatic" 7), and stylistic excess was then treated as the source of the genre's politics. This problematic approach to melodrama relies on a Brechtian, avant-garde value system to evaluate a popular form, implying that irony is more subversive than sentimentality. This stance also elevates formal style above narrative as a locus for subversion, as did the modernists and the Marxist Frankfurt School. Implicit in these arguments is the assumption that melodramatic narratives are essentially regressive and unworthy of intellectual scrutiny. More defensible critical approaches to melodrama link its politics to its manipulations of affect and identification, precisely because these strategies have a strong impact upon audiences. Whereas film critics may be able to appreciate Sirk's ironic formalist critique, it is unlikely that popular audiences would have been moved ideologically by such strategies. Barbara Klinger makes this point by comparing the popular reception history of Sirk's *Written on the Wind* with its appraisal by *auteur* critics as a critique of bourgeois capitalism (Klinger 5). Marketing and reviews reveal that the film reinforced rather than disrupted the capitalist orientation of its viewers, who were attracted by the "presentation of class and sexuality as pure 'consumable' spectacles" (Klinger 19). Paying attention to how narratives were read by popular audiences, however, does not necessarily lead to the conclusion that melodrama always reinforces the status quo. Feminist critics have seen subversion within women's films of the 1930s (and even in the more conservative 1950s domestic melodramas) because they provide female viewers with a sorely needed space for the serious exploration of women's emotional concerns. By allowing female audiences to recognize their own suffering in that of the heroine, these films offer a protest against the impossible demands that patriarchy places upon women. E. Ann Kaplan, for example, argues that some women's films such as *Stella Dallas* (1937) could be called resistant for their "questioning of woman's position as Mother" and their attempt to strengthen mother-daughter bonds that are often thwarted by patriarchy (126). While Laura Mulvey believes that 1950s melodramas ultimately refuse satisfaction for their female characters, she finds it "socially and ideologically beneficial" that they allow a "dramatic rendering of women's frustrations" and of the repression of female desires under bourgeois patriarchy ("Notes on

Sirk" 40). These feminist critics locate melodrama's politics in its ability to foster identifications that allow women to recognize the emotional conflicts engendered by their social positioning.

Attributing a singular politics to melodrama is fraught with difficulty, for it depends on what aspects of the genre one chooses to emphasize, such as the realistic depiction of female suffering, the complicit happy endings, or the excessive *mise en scène*. Critics' generalizations about melodrama's politics also depend on their choice of examples—Sirk's films vs. 1930s women's pictures, or even particular texts within a given time period. As with any kind of political critique, the danger is that "critics' own ideological positions" may "lead them to predetermined conclusions" (Byars, *All That Hollywood* 259). It would be unwise to attach a static ideological position to a genre that has spanned so many different cultures and historical moments, and whose target audiences have shifted considerably since its inception in 18th-century popular theatricals. Furthermore, the emotional volatility of melodrama also renders its politics unstable and mutable. Cvetkovich reminds us that "the politics of affect is double-edged" (5) in that it is "as much a way to dominate as it is a way to resist domination" (10). Sentimentality and melodrama should be considered transideological, because they may "function either subversively or as escapism—categories which are always relative to the given social and historical context" (Elsaesser 47; see also Dana Nelson). It is useful to keep in mind Stuart Hall's insightful argument that all popular texts are complex negotiations between dominant cultural values and resistant urges: "if the forms of provided commercial popular culture are not purely manipulative, then it is because, alongside the false appeals, the foreshortenings, the trivialisation and shortcircuits, there are also elements of recognition and identification" ("Notes" 233).

Melodrama and sentimentality have the potential to offer just such a dynamic negotiation between patriarchal, middle-class values and a resistance to those norms from the perspective of women, racial and ethnic minorities, and other socially marginalized people. In my analysis of the politics of postmodern melodrama, for example, I see melodramatic and sentimental narrative strategies working toward both conservative and progressive ends. These texts' invocation of essentialist identities and stereotypes could be read as regressive, but they also offer an important counterpoint to the overzealous poststructuralist dismissal of identity politics. One could read their acknowledgment of the desires for comfort and tradition to be nostalgic and escapist, or one could see it as a critique of the destructive tendencies of radicalism. By using sentimentality to depict the plight of homosexuals, women, and ethnic minorities, these hybrid texts could foster a progressive empathetic identification or they could result only in a complacent form of pity. I contend that the politics of a text or a genre cannot be determined by textual analysis alone. The question of whether postmodern melodramas foster progressive empathy or conservative pity can best be answered by studying how actual audiences have received these particular texts. The need for audience studies is particularly important when dealing with affective genres since emotions are so volatile and hard to predict. For example, while many feminist critics and viewers celebrated *The Piano* as a subversive text, many other female viewers were enraged by what they saw as an anti-feminist film. Although many studies of sentimentality and melodrama locate the politics of these genres in their affective strategies, they neglect to consider that emotional effects cannot be totally determined by the text. Psychoanalytic readings, which have tended to dominate melodrama criticism, suffer from both ahistoricism and textual determinism. In contrast, I treat local moments of reception as the scene of a text's political articulation, by studying audiences in the process of constructing political meanings out of postmodern melodramas.

In using the term "political" to describe the effects of sentimental postmodernism on its audiences, this study begs a question that has preoccupied scholars in cultural studies: what is the relationship between the consumption of popular texts and the arena of political change? Lauren Berlant explicitly addresses this question in her numerous articles on the sentimental strategy of "privatizing the political," which she views as a "legitimating device for sustaining the hegemonic field" ("Subject" 54). Berlant's Marxist critical emphasis on the commodification of feeling within capitalism leaves little hope for sentimentality to accomplish its "unrealized" radical potential to "move people . . . into identifying against their own interests" ("Poor Eliza" 640) and protesting against the status quo. In "Poor Eliza," she concludes that sentiment's "ethical imperative toward social transformation is replaced by a civic-minded but passive ideal of empathy. The political as a place of acts oriented towards publicness becomes replaced by a world of private thoughts, leanings, and gestures" (641). Opposing Jane Tompkins and Harriet Beecher Stowe, Berlant sees in sentimental discourse a "confusion . . . between changed minds and changed worlds" ("Poor Eliza" 644) and doubts whether "changes in feeling, even on a mass scale, amount to substantial social change" ("The Subject" 53). Given her Marxist leanings, Berlant figures sentimental culture as a consumer distraction, a form of compensatory fantasy that inhibits political action. Scholars have similarly asserted that melodramas enforce the status quo by "encouraging [a misguided] belief in the power of the individual and ignoring the necessity for social change" (Byars, *All That Hollywood* 253; see also Torres).

Rather than viewing sentimental culture as a "passive ideal" or an impediment to political change, I argue that the empathetic feelings and self-reckoning fostered by such texts can play an important role in catalyzing action. Implicit in Berlant's argument is a familiar hierarchy of emotions, in which the power of rage reigns supreme. Despairing about the ability of sentimentality and sympathy to foster structural change in the public sphere, she places hope only in "political rage, a discourse of demand and radical critique" ("The Subject" 83). I agree that rage is central to radical action, but anger is difficult to sustain over time, and political movements would quickly burn out without reserves of hope. Among the emotions motivating political action, sociologists include not only outrage, but also moral shock, guilt, shame, and pride, all of which can be stimulated by sympathetic feeling (Goodwin, Jasper, and Polletta 10, 16). AIDS activists, for example, were quick to recognize the political efficacy of sentimental appeals such as the names quilt project and the melodramatic protest film *And the Band Played On.* As Mouffe reminds us, the Left has for too long ignored the political power of affect to engender and sustain radical movements (Mouffe, "Politics and Passion"). Berlant's work on Reaganite national sentimentality diagnoses the problem as one of reducing the political to the realm of private feeling (see *The Queen of America*), but the inverse phenomenon is perhaps even more troubling—a lack of personal engagement in politics, evidenced by the paltry percentage of Americans who vote. Sentimental postmodernism aims to politicize the private sphere, but in the opposite ideological direction of Reaganite conservatism. These emotion-laden works encourage audiences to form counterhegemonic identities and alliances, and such a strategy must be read within a historical context in which capitalist and bureaucratic networks have contributed to feelings of powerlessness and a cynicism about democracy. By insisting that individuals can change themselves and their interactions with marginalized social others, postmodern melodramas counteract a pervasive political apathy. The fact that these moments of radical empathy are fostered by popular texts produced within a capitalist culture industry, I contend, does not completely negate their oppositional effect.

While Berlant aims to pry apart the private and the political spheres with her definition of the "political as a place of acts oriented toward publicness" ("Poor Eliza" 641), my work emphasizes the interdependence and mutually reinforcing relationship between the private consumption of emotional popular culture and the public sphere of political praxis. As Gayle Wald and You-Me Park argue, post-Habermasian theory underscores that "public and private are not stable, unchangeable, or natural polarities" (612). On a symbolic level, private scenes of interpersonal exchange—a central feature of narrative fiction and film—can be as politically charged as any public action on a collective scale. More importantly, my ethnographic study revealed the existence of a feedback loop between the consumption of politicized culture and political attitudes and actions. Although Berlant is right that experiences of empathy provided by cultural texts may not often lead a previously apolitical reader or viewer to take public action, she neglects to consider that affect can be crucial to *sustaining*, rather than simply giving birth to, a desire for systemic change. Many of the people I interviewed were already politically active to some degree, and encountering these texts nourished and galvanized their ideological commitments. Rather than relying on the specious causal logic that private feeling experienced via culture leads directly to public political praxis, my study emphasizes their mutually sustaining relationship.

While I am using sentimental postmodernism to challenge assumptions about the politics of sentimental culture, it is important to remember that the texts I address here mix the rhetoric of sentimentality with that of postmodernism. As hybrid texts, they both employ and critique sentimental strategies simultaneously. Sentimental postmodernism thus bears some relation to what Berlant describes in "Poor Eliza" as a more promising strain of the "postsentimental," exemplified by Toni Morrison's novel *Beloved.* In Berlant's analysis, Morrison's text relies on affect yet challenges the "too-quick gratification after the none-too-brief knowledge of pain" ("Poor Eliza" 665) by disrupting the desire for "unconflictedness" (656), easy resolution, and universal connection. The texts in my study register a similar ambivalence towards the sentimental. By combining postmodern aesthetic values and models of subjectivity with the emotive strategies of sentimentality and melodrama, these texts ask "us to demand of the sentimental project that its protests and complaints be taken seriously in themselves" and to stop deferring action ("Poor Eliza" 666). These hybrid texts induce empathy in the service of utopic goals but do not suppress difference and dissent; they value the role of emotion in coalition-building but also critique the sentimental fantasy of universal harmony. The texts in my study owe their critical edge to postmodern concepts of pluralism, anti-foundationalism, and anti-essentialism, but they also draw subversive power from their invocation of sentimental emotions. While I am suggesting that this particular dialectic of rhetorical forms and narrative preoccupations conveys a certain political orientation, any discussion of the "politics" of sentimental postmodernism, or of any cultural product, must take into consideration how such ideological textual strategies impact the psyches and political commitments of audience members.

The Birmingham School Meets Psychoanalytic Theory

While the postmodern melodramas I analyze offer a hybrid of two competing worldviews and aesthetics, the hybrid methodology of this book offers another important mediation between textual analysis and reception study. Textual critics and audience researchers often view themselves as antagonists propounding antithetical knowledge claims about cultural forms. One of the essays that inaugurated the rift was David Morley's "Texts, Readers, Subjects" (1980), in which he critiques psychoanalytic film theory, typified by the journal *Screen*, from the position of the Birmingham Centre for Contemporary Cultural Studies. As Morley describes, psychoanalytic film critics locate meaning in the text, arguing that identification is a function of textually embedded codes that suture the spectator into particular subject positions. Complaining that such a deterministic theory treats readers merely as "bearers or puppets of their unconscious positionings" (167), Morley instead describes the reader as an active participant in the construction of meaning and the "struggle in ideology" (165). As a consequence of this debate over whether to give primacy to texts or readers as producers of meaning, an antagonism developed between cultural studies ethnographers and psychoanalytic textual critics and theorists. Even though both bodies of work are explicitly concerned with the politics of culture, and with the relationship between identity and interpretation, this disciplinary enmity has prevented a fertile exchange of ideas about the process of identification.

By synthesizing the insights of cultural studies ethnographic work and psychoanalytic theories of identification, this book aims to enrich both subfields. Although I engage in an ethnographic study of audiences in order to address some of the limitations of textual criticism, I do not underestimate the role of the text in suggesting various ideological positions for readers. While I invoke psychoanalytic and poststructuralist theories concerning spectatorship and identification to explain the audience responses, I also use the ethnographic findings to question and revise existing theory. The major risk of such an interdisciplinary strategy is that it will alienate and frustrate scholars from both the humanities and the social sciences. Although I learned the skills to conduct ethnography from extensive reading and consultation with sociologists, social scientists will undoubtedly find my approach too text-focused. Anthropologists and some cultural studies scholars may wish that I had replaced my textual analysis with more "fieldwork" and a fuller attention to the everyday lives of the research subjects (McRobbie, "Post-Marxism" 730). Literary and film critics may feel threatened by the decentering of the critic's role as sole interpretive authority, a decentering that results from an attention to the meaning-production of other readers and viewers. Yet the project itself—an investigation of the socio-political effects of reading and viewing a hybrid textual style—necessitated a deviation from the traditional humanities and social science protocols. Rather than delegitimating these traditional methods, my interdisciplinary approach aims to uncover aspects of reading and spectatorship that have been obscured by disciplinary schisms.

In anticipation of the concerns of a multidisciplinary readership, the remainder of the chapter situates my project in relation to key methodological and critical debates emerging from within text-oriented and audience-oriented scholarly camps. I address reception scholars' debates about the pursuit of objective truth, the power dynamic between researchers and subjects, and the problem of "sociological determinism" (Morley, "Texts" 173). My qualitative study of audiences acknowledges the complexity of individual subjectivity rather than reducing people to mere representatives of demographic categories. While I offer a critique of the essentialism that undergirds many audience studies, I uncover similar flaws or limitations in textually-based, psychoanalytic theories concerning reader and viewer identification. The psychoanalytic theories associated with the journal *Screen* treat identification as an unconscious process of self-recognition that works to solidify unitary identities. I argue that "screen theory" is inadequate to explain how audiences respond to postmodern melodramas, which complicate identity and encourage fluid and multiple identifications. As opposed to the psychoanalytic view of identification as an unconscious process of "suturing," this study treats identification as a social process that can involve a conscious and active negotiation between self and other, a negotiation that fosters an awareness of the political nature of identity and social relationships. While my ethnographic work challenges "suture" theory, it corroborates more recent anti-essentialist contributions to identification theory. Interviews with actual audiences have revealed that identification can be fluid, multiple, ambivalent, and politicized, as Kaja Silverman and Judith Butler have theorized. Many of these viewers and readers of postmodern melodramas were able to identify across divisions of gender, sexuality, and race, and to align their sympathies against the interests of their own social group. These findings suggest a need to rethink the ruling critical attitudes about the politics of identifying with the "Other." Critics within gender studies and race studies have tended to treat cross-group identification as a problematic appropriation and incorporation with retrograde political consequences. As such, their arguments echo those waged against sympathy as a structure of feeling. This chapter closes with an argument for the subversive potential of empathetic identification, as a means of destabilizing entrenched identities and enabling left-leaning political alliances.

The Text/Audience Interface

My decision to learn the skills to conduct ethnographic research came from my dissatisfaction with literary and film scholarship which grants absolute power to the text and ignores the agency of audiences. Even when literary and film critics are concerned with the ideological effects of a text upon audiences, they often place the text at the center of meaning, invest its structural elements with the ability to produce univocal readings, and assume audiences to be passive. Rather than investigating the responses of actual readers, theorists of reception and spectatorship speculate about an "implied reader" (see Iser) or "implied spectator" (see Doane) that represents the supposedly normal response elicited by a text. This indifference to the diverse responses of audiences signals a problematic understanding of how meaning and ideological effects are produced. Film studies, in particular, has been heavily influenced by Louis Althusser's concept of interpellation, which focuses on the power of mass-media texts to reproduce the viewer as a subject of ideology. Althusser's model underestimates the polysemic nature of popular texts. He assumes that mass culture always inscribes a conservative ideology, and ignores that readers and viewers often construct widely different interpretations of texts, depending on their social positioning, their discourses for making sense of the world, and their "background assumptions" (Freundlieb 126). Even those film critics dissatisfied with textual determinism find it difficult to buck the dominant paradigm. Gledhill, for example, concludes that "the text alone does not provide sufficient evidence for conclusions" concerning the "political effects of textual ideologies," but she continues to offer only textual readings, claiming that she lacks "ethnographic skills" ("Pleasurable Negotiations" 73). Instead of persisting in a method I find insufficient, I acquired the skills necessary to answer the questions I wanted to ask.

In challenging the assumption that politics is textually determined, I draw on the work of cultural studies theorist Stuart Hall. In the 1970s, Hall and the Birmingham Centre for Contemporary Cultural Studies offered a corrective to Althusser and communication theories by discussing the reader as an active participant in the process of meaning-production. Hall's groundbreaking 1973 essay "Encoding/Decoding" sparked a flurry of ethnographic work, most notably Morley's study of audience responses to the television news program *Nationwide*. In "Encoding/Decoding," Hall argues for the "'relative autonomy' but 'determinateness,' of the entry and exit of the message" from text to audience, stressing that audiences do "interpretive work" (134) and can make different ideological interpretations of the codes they see in texts. While this theory grants agency to the viewer, Hall recognizes the power of the text to construct "some of the limits and parameters within which decodings will operate" (135). By pointing out that audiences tend to fall into clusters or patterns of interpretation, his theories offer an important warning against the "subjective relativism" of some ethnographic work; Dorothy Hobson's *Crossroads*, for example, suggests that each viewer produces a totally individualized response, thereby rendering the textual codes irrelevant. Some reader-response literary critics have also given too much power to the reader to construct the text. Umberto Eco argues that all texts are "open," inviting an infinite number of interpretations. Norman Holland also takes the subjective approach too far, arguing that readers use "the literary work to symbolize and finally to replicate ourselves" (816). While Hall rightly encourages equal attention to both text and audience in the production of ideological effects, his division of audience response into preferred, negotiated, and oppositional readings is overly schematic. Using an example of television news, Hall argues that a preferred or "dominant" reading accepts the hegemonic "institutional/political/ideological order" that has been encoded into the newscast ("Encoding/Decoding" 134), while readers also have the ability to construct a resistant reading or a negotiated one which allows both "adaptive and oppositional elements" (137). Several problems arise, however, if one attempts to apply this model to fictional texts. The labels dominant and oppositional are too dependent upon a critic's own reading of the text's ideological stance, which he or she claims to be the preferred reading. Furthermore, the concept of a dominant reading falsely implies that texts have a stable and unified ideological meaning that necessarily reproduces the dominant cultural order (Christie 52). What would be the dominant or preferred reading of a sentimental postmodernist text, where two worldviews are juxtaposed, resulting in ambiguous and ambivalent political messages? Since the texts I examine negotiate between two cultural orders, and depict moments of both resistance and containment, it would be impossible to assign the binary labels "dominant" or "oppositional" to interpretations made by my interview subjects.

Adopting the model of dominant vs. resistant readings has led reception researchers to focus mainly on audience populations who seem to be resisting the values of ideologically conservative mass-culture texts. The reader is only granted agency if he or she can resist the dominant encoding of the text by reading "against the grain." Since postmodern melodramas contain oppositional discourses within them—feminism and queer theory, for example—the audiences I interviewed often worked with rather than against the grain of the text. To search for pure "resistance" would be beside the point, since almost all of the readings involved some form of negotiation with the text's multiple codes. As Chris Christie complains of much cultural studies work, "the focus is not on how interpretation occurs, but on how resistance occurs" (53). Following tenets of the "empirical study of literature," my study sheds light on the process of interpretation itself, investigating how "the audience's interpretation of a text and their cultural background are connected" (Christie 54; on the empirical study of literature, see Freundlieb; Nardocchio; László; Larsen; Schmidt; Tötösy, "The Empirical Science of Literature"). Since my hybrid texts invoke multiple and contradictory worldviews, they make audiences work to reach a political interpretation. Although the dominant/resistant reading paradigm did not hold for my study, I did see more subtle clusters of response influenced by the viewers' ideologies. For example, some of the interpretive patterns correlated with viewers' sympathies for difference-based feminism or postmodern feminism, or gay-liberationist or queer ideologies. While these clusters revealed much about the process of political interpretation, I paid special attention to the viewers and readers who produced "negotiated" or ambivalent readings that focused on the contradictions and tensions, on the space in between the sentimental and the postmodern threads of the narratives.

Much more useful for my project is Hall's later elaboration of Gramsci's concept of articulation, which treats texts and reading practices as complex negotiations whose ideological significance is contingent upon social forces. In "Notes on Deconstructing the Popular," Hall takes a clearer stand against textual determinism, arguing that "the meaning of a cultural form and its place or position in the cultural field is not inscribed inside its form. Nor is its position fixed once and forever. . . . The meaning of a cultural symbol is given in part by the social field into which it is incorporated, the practices with which it articulates and is made to resonate" (235). In the interview "On Postmodernism and Articulation," Hall argues that cultural products are "never whole, never fully closed or 'sutured'" (Grossberg 56) because their meaning depends on surrounding social contexts and the audiences that interpret them. My project investigates how postmodern melodramas are articulated in relation to contemporary discourses about the politics of identity, and how audiences then use these texts to articulate their own ideologies and identities. Further, I examine representation and consumption as a complex negotiation rather than separable processes. By adopting the theory of articulation, I reject the "assumption that the two moments [of encoding and decoding] are, even analytically, separable, as if each were completed or complete" (Grossberg, "Putting the Pop" 169). Models for my approach include Jackie Stacey's *Star Gazing*, Miriam Hansen's *Babel and Babylon*, Ien Ang's *Watching Dallas*, and Janice Radway's *Reading the Romance*, all of which study female audiences or cultural forms aimed at women. Stacey and Hansen attempt to historicize spectatorship by looking at the social and public context of cinema-watching for fans of female stars in the 1940s and 1950s, and for female viewers of the spectacle of the male body in early silent film. Ang and Radway locate politics in the processes of reading and viewing, but analyze the text as setting limits on the range of interpretations. My project synthesizes their approaches by examining the symbiotic relation between text, sociohistorical context, and audience response. I concur with Janice Radway's belief that ethnographic studies of reading should not be a replacement for textual studies but should be part of a multilayered approach (*Reading the Romance* 5–6).

Many psychoanalytic and formalist critics have reacted defensively against the cultural studies' call to investigate consumption. Mary Ann Doane voices the general disdain of psychoanalytic critics for the practice of ethnography because it is based on the "working assumption that the primary effects of the media concern consciousness" rather than the unconscious (*Camera Obscura* 146). Psychoanalytic critics complain that audience research reveals only easily articulated responses rather than hard-to-access unconscious reactions. By adhering to the common critical practice of viewing the female spectator as "a concept, not a person" (*Camera Obscura* 142), Doane neglects to consider the possibility that human audiences could offer any knowledge about the process of spectatorship, or even the functionings of the unconscious. Her logic—that viewers have nothing useful to tell us about the workings of the human mind—ignores the fact that the principles of psychoanalysis were predicated upon case studies of patients. Despite her condescending attitude toward real viewers, Doane makes an important defense of theory, arguing that "forms of abstraction are crucial to thought itself and are not necessarily in conflict with the 'real.' Our abstractions are our realities. We live them every day" (*Femmes Fatales* 10). This insightful point should not, however, be used as a defense against testing one's theories in real-life situations or on real human subjects. People need abstractions, but theories can also become untethered from reality.

Just as the researchers of the Birmingham Centre for Cultural Studies use ethnography to "develop and internally test" Marxist theory (Grimshaw, Hobson, and Willis 76), I use interviews with audiences to test and revise the suppositions of identification theory. Psychoanalytic critics like Doane might complain that my work privileges easy-to-access conscious responses and ignores the unconscious. Yet such an argument underestimates the fluid connections that can be forged between the unconscious and conscious minds, and between the psychic and the socio-political, particularly through the process of identification. In *The Threshold of the Visible World*, Kaja Silverman underscores the ability of the conscious mind to access and change the process of the unconscious (3–5). Although film viewers often unconsciously identify with dominant social positions portrayed on screen, Silverman argues that they can be reeducated by radical films to identify with and idealize "disprized bodies" in subordinate social positions (26). She concludes: "These are not lessons that we can ever unconsciously learn, they must be taught to us over and over again at the only site at which knowledge is possible—at the site, that is, of consciousness" (226–27). Although Silverman analyzes textual codes with the use of psychoanalytic theory rather than focusing on reception (other than her own), her insights resonate with my work on the political identifications of audiences of postmodern melodrama. I investigate the moments at which subconscious identifications surface into the conscious mind and thus become open to politicization. Like the experimental films Silverman analyzes, postmodern melodramas aim to push identifications out of the unconscious and into the light, where they can be consciously considered and perhaps influence political praxis. And as Silverman implies, such texts may have the power to alter our unconscious psychic investments and alignments as well.

Many textualist critics of audience research also voice concerns about the status of the evidence. Literary critics, wary of social scientific methodology, rightly question the idea that "objective truth" about consumption can be found in empirical data. Audience researchers trained in the humanities express similar concerns about some of the scientific suppositions of ethnographic work (Ang, "Wanted" 103). Janice Radway criticizes her own search for empirical truth, in a 1991 retrospective introduction to *Reading the Romance*. In what she calls a misguided attempt to avoid subjective interpretation, her book employed multiple-choice questions and broke down the responses of her subjects into statistical data. As ethnographer Valerie Walkerdine notes, "there are no easy matters of facts and comforts that may be drawn from statistics" (*Daddy's Girl* 70). Indeed, my interview groups of 31, 44, and 30 people may not be "statistically significant" samples by the standards of hard-scientific research, but social scientists have themselves begun to question the validity of a quantitative approach that strives for objective "facts" via statistical analysis (see Porter; Longino; Mark Smith). My own approach to ethnography is informed by my humanities training in textual analysis, accompanied by a suspicion of the drive for objective truth that still lurks in the social sciences. I examine audience responses as narratives, paying attention to the discourses that audiences use to describe their reactions and interpretations, and placing emphasis on the contradictions and complexities of those narratives. I do not view these narratives as offering a totalizing truth about the reception of sentimental postmodernism. Yet the reception story that I uncovered reveals some important detail about the socio-political significance of these texts, and about the process of identification at this particular historical moment. We can never hope to explain how reception works in any universal manner, but can only work to produce local histories and to measure them against one another. An ethnographer working in psychology and cultural analysis, Valerie Walkerdine suggests that a postmodern questioning of Truth need not make empirical work impossible (*Daddy's Girl* 60). Nonetheless, she underscores the difficulty of producing knowledge without recourse to truth claims: "how can we present stories in all their complexity when the rest of the world is still sold on truth?" (*Daddy's Girl* 75). In her essay "Situated Knowledges," Donna Haraway has similarly encouraged scientific researchers to treat knowledge as partial and situated. Like Walkerdine and Haraway, I present my ethnographic work as a form of knowledge about reception, but as a story that explicitly acknowledges the contingency of "truth" by highlighting the diverse and conflicting interpretations of audiences.

While my study distances itself from a scientific search for "hard facts" about reception (Nardocchio 2), I am nonetheless seeking a better understanding of how some individuals have used cultural texts to make sense of their world. To this end, I employed a mixture of qualitative interviews and quantitative surveys, and adopted "naturalistic" as well as "interventionist" methods (de Beaugrande 197). Like many cultural studies reception scholars, I prefer qualitative interviews because they allow attention to discourses and to individual difference. David Morley and others have criticized the empiricism of quantitative mass-communications research, which uses multiple-choice questionnaires to obtain objectified knowledge. As he rightly points out, multiple-choice questions do not tell the whole story, since a "yes" answer may mean different things for different people (Morley, *Nationwide* 31). However, I chose the questionnaire method for my study of the *Northern Exposure* Internet fanclub because of the geographic dispersal of the group, and because they also interact via the written word in their online posts. In addition to the interventionist methods of the survey, I also employed the "naturalistic" technique of analyzing posts to the *Northern Exposure* Internet newsgroup. Although the study that follows does present some statistical information, such as percentages of similar responses and correlations between interpretations and social backgrounds, I focus primarily on the language used to express interpretations and responses. In the *Northern Exposure* survey, multiple-choice questions were always followed by broader short-answer questions which asked the respondents to use their own words, so that I could compare the two answers for qualification. Discrepancies between my constructed choices and the respondents' own explanations were revealing because they highlighted the subjective nature of interpretation and its connection to the cultural discourses available to the viewer.

My research protocol—soliciting audience responses well after the respondents had initially encountered the texts—differs from a model employed by empirical researchers in the social sciences. Social science experiments are often constructed to solicit responses during or immediately after reading or viewing, to get a "temporally unfolding *experience* of a text rather than its consummating *interpretation*" (Miall and Kuiken 239). While the goals of psychologists are often to ascertain general principles of cognitive functioning, I am more interested in how an experience of a cultural product is remembered, shaped in dialogue with others, and solidified over time into an interpretation that is lasting rather than fleeting. Particularly in my study of *Kiss of the Spider Woman*, some readers and viewers had not "experienced" the text in years, but they still retained potent memories of their responses. The ability of these responses and interpretations to endure the test of time is precisely what made them interesting to me. Since the goal of my research was to gain access to how people make sense and make use of texts, both my interviews and questionnaires employed open-ended questions that engendered long and complex responses (see the appendices for sample questionnaires and interview transcripts). Throughout the book, I read these response narratives as intricate texts in themselves. Jane Feuer has criticized this treatment of the "audience as text," on the grounds that it endlessly defers meaning and displaces interest away from people and once again onto texts. Feuer also argues that if audience responses are read as representations, then "the reception theorist constantly risks falling back into an empiricism of the subject, by granting a privileged status to the interpretations of the audience over those of the critic" (qtd. in Morley, "Changing Paradigms" 24). Her conclusion, then, is that discourse-based audience studies offer no greater insight than speculative textual readings done by psychoanalytic film theorists, which she prefers. By implying that viewers are mere dupes who are totally unable to analyze themselves, Feuer's conclusions ultimately serve to legitimate the elitism of critics. Feminist film historian Miriam Hansen counters such theoretical elitism by arguing that "we need to grant the 'ordinary' female viewer a certain interpretive capability, a reflective distance in relation to the roles she is expected to assume" (*Camera Obscura* 172). Siegfried J. Schmidt, a key theorist of the systemic and empirical approach to literature, urges empirical researchers to "de-trivialize" their research subjects by treating them as "self-organizing, creative, and autonomous" individuals (146). Since all people are informed by the language and discourses that we have acquired to describe our lived experience, I contend that a study of response narratives produced by individuals can provide valuable insight into the process of textual reception.

While Feuer believes that audience interpretations are taking precedence over critics' interpretations in the field of reception studies, the reverse tendency is far more prevalent. Critics often "read against the grain" of respondents' discourses in an ethically problematic manner. As Walkerdine reminds, the privileged, educated researcher can perpetuate hierarchies of power through a voyeuristic desire for mastery over the "mass audience" ("Video Replay" 181). Ang also worries that the gaze of the researcher often objectifies audiences into an exotic "other," and she calls for more "audience research which is on the side of the audience" ("Wanted" 104). In my research, I strived to emulate Janice Radway's respectful attitude toward her research subjects, female fans of romance novels. Radway listens to what these women say about the meaning of reading in their own lives, and amplifies their own analyses, rather than merely reading against the grain of their responses. She argues that their reading of romances functions as a "minimal but nonetheless legitimate form of protest" against patriarchy (*Reading the Romance* 222). In short, Radway treats her subjects with the respect that McRobbie notes is lacking among academic feminists, who tend to "underestimate the resources and capacities of 'ordinary' women and girls . . . to participate in their own struggles as women but quite autonomously" (McRobbie, "Politics" 53). Likewise, I have attempted to learn *from* the audiences in my study, rather than merely learning *about* them, like butterflies under a microscope. While attending to inconsistencies in their interpretations, I have nonetheless tried to respect each person's response. Rather than dismissing them as confused, I underscore the difficulty of navigating mixed-code texts and stress that no one's ideology is ever seamless or unitary. My goal was not to weigh their interpretations against my own, but to investigate what these texts do for them and to uncover what influenced them to respond as they did. In conducting empirical research, Morley and Ang insist on the importance of being open to surprises "not prefigured in one's starting paradigm" (Morley, "Changing" 25), and this advice turned out to be crucial for my project. When I began the research, I did not expect to find such frequent instances of cross-group identification among these audiences, and this finding opened up a much richer line of analysis.

All ethnographers must acknowledge the power that academic researchers wield over their subjects, especially since this power differential can interfere with one's results. If subjects are intimidated, they may alter their responses to try to sound more educated, or to tell the researcher what they think he or she wants to hear (see Seiter, "Making Distinctions"). While it is impossible to construct a power-free interview situation, I adopted several strategies to address the power imbalance that can render ethnographic work politically suspect. Fortunately, my status as a female graduate student helped to reduce the intimidation factor. I also attempted to alleviate anxieties by first answering the respondent's questions about my research goals. I asked them direct questions about whether they felt their gender or sexual identity influenced their readings, so that they could participate in turning a critical lens on themselves. When a person's interpretations or emotional responses echoed my own, I often said so, which created a feeling of solidarity and affirmation that made the interchange more like a friendly conversation. If I felt the person was not easily threatened, I occasionally played devil's advocate, presenting an alternative point of view to which they could respond. David Morley might argue that I talked too much, and that my words pushed audiences into taking up particular stances. In *The "Nationwide" Audience,* Morley contends that by saying little in the interviews, he avoided unduly influencing his respondents. However, I believe that an interchange between two people who each express their thoughts is ultimately much more revealing because it resembles the negotiations that take place in a real conversation, the kind people might have with their friends outside of a movie theater. I tried to maintain a balance between giving the respondents some sense of me as an individual, and muting my own political views so as not to prejudice their responses or provoke them unnecessarily. Adopting a relatively neutral stance was sometimes useful in putting people at ease to express their true thoughts; some even felt comfortable enough to voice anti-semitic or anti-feminist views, which they might not have done had they known my politics or religious affiliation. I only mentioned my own political leanings, such as my feminism, if they were in accord with those of the respondent. Despite these precautions, a few moments of tension did occur, but I view those misunderstandings as productive rather than detrimental to the interviews because they resulted in frank dialogue. I was able to address and partially allay the suspicions of a black man who made assumptions about me because I am white, and of a gay man who wondered why a heterosexual woman was interested in gay culture. (See Appendix A for an annotated transcript of my interview with a queer black man.) During the interviews, I acknowledged my own locatedness at moments when it would serve to open up honest dialogue rather than close it down.

Critics might counter that such interviewing strategies could not wipe away the differences between an academic researcher and a mass-culture fan with little cultural capital (Seiter, "Making Distinctions"). For example, Morley argues that claiming a shared kinship as a fan (as does John Fiske) "merely obscures the researchers' dominant relation to their subjects in terms of access to cultural capital" (*Television* 32). The goal of my interview strategies, however, was not to erase or ignore difference, but rather to prevent differences from impeding communication. Furthermore, a significant difference between my project and many other audience studies is that nearly all of my respondents are middle-class, college-educated, and liberal. Our similar class status and political orientation granted me the position of "insider" and alleviated some of the power differential common to ethnographic work. Differences other than class, however, sometimes moved me to the margins, as in my conversations with gay male fans of *Kiss of the Spider Woman*. My point is that class difference is certainly not the only hurdle to overcome in conducting ethnographic work. Difference comes in many forms and must always be negotiated sensitively. Because I was simultaneously an insider and an outsider among all of the audience groups that I interviewed, I tried to remain aware of how such moments of inclusion and exclusion might impact my analysis. One might assume that I felt a comfortable "insider status" while interviewing academic feminists responding to *The Piano*, since I am one myself. However, since I feel very passionately about my own particular feminist ideology, it was in fact harder for me to analyze without prejudice the responses of those who disagreed with me about feminism and about my favorite film. Walkerdine contends that "[since] it is an impossible task to avoid the place of the subjective in research . . . we should think more carefully about how to utilize our subjectivity as a feature of the research process" (*Daddy's Girl* 59). Instead of striving for impartial detachment, I heeded Walkerdine's advice to record my emotions during the interviews, and to turn an analytical eye upon my own responses to my interview subjects (65). This strategy was particularly relevant given my focus on emotional genres and the unpredictability of identification. Ultimately, by remaining aware of my emotional responses and critical reactions during the interviews, I was able to gain further insight into the role of affect in political identification. Acknowledging one's own subjective investment in the research is crucial if one hopes to negotiate the myriad of possible differences between researcher and subject. Since I was studying audience groups with whom I share ideologies, identities, or simply the position of being a "fan" of a particular text, it was particularly instructive to take note of differences of opinion between myself and the interviewees. Paying attention to moments of chafing and disagreement thus helped to illuminate the very subject of my research—differences in interpretation that abound within supposedly unified or homogeneous groups.

As noted earlier, the readers and viewers that I studied are homogeneous in their class status and educational background (middle-class and college-educated). Studying audience groups with cultural capital gives me the opportunity to fill a gap in cultural studies analyses of reception. Because of cultural studies' origins in Marxist social theory, ethnographers tend to focus on the "subordinate and the disempowered" (Fiske 5), the uneducated consumers of lowbrow mass cultural texts, typified in the figure of the housewife (see Hobson, "Housewives"). Few researchers have studied educated audiences, as if the critic's own reading could stand in for that diverse class of viewers and readers. This bias indicates a false assumption that elite or middle-class people do not consume mass-cultural texts, or that their responses are univocal. Ethnographers often falsely imply that the television-watching masses are somehow separate from the class of the observer. The diverse readings that I encountered among people of similar class backgrounds also make it necessary to question the assumption that class predicts interpretation and taste. In his study of *Nationwide*, Morley organizes his audience groups according to similar socioeconomic positioning, and categorizes each group's interpretations as either dominant, negotiated, or oppositional. By crafting such a neat and schematic grid, Morley reifies essentialist beliefs about class difference, suppressing individual difference and the potential influence of other identities. (Morley reconsiders his class essentialism in *Television, Audiences and Cultural Studies.*) A similar bias can be found in *Distinction*, Bourdieu's study of taste stratification in France, in which he implies that taste for high or low culture necessarily devolves from class. How would Morley and Bourdieu explain the fact that middle-class people with cultural capital enjoy popular sentimentalism as well as the "writerly" qualities of highbrow texts? Rather than focusing solely on class (and education) as a predictor of interpretation and taste, as do many ethnographers, my study examines the impact of a variety of identities—gender, race, religion, ethnicity, sexuality, and political affiliations—upon the process of reading. Instead of simply categorizing people according to "different sectors" (Morley, "Texts" 173), I emphasize differences *within* such sectors and attend to the ways in which individuals are multiply positioned. Regardless of what social identities a researcher may emphasize, one is still faced with the problem of the "creeping essentialism that lurks behind the classificatory move" (Ang, *Living* 116). As Ang argues, by boxing people into social categories, the "inconsistencies and variances within informants' accounts . . . remain unaccounted for, or are even actively repressed" (*Living* 117). This problem rears its head in many studies of reading that focus on a single axis of identity, thereby reducing audiences to their gender, race, or class. For example, Radway's single-axis study of female romance readers could have benefited from a consideration of how class, religion, race, and educational background could result in more diverse patterns of interpretation. By looking at differences among women (e.g., differing feminist ideologies and educational backgrounds), the essay collection *Gendering the Reader*, edited by Sara Mills, moves successfully beyond the essentialism of earlier work on "the woman reader." Such anti-essentialist studies of audience consumption, however, are rare.

I speculate that the history of disciplinary enmities between ethnographers and psychoanalytic critics has unfortunately led audience researchers to ignore new psychoanalytic theories of subjectivity focused on the fluidity and intersectionality of identity. Walkerdine, one of the few ethnographers who is also interested in psychoanalytic theories of subjectivity, laments that "cultural studies has shied away from psychology since the former's inception" (*Daddy's Girl* 7). Walkerdine contends that "cultural studies desperately needs the very work on subjectivity that it rejected along with Screen Theory" (56), and my work responds to this need. My audience ethnographies are informed by anti-essentialist theories of subjectivity, in that I investigate how multiple axes of identity can complicate a viewer or reader's positioning. For example, my chapter on *Kiss of the Spider Woman* investigates differences of interpretation among a group of gay men, differences influenced by political affiliations, gender-identifications as effeminate or macho, and adherence to either an essentialist gay identity or an anti-essentialist queer model. While it is important to disrupt facile, essentializing equations of identities with a particular interpretation, taking a non-essentialist approach does not mean that ethnographers should ignore social groupings altogether. Morley suggests that even if class does not totally determine one's ideologies and interpretations, it does not follow that "any relationship between discursive formations and class formations must be, by definition, 'reductionist'" ("Texts" 172). Although there is no simple one-to-one correspondence between identity and reading, that does not mean that such linkages never occur. My ethnographic work offers a critique of essentialism at the same time as it acknowledges the ways in which we may be situated as raced and gendered people. The social positioning of audience members can influence their interpretation of texts, but we need a less deterministic understanding of the concept of social positioning. Stanley Fish's concept of "interpretive community" remains useful, but the communities he discusses, such as college students and literary critics, are too broadly conceived (see *Is There a Text in This Class?*). In the journal *Poetics*, Birgitta Höijer offers an exemplary model for studying reception that mediates between the psychological and the sociological. Employing the flexible concept of "schemas" from cognitive psychology—the idea that people develop interpretive models based on repetitive life experience—Höijer theorizes that interpretive schemas can be individualized as well as influenced by social groups and cultural conventions. Her multi-layered analysis of television viewers thus takes into account the "private, occupational, educational, and media spheres" that may influence a viewer's interpretation (289).

Merging Fish's interpretive communities and Höijer's concept of "schemas" in my own audience study, I examine subtle shadings within the umbrella categories of race, gender, and sexuality, and even within interpretive communities such as academic feminists, breaking down such identities and social locations into smaller components, subcommunities, and individualized schemas. For example, all the women I interviewed did not interpret *The Piano* in the same way, but those who espoused gender-essentialist, difference-feminist beliefs did tend to produce similar readings; those women were also influenced by their occupations as sexual assault counselors or by their personal experience as victims of assault. My ethnographic study thus avoids sociological determinism by emphasizing that identities are ideological rather than biological, and multiplicitous rather than unitary. Despite the resistance of identification theorists to such empirical work, I contend that ethnography can be an important means of opening up new theoretical ground about subjectivity and identification.

Political Identification

The concept of identification has preoccupied a wide range of thinkers because of its social and psychic importance as a means by which our identities and ideologies are constructed and reinforced. Psychoanalysts Laplanche and Pontalis define identification as the "psychological process whereby the subject assimilates an aspect, property or attribute of the other and is transformed, wholly or partially, after the model the other provides. It is by means of a series of identifications that the personality is constituted and specified" (205). Building on psychoanalytic principles as well as Althusser's theory of interpellation, "apparatus" film theorists treat identification as an unconscious process of self-recognition that works to solidify unitary identities among film viewers. They argue that film structures repeatedly place or "suture" the viewer into the same subject positions, "thereby giving the subject the illusion of a stable and continuous identity" (Silverman, *The Subject of Semiotics* 221). Although apparatus film theory has waned in influence since its advent in the 1970s, this view of identification still predominates in film criticism, as Silverman argued in 1996: "we are far from being liberated of this assumption today—that the pleasure of identifying with a fictional character always turns on the spectator's rediscovery of his or her preordained place within gender, class, and race. Secondary identification, in other words, is frequently equated with interpellation in the dominant fiction" (*Threshold* 85).

Few audience researchers have attempted to evaluate the usefulness of such theories by investigating the identification patterns of actual viewers, as opposed to theoretical spectators. Empirical studies that address identification tend to adopt the "commonsense" view that men simply identify with men, whites with whites, etc., and thus their sociological determinism echoes the essentialist premises of the apparatus film critics. A notable exception is Jackie Stacey's fine book *Star Gazing*, in which she uses empirical work with female fans of classic Hollywood stars to re-evaluate identification theory. Through her research with fans, Stacey presents identification as a more active and diverse process than psychoanalysts admit. I argue that such a reconsideration has become increasingly necessary given the recent sea-change in representations of identity in postmodern texts, and in the conscious self-constructions of audiences. Developed to explain the spectator's relationship to classical films that rely upon essentialist identity categories, the "suture" model of apparatus film theory is inadequate to explain how audiences identify with texts that reflect and encourage a postmodern questioning of identity politics. My work with audiences thus contributes to recent efforts, in feminist and queer studies, to rethink identification in order to take into account a poststructuralist understanding of the subject as mobile, "contradictory, divided, and fragmented" (Mayne 100).

A crucial difference between my ethnographic approach and these recent poststructuralist theories is that many of them continue to base their arguments upon psychoanalytic premises and therefore only discuss identification as an unconscious process. My study argues, on the other hand, that identification is a form of articulation that can also involve a conscious process of negotiation between self and other. For example, feminist audiences of *The Piano* recognized that their identification and/or disidentification with Ada was influenced by their particular feminist ideologies. Their identification process included a conscious understanding of the politics of gender identity, a possibility often ignored by psychoanalytic theorists such as Anne Friedberg, who contends that "identification with a film star does not entail a cognitive choice" ("Denial of Difference" 36). Furthermore, the texts I have chosen pose a challenge to this body of theory because they explicitly aim to move identity formation out of the realm of the unconscious and into the conscious mind of viewers, where it can be analyzed as a social process with political significance. Silverman is one of the few psychoanalytic theorists interested in conscious identifications and their relationship to political concerns. As I have discussed earlier in this chapter, she theorizes a feedback look between the conscious and unconscious minds. Like the postmodern melodramas I address, the radical films Silverman analyzes push identification into the realm of the conscious mind, facilitating an "opening up of the unconscious to otherness" (*Threshold* 184). By presenting audiences with conflicted representations of identity (as either essentialist or anti-essentialist), postmodern melodramas upset an unconscious process of sliding into familiar and stable subject positions. These texts aim to produce critical distance, but they avoid the avant-garde strategy of disrupting identification altogether, a tactic that has been criticized by some feminist film scholars (see Silverman, *Threshold* 85; and Gaines, "Women and Representation" 81). Instead, postmodern melodramas encourage identification as do most melodramas, but they work to bring identification into consciousness, to make audiences aware of the process and its potential political significance. As Silverman argues, the capacity to provoke identification may be "one of [film's] greatest political assets, since it represents the potential vehicle for a spectatorial self-estrangement" (*Threshold* 85). Although she links this capacity to film's visual properties, I also examine the ways in which literary texts foster self-alienating identifications with subversive political effect.

In addition to an unwillingness to discuss conscious, ideological identifications, another drawback of some psychoanalytic theories is their reliance on universalizing and essentialist models for understanding gender. While psychoanalysis is a theory of the social construction of the psyche, Freud nonetheless based many of his ideas about gender on the recognition of biological difference (e.g., woman as castrated). As Jane Gaines argues, because Freud "strikes a mean between the biological and the social" ("Women" 80), his ideas have been used to support biological essentialism. On the other hand, Lacan has been hailed as an anti-essentialist who focuses on discourses rather than bodies (Doane, *Femmes Fatales* 172), but his notion of the "subject position" nonetheless relies on essentialist underpinnings (Fuss, *Essentially* 29). Even more problematic, Diana Fuss argues, is his universalizing treatment of woman as lack (12). Feminist identification theorists who adopt Freudian and Lacanian notions often end up reifying gender difference. Spectatorship theorists Mulvey and Doane, for example, neglect to consider female viewers as actively desiring subjects and voyeurs for whom gender is only one of many identity formations. The women in my study groups did not always identify with other women, since their sense of gender identity varies widely. These apparatus theorists of the "male gaze" also adopt an essentialist view of masculinity, ignoring that men may identify with rather than objectify female characters. Their exclusive focus on gender difference leads them to underestimate the differences *within* each gender, caused by other social identities such as race and class, or by political ideologies such as anti-racism or feminism. In my view, any current study of identification needs to acknowledge that "subjectivity does not devolve from the body; . . . [but] is defined by social and historical processes that are irreducible to singular categories" (Rodowick 139–40).

Theorists in the 1970s and 1980s often viewed identification as a means of solidifying unitary identities among spectators. This idea, which conflates identity with identification, has also been referred to as the "folk" or common-sense view of identification—that women identify with women, blacks with blacks., etc. Such a limiting definition does not address the complexity of identity and the ways in which people are multiply located. The problem begins with Freud, who theorized in *Group Psychology* that identification is "typically masculine" and phallic, serving to solidify and erect the subject (105). Building on this idea, Friedberg argued that classical film offers fixed gender identities, encouraging the viewer to solidify one's own identity as an existing type of femininity or masculinity as a result (Friedberg, "A Denial of Difference"). The related notion of "suture" is based on the idea that spectators are stitched into static subject positions within the narrative fabric. The belief that identification shores up and rigidifies socially conservative identities has led many feminist critics to view it negatively. Mulvey and Doane focus on identification as a form of entrapment that seduces female spectators of classical film to acquiesce to their "proper" feminine role (see Doane, *The Desire to Desire*). While most identification theories concern gender identity, many critics within race studies treat identification as a means of solidifying racial identity. Jacqueline Bobo's study of "the black female audience" for *The Color Purple* portrays this group as a unified block identifying with the film and novel in the same basic way; little attention is paid to exceptions that might complicate the picture. Manthia Diawara simply grafts Mulvey's theories onto a race model, arguing that film is created for a white spectator, so a black spectator's only resort is to resist identification. While bell hooks agrees that black women often take an oppositional stance to mainstream films, she rightly questions the essentialist assumption (made by Bobo and Diawara) that African Americans, male or female, have an "inherently different field of vision" ("Oppositional Gaze" 128). She reasons that black individuals respond differently to the pressures of dominant cultural values. However, while hooks is attentive to differences among black women, she unfortunately tends to essentialize white spectators as a monolithic block (see "Dreams Conquest"). On the basis of reading negative reviews of *Daughters of the Dust* by white men, hooks concludes that "the impact of racism and sexism so over-determines spectatorship—not only what we look at but who we identify with—that viewers who are not black females find it hard to empathize with the central characters in the movie. They are adrift without a white presence in the film" ("Oppositional Gaze" 130). Although racial identification theory does not often invoke a psychoanalytic model, a reliance on identity politics results in a similar oversimplification of reception that fails to account for differences within a racial group.

Among African American critics such as Barbara Christian and Joyce A. Joyce, the resistance to poststructuralist anti-identitarian theory is a consequence of a desire for empowering notions of racial solidarity (Gates, "Criticism in the Jungle"). As

Fuss points out, "the Afro-American subject . . . begins fragmented and dispersed" (*Essentially* 95), so fragmentation is seen as something to be overcome rather than embraced. Although essentialist principles are a problematic basis for identification theory, I respect the desire for the political empowerment that identity politics can enable. Identification can certainly work to foster group solidarity, but it is also important to consider its potential to destabilize identity boundaries for progressive ends. A key problem with essentialist models is that they define identification as a process of recognizing sameness, disallowing that identification may also entail an awareness of difference. Working with Lacan's concept of the mirror stage in "Visual Pleasure and Narrative Cinema," Mulvey reduces identification to the simple pleasure of recognizing oneself as in a mirror (17–18). Freud's identification theories have generally emphasized sameness over difference: "identification endeavors to mould a person's ego after the fashion of the one that has been taken as a model" (*Group Psychology* 106). Claiming that identification "disallows difference" (36), Friedberg asserts that "identification can only be made through recognition, and all recognition is itself an implicit confirmation of the ideology of the status quo" ("Denial of Difference" 45). Hinton echoes these theorists by focusing on "identification as resemblance," or a search for one's own "self-ideality" (26). Stacey has criticized those who view identification as a process of recognizing similarity and thereby perpetuating static views of the self; in contrast, she looks at fans whose identifications with female stars "involve the productive recognition of differences between femininities" (*Star* 171). She writes: "the identifications represented in these letters [from fans] speak as much about partial recognitions and fragmented replications as they do about the misrecognition of a unified subjectivity in an ego ideal on the screen" ("Feminine Fascinations" 208). My study also focuses on people identifying with subjects whom they recognize to be different than themselves. Many of the gay men in my study of *Kiss of the Spider Woman*, for example, identified with the gay character while simultaneously asserting that they are not as effeminate and apolitical as he is. The concept of a singular identity is simply a fallacy, since there are many ways of experiencing any identity. As Butler reminds, "femininity itself might offer an array of identificatory sites" rather than a single one (*Bodies* 239). Likewise, many women identified with Ada McGrath in *The Piano* "as a woman," but experienced that identity in multitudinous ways.

Freud's theory of identification is particularly problematic, I argue, because it relies on a notion of "incorporation." Identification, Freud reasons, operates like a hostile, colonizing incorporation that "behaves like a derivative of the first, oral phase . . . in which the object that we long for and prize is assimilated by eating and is in that way annihilated as such" (*Group Psychology* 105). Freud wrongly assumes that identification always involves turning the other into the same, thereby erasing difference. This theory cannot account for the fact that many members of my audience group experienced a more ambivalent identification process, which involved a recognition of incongruities and a respect for difference rather than a desire for assimilation. My ethnographic work underscores that identification is often ambivalent and partial because of the contradictory, multiple, and fractured nature of subjectivity. Among my audience group, I saw many instances of ambivalence in which people both identified and disidentified with the same character. Their selves were not completely swallowed up by the other, and vice versa. Television critic Liebes describes several kinds of ambivalent identifications: wanting to be like someone but knowing that you could never be; hating someone but fearing you are like them; identifying with someone but wishing that you were different from them. Cognitive film theorist Berys Gaut persuasively argues that identification is partial or "aspectual" rather than whole, since two subjects are never equivalent. Some empirical research in psychology suggests that "witnessing" and/or "empathy" may be better terms for what film spectators do than "identification" because these terms recognize the boundary between viewer and character (see Tan; Zillmann). As Ed Tan reminds, "total identification, in a literal sense, would end in delusion" (*Emotion* 190).

Although some theorists have addressed ambivalence in identification, I use the term "ambivalent" differently. A common argument is that an ambivalent identification involves both a connection and a refusal, sympathy as well as hatred. Freud's theory of incorporation admits this kind of ambivalence, since identification "can turn into an expression of tenderness as easily as a wish for someone's removal" (*Group Psychology* 105). In *Totem and Taboo*, he argues that the "sons hate their father but they also simultaneously love and admire him" (Fuss, *Identification* 34). Likewise, Butler notes that "identification is always an ambivalent process" (*Bodies* 126), since it can include "unresolved aggression" (143). However, I do not read the ambivalent identifications among my audience groups as necessarily indicative of hatred or aggression lying beneath outward sympathy. Many of these people were able to identify while also recognizing their differences in respectful and non-hostile ways, in the ethic of "live and let live." Instead of reading ambivalence as reflective of the aggressive and violent underpinnings of the universal human psyche, as do these psychoanalytic theorists, I see ambivalent identification as a positive social development, an awareness of difference that prevents a colonizing incorporation yet leaves room for sympathy and connection. More so than Freud, Lacan acknowledges that identification involves the recognition of difference, but he sees these moments as frustrating for the individual, who despairs that he can never equal his ideal other. Lacan argues that the subject is always alienated and split between self and an ideal image/other. While Lacan's concept of the split subject prefigures poststructuralist notions of identity as contradictory and unstable, I find it problematic because it is predicated on a premise of psychic hostility just like Freud's theories—that the self and other are "rivals" rather than teachers or potential allies (Lacan, *Ecrits* 22). There is no consideration in Lacan's theories that encounters with the other could help to broaden and enrich the self.

Jessica Benjamin's theory of intersubjective "identificatory love" offers a welcome alternative to Freud and Lacan's view of identification as a hostile take-over. Her theory aptly describes the ambivalent identifications I found among my audience groups. A theorist of the school of relational psychology, Benjamin argues that Freud's theory of "internalization implies that the other is consumed, incorporated, digested by the subject self. . . . The joy of discovering the other, the agency of the self, and the outsideness of the other—these are at best only fuzzily apprehended by internalization theory" (*Bonds* 43) which cannot "comprehend the simultaneous process of transforming and being transformed by the other" (49). Her theory of "identificatory love" describes a relation that involves the "ability to share feelings and intentions without demanding control, to experience sameness without obliterating difference" (*Bonds* 48). She posits that such a "mutual recognition" of the subjecthood of the Other could lead to a transformation of the self, and she explicitly connects identificatory love to the political projects of feminism and anti-racism. Instead of looking at ambivalent identification as a form of unconscious hostility or alienation, I read it along with Benjamin as a sign of mutual recognition—a positive form of co-feeling or "double identification" that fosters respect for the unknowable difference of the Other (Benjamin, *Shadow* 107). Such ambivalent identifications also illuminate "the possibility of multiple and contradictory identities coexisting in the same subject at the same time" (Fuss, *Identification* 34). By pointing out subtle differences between themselves and characters that they identified with, these audience members were attesting to the complexity of subjectivity. Furthermore, many of the people in my audience study identified with two seemingly opposed subject positions at once—both male and female, both racial minorities and whites, or both gay and heterosexual characters.

Several theorists have attempted to address this kind of identificatory oscillation, but they tend to focus only on vacillation between gender polarities (see de Lauretis; Clover; Silverman; Cora Kaplan; Hansen, "Pleasure"; Mulvey, "Afterthoughts"). Teresa de Lauretis has discussed a "double or split identification" of the female spectator with both the active male gaze and the passive feminine image. Her theory of the ambivalence of women's cinematic identification is predicated on Freud's notion that some women are "bisexual," experiencing a "repeated alternation between periods in which femininity or masculinity gain the upper hand" (Freud, "Femininity" 131). Like Lacan, de Lauretis views this ambivalence or split identification negatively. She sees it as a trap that seduces women into consenting to femininity by allowing a compensatory but illusory identification with the power of the male hero. De Lauretis does not consider the liberatory possibilities of such gender oscillation; nor does she allow that men may also experience double identifications with masculinity and femininity, as did many of the men in my study. Her overemphasis on binary gender difference blinds her to the fact that women may identify with men (or vice versa) because they share other identities (such as race) or ideologies. Because it is too narrowly conceived, her theory cannot explain the wide variety of ambivalent and fluid identifications that both men and women in my audience groups experienced.

My research findings corroborate recent theories that move beyond unitary and binary models to assert the multiplicity of identity. Lesbian theorist Sallie Munt describes a "multivalent self" based on a useful model of "intersecting plates, so that the ground of the self shifts and recombines with the intervention and chafing of other selves, which sculpt a new self based on intersubjectivity" (2). Butler uses a similar figure to describe the subject as a series of intersecting "vectors of power" (*Bodies* 167) that can include sexuality, gender, and race (see Gaines's "White Privilege" and Wiegman for similar analyses of intersectionality). An understanding of the self as intersubjective and dialogic helps to explain how it could be possible to identify with many seemingly distinct or even antagonistic subject positions in a narrative, as did many of my interview subjects. My interviews revealed the intersubjectivity of these audience members, uncovering interconnecting vectors of affiliations and experiences that resist efforts to place these subjects into tidy identity boxes. I also contend that recognizing one's multiple identifications may have crucial political consequences. As Butler suggests: "if that very subject produces its coherence at the cost of its own complexity, the crossings of identifications of which it is itself composed, then that subject forecloses the kinds of contestatory connections that might democratize the field of its own operation" (*Bodies* 115). Wary of the "violence of exclusion" that can result from identity politics, Butler instead favors an "expansive set of connections" that allow political coalitions (*Bodies* 118). As Benjamin suggests, recognizing intersubjectivity is crucial to any politics of inclusion, where "the self as subject can and will allow all its voices to speak, including the voice of the other within" (*Shadow* 108). In studying the identifications of audience members, I have seen many examples of what Munt calls the "visiting self, which leans into the experience of others and listens and learns" (4). For many of the people I interviewed, identification is "an amalgam of experience and desire, a process not of exclusion, but of 'pivoting.' This sensibility produces a sense of belonging, a sense of 'we,' which is not an attempt to universalize" (Munt 4).

Cross-group identification has been a key concern for feminist critics, who fall into two camps—those who view identification across gender lines as illusory, and those who view it as potentially subversive. These two camps are distinguished by essentialist versus anti-essentialist views of gender identity. In "Afterthoughts on 'Visual Pleasure'," Mulvey admits that female spectators may identify with an active male protagonist, but she calls such an identification a sad act of transvestitism that leaves female spectators without a "stable sexual identity" (30); de Lauretis takes a similar attitude in her description of double identification. Doane also views the pursuit of a "well-defined subjectivity" (*Desire* 177) as a positive goal for women that is often thwarted by film, rather than considering the liberatory possibilities of a blurring of the boundaries of the subject via destabilizing identifications. I take issue with the suggestion that "transvestite" cross-gender identification is to be lamented as illusory, a kind of false consciousness for women. Women viewers identifying with male characters could be read as a progressive rather than a regressive political development, a reflection of a growing anti-essentialist feminist sensibility and a rejection of female stereotypes. Instead, I align myself with such scholars as Silverman, Carol Clover, and Eve Sedgwick, who have explored the potentially subversive effects of a loosening of the boundaries of the self through cross-gender identification. Clover, Silverman, and Gaylyn Studlar have all examined male identification with women as a destabilizing process with progressive political effects. Studlar sees her work on male masochism and submission to the female gaze as a corrective to that of Mulvey and Doane, who neglect the "possibilities of male identification with the female (even as an ego ideal) or his identification with a 'feminized' masculine character" (278). Similarly, in her book *Men, Women, and Chain Saws*, Clover discusses the "Final Girl" survivor in slasher horror films as an androgynous figure, both hero and victim; this narrative device allows young male viewers to identify with the position of victimized femininity. While Studlar's generalizing psychoanalytic model unequivocally celebrates male masochism, Clover qualifies the subversion that she finds in this gender-bending identification, since it still involves a projection and deflection of male fears onto a girl. Despite the masculine address of the genre, Clover finds slasher films to be transgressive because they play with gender, allowing males to explore "an imaginative curiosity about the feminine" (55).

Silverman's work on the radical potential of "excorporative" identifications has been the strongest influence on my own perspective. Her book *Male Subjectivity at the Margins* avoids assigning a fixed political significance to a cross-over identification with the feminine. Looking at a range of texts, Silverman considers the regressive, imperialistic elements of Lawrence of Arabia's masochistic identifications as well as the radical aspects of Fassbinder's films, which involve an "assault on male subjectivity" (265) and a total loss of self in the feminine other. Similarly, I locate my arguments about cross-group identification in the local context of each particular text/audience interface. Silverman's work also challenges Freud's theory of "identificatory incorporation" by focusing on excorporative or "heteropathic identification" as a "lifting of the psyche up and out of the body . . . into other sites of suffering" (275). This masochistic or empathetic form of identification "works against the consolidation of the isolated ego" (275) and against the "imperialism of the self" (265), thus offering a powerful political attack on masculinity and violence. In her more recent work, *The Threshold of the Visible World*, Silverman discusses excorporative identification as an "active gift of love" (74) that involves "forming an imaginary alignment with bodily coordinates which cannot be assimilated to one's own" (71) and that may in fact be culturally devalued. She builds her theory upon analysis of political films such as Isaac Julien's *Looking for Langston*, which encourages spectators to idealize black, gay bodies. Echoing Silverman's hope that cross-group identification can work as an agent of "psychic and social change" (85), this study locates such potential not only in experimental political cinema, but also in the realm of popular culture.

In the field of queer studies, theorists striving for a politics of coalition have also been interested in the radical potential of cross-group identification. Critical race theorists, in contrast, tend to be more skeptical of cross-racial empathy. Gay male identification with women has long been a focus for theorists of camp and drag; in his book *Heavenly Bodies*, Richard Dyer discusses Marilyn Monroe and Judy Garland as stars whom gay men have seen as sympaticos in suffering. Silverman makes the important point that a gay male identification with the feminine has been too quickly dismissed in the backlash against the "inversion" theory of homosexuality, and she argues that it still offers a subversive "phallic divestiture, as a way of saying 'no' to power" (*Male Subjectivity* 389). Eve Sedgwick has inverted this familiar identification by discussing her own cross-group fascination with gay male culture. In *Tendencies*, Sedgwick notes that "the word 'queer' itself means across" (xii) and proposes her book as a study of the "passionate queer things that happen across the lines that divide genders, discourses, and 'perversions'" (xiii). Challenging the idea that sexual identity necessarily predicts one's identifications, Sedgwick sees queerness as an affiliation, a boundary-breaking coalition that embraces once-excluded bisexuals and transgendered people. The queer coalition has even made room for anti-homophobic heterosexuals such as critics Lauren Berlant and Michael Warner, although the politics of this particular cross-group identification has been the subject of some debate (see Bersani; Thomas; Sedgwick).

Scholars and critics who explore the politics of identification across racial and ethnic lines, rather than across gender and sexual boundaries, take a much more negative view of the process, particularly when members of the dominant culture claim to identify with minority others in a text. Because of the recent influence of postcolonial theory, such crossings are now disdained as a form of appropriation akin to Freud's incorporation concept, as bell hooks implies in her essay "Eating the Other." Postcolonial theory has rightly led critics such as Chow to be wary of the assimilationist desires lurking behind facile identifications with "the native, the oppressed, the savage;" this fascination and drive for knowledge of the other can mask a "not-too-innocent desire to seize control" (Chow 53). In a chapter on Fanon, Fuss concludes that "identification . . . is an imperial process, a form of violent appropriation in which the Other is deposed and assimilated into the lordly domain of self" (*Identification* 145). While there was clearly need for a correction to the rosy picture of cross-cultural identification drawn by advocates of multicultural harmony, critics have gone too far to the other extreme, dismissing such crossings as necessarily colonizing and politically retrograde. We need the cautionary tales offered by Michael Rogin and Karen Sanchez-Eppler, who critique the appropriative nature of white identifications with blackness, but other sides to this story are often neglected or suppressed by politically leftist critics. A typical rhetorical move made by studies of cross-racial identification is to lament that the liberating potential of such boundary-blurring exchanges is almost never realized in cultural representation. In her study of abolitionist fiction and rhetoric, Sanchez-Eppler was thwarted in her aim "to tell a happier story about the insight and strength to be found in strategies of coalition" (13) when she found so much evidence of the exploitation of black slave women by abolitionist white women. Despite her confessed "utopic hopes," Robyn Wiegman reads integrationist literature and film as ultimately wedded to white authority, and concludes that "the transformatory hope of identifying with the pain and suffering of others seems ever more bound to an imperialistic cast" (200). In her book *Racechanges*, Susan Gubar sees visual images of cross-racial imitation, masquerade, and identification as potentially radical in their denaturalizing function, but concludes that they so "rarely find egalitarian expression" (241). Gubar theorizes that mimetic representation always "poses the threat of violation" and "inevitably leads to the disappearance of the other's otherness" (245). It is notable that these similar stances and conclusions are reached by white anti-racist scholars whose own critical work attests to the radical potential of some acts of cross-racial affiliation. In our zeal to avoid celebratory analyses that underestimate the power of white hegemony, is the only possible critical stance one of despair?

While these writers take a despairing tone, Doris Sommer stridently condemns cross-racial identification and empathy. Focusing on the narrative strategies that ethnic writers use to refuse access to white readers, Sommer dismisses the sympathy of white liberals as an "appropriation in the guise of an embrace" ("Resistant Texts" 543) and a "violation by sentimentality" (*Proceed with Caution* 22). Arguing that "empathy is the egocentric energy that drives one subject to impersonate another, the calamitous dismissal of politics by feeling" (*Proceed* 22), she echoes Freud's view of identification as a hostile form of envy and a "metaphoric" substitution of the self for the other that erases difference. Sommer's disdain for a sentimental "politics of feeling" replicates the stance of the modernist Frankfurt School and inadvertently castigates the many minority writers who have relied heavily on affective strategies to further their political goals. While Sommer calls the distancing strategy of some minority writers a "life and death game to stop us short" (*Proceed* 30), it seems to me that a lack of identification between racial groups is much more likely to lead to life-and-death crises such as the Holocaust, "ethnic cleansing" in Serbia, or the ongoing hostilities between Israelis and Palestinians. A useful counterpoint to Sommer can be found in Andreas Huyssen's article concerning the airing of the television miniseries *Holocaust* in Germany, a program which offered German viewers the opportunity to identify emotionally with a family of Jewish victims. Huyssen argues that this mass-culture television text accomplished more important political work among the German populace, resulting in a national "collective mourning" ("Politics of Identification" 135), than had all the avant-garde Brechtian theater and rationalist political dialogue of the postwar years. By allowing Germans to remain at a distance, these avant-garde treatments of the Holocaust fostered a repression of guilt and responsibility, and were powerless to combat the recurrence of anti-semitic sentiments. Clearly, critics ought to consider cross-group identification in local context when analyzing its political effects.

Although Sommer dismisses identification as a metaphoric erasure of difference, she nonetheless offers a useful model for potential alliances between members of dominant and subordinate cultures, calling for a "metonymic association rather than a metaphoric" substitution of self for other ("Resistant Texts" 539). My work with audiences underscores the metonymic qualities of identification and its ability to foster respect for difference. This study reminds that identification can operate much like Audre Lorde's figure of the erotic as a "longing for the other, not to colonize, but to understand" (Munt 24). While identification can allow a facile form of sympathy that does little to destabilize the viewer's own subjectivity, it also allows the possibility of a more radically unsettling form of empathy. Paul Ricoeur writes of the power of empathy: "It is always through some transfer from Same to Other, in empathy and imagination, that the Other that is foreign to me is brought closer" (184). Even as Susan Gubar documents the murderous consequences of so many cultural experiments with racial "crossing," she concludes with a hope for an ethic of "transraciality" in which people "seek neither to become the Other . . . nor to flaunt their alienation from the other" but rather to dwell "in racial borderlands" (248). By underscoring the multiplicity of identity and fostering "ambivalent" identifications, postmodern melodramas similarly adopt the borderlands ethic of the "trans," rather than the "crossing over" model which reifies the boundaries between self and other. My study of audience responses to postmodern melodrama highlights the "excorporative" potential of identification to shake people from the moorings of their identities and steer them in a progressive direction. The chapters that follow challenge the commonly held assumption that identification merely reinforces the status quo.

As my ethnographic case studies demonstrate, these sentimental and melodramatic postmodern texts nourished the political commitments of viewers and readers, helping them to strengthen their identifications as left-leaning political subjects—as feminists, anti-racists, multiculturalists, and critics of heteronormativity. A cultural pessimist might conclude that these popular texts merely satisfy a consumer longing for the emotional experience of coalition, providing a commodified compensation for the loss of a meaningful sphere of political engagement. I contend, however, that literary and visual culture offers a crucial space for keeping alive the notion that social change is possible, by imagining what it might look and feel like to inhabit a world where men and women, gays and straights, whites and ethnic minorities, could be transformed by their identifications with one another.

Chapter Three

The Piano and Feminist Political Identification

One of the most "talked about" feminist films of the 1990s, Jane Campion's *The Piano* provoked vehement debate among both film critics and female viewers. At one otherwise tame New Year's Eve party in 1996, as I described my research to a woman I had just met, she launched into a violent diatribe against the film, which soon attracted five or six others, who began shouting out their own reviews. The fiery conversation ended when another woman stormed off, declaring that she couldn't bear to see her favorite film so maligned, to see Ada "dragged through the mud" once again. Despite critical acclaim that included several Oscars and the prestigious Palme d'Or at Cannes, as well as high box-office gross for an art-house film ($40 million in the U.S.), *The Piano* was a polarizing text; viewers tended to either love it or hate it. Campion's story of Ada McGrath—a mute Victorian woman struggling with expression, sexuality, her prescribed gender role, and her own powerful will—received thoroughly mixed reviews. Some hailed it as a feminist masterpiece, while others contended that it merely perpetuated women's victimization and oppression. In addition to the debate over its ambiguous feminist politics, its aesthetic strategies and generic roots also caused much confusion and disagreement, particularly among reviewers. Some reviewers and audience members thought it pretentious, arty, and overly symbolic, while others disparaged its melodramatic tone and romantic happy ending.

Audience confusion about the film's feminist politics was partly caused by *The Piano*'s formal hybridity—its mixture of art-house and experimental cinematic technique influenced by surrealism and postmodernism, along with the generic strategies of low cultural forms usually associated with women, i.e., melodrama, romance, and the Gothic. Since different genres construct or imply different relationships between text and audience, from melodrama's emotional engagement to the avant-garde's critical distance, audience members' interpretations are usually influenced by what genre or type of narrative they think they are viewing. When these kinds of cultural codes are confounded as in *The Piano*, the process of spectator identification with the text is complicated and results in a multitude of political readings and emotional responses. Because one woman at the New Year's Eve party had expected to see an intellectual, subversive art-house film, she had been annoyed to find instead what she called a "manipulative piece of trite pop culture" with an "insidiously anti-feminist" message. Although postmodern culture has been lauded by critics for its freeing mixture of high and popular cultural aesthetics, such a mixture still provokes anxiety among some viewers and creates confusion about the politics of such a hybrid text. In explicating the dense complexity of the film's meanings, this analysis resists a simplistic equation of high art with subversion and popular culture with retrograde conservatism. The film's generic and narrative hybridity also raises questions that cannot be answered by psychoanalytic theory, the preferred tool of film theorists for understanding spectator identification. A textual reading assuming an "implied spectator" underestimates the social factors influencing viewer responses and cannot fully explain the process of identifying with a text *politically*. To shed light on how viewers respond to such a conflicted text, I interviewed thirty-one self-identified feminists at the University of Virginia (professors, graduate students, and undergraduates). The viewers' interpretations of this film were clearly affected by their previous connections to feminism as a discourse, and by their own identities as sociologists, literary critics, anthropologists, victims of sexual assault, spouses, lovers, women and men. I argue that highly variable audience responses to *The Piano* are a function of its textual hybridity, of the viewers' own intellectual and personal histories, and of shifts in feminism in the 1990s.

Although this film is centrally concerned with gender as a defining aspect of human experience in the 19th century, it simultaneously engages with a postmodern questioning of gender identity. This historical period film about gender and power hit a contemporary nerve, since interrogation of gender as a social category has moved beyond feminist circles to become part of the general public consciousness. Crucial to the reception history of *The Piano* is the extreme fissuring of feminist discourse in the 1990s, as essentialist identity structures faced challenges from postmodern critics. Among the thirty-one respondents in my study, the diversity of feminisms was quite striking, as each expressed an allegiance to one or several of the following particular feminist "identities:" postmodern, anti-essentialist, materialist, psychoanalytic, essentialist, pro-sex, difference-based, lesbian, victims' rights, Marxist, radical separatist, practical or liberal, equal-rights, French feminist, and even postfeminist. These identities informed viewers' interpretations of the text, but did not necessarily predict their responses, because the film invokes or critiques many of these conflicting feminisms. Contemporary debates in feminism are highlighted by this film, because it enacts a conflict between depth and surface models of the self—between essential gendered identity and a deconstruction of gender as socially constructed and mutable. This duality resonated with audiences who struggle to reconcile varied conceptions of gender in their daily lives. This film engages in the postmodern debate about gender identity, but it stages that debate within an intensely emotional realm not usually associated with postmodernism, but rather with melodramatic popular culture. No longer just an obscure academic debate, the postmodern theoretical questioning of identity has become central to our personal lives and our popular texts. Furthermore, the highly political nature of my audience group's emotional reactions underscores an important and often ignored relationship between affect and political identification. What *The Piano* does so effectively is provoke audiences to feel—anger, empathy, fear, sexual desire, love, frustration—and to use those feelings in the service of their ideologies. The film's use of the affective strategies of melodrama makes its postmodern interrogation of gender identity more powerful, bringing politics into the realm of the popular and the everyday.

Psychoanalytic Film Theory versus Reception Theory

Psychoanalytic textual analysis, typified by the journal *Screen*, has been the privileged tool for discussing how women's relationship to language, desire, and to the camera's gaze affects their identification with film texts. This chapter uses interviews with feminist audiences to question some of the premises of feminist "apparatus" film theory. Mulvey began a lengthy debate about the "male gaze of cinema" when she argued that classical film represents woman as lack and above all as an object to be looked at. Classical cinema, she argued in "Visual Pleasure and Narrative Cinema," constructs the viewer as a male attempting to control the enigmatic figure of woman and to ward off fears of castration. Mulvey's use of the Lacanian premise that women are always passive objects of the male gaze rather than active voyeurs launched much theorizing in the 1970s and 1980s about how women enjoy film. Revising her earlier viewpoint in "Afterthoughts on 'Visual Pleasure,'" Mulvey suggested that women can assume the active male spectator position in an act of transvestitism; de Lauretis made a similar point in her theory of women's "double identification" (143–44). Doane, in her books *The Desire to Desire* and *Femmes Fatales,* argued that female spectators have the choice to identify masochistically with a degraded female image on screen, or to distance themselves from the image through the act of masquerade. While these feminist critics are sensitive to the ways that classical film may constrain female spectators, they fail to consider female viewers as actively desiring subjects who are not solely defined by their gender. Not only do these theorists accept a Lacanian equation of passivity and lack with femininity, but they also reduce the male viewer to a voyeuristic eye. Thus they neglect to consider that men may identify with rather than objectify female characters in film, as many of the feminist men I interviewed identified with Ada McGrath in *The Piano.* My findings also challenge Doane's contention that identifying with a woman character who is objectified by men is primarily a masochistic process for the female spectator. For many in this audience group, their identification process was a more empathetic or sympathetic one, involving a connection to Ada but also a recognition of their difference from this nineteenth-century woman with far more limited choices. While psychoanalytic critics pay important attention to the ways that media construct women differently from men, their essentialist approach ignores the socio-historical roots of such female "difference," and obscures the fact that viewer identification is a hugely variable social process. Some psychoanalytic critics such as Pollan and Silverman are responding to these charges of ahistoricism, and are doing excellent work that historicizes particular desires and psychic formations (see Pollan; Silverman, "Fragments of a Fashionable Discourse"). Despite this promising work, most psychoanalytic textual critics remain largely wedded to a master-key system of reading, based on Freud's Oedipal scenarios, that essentializes female sexuality and thus women's relationship to language, looking, and desire. The rigid spectator positions envisioned by these critics simplify and may in fact obscure the processes of viewer interpretation by reducing audiences to sameness. Furthermore, psychoanalytic film criticism tends to ignore the social context in which textual codes are articulated, such as the feminist debates that clearly influenced these viewers of *The Piano.*

This study of film audiences enacts a cultural studies critique of psychoanalytic film criticism, but it also differs in one important aspect from other feminist studies of audiences. Stacey and Radway, in particular, see feminism as their own privileged discourse, a critical model of reading that their interview subjects lack. Unlike Stacey's and Radway's work with apolitical and conservative women, I examine the ways in which these film viewers use popular culture to forge a political and leftist sense of self. Thus feminism is not just the framework of my analysis, but it is also the object of analysis. I am interested in how feminism as a public discourse has shaped people's everyday identities and the way they interpret popular texts. This chapter treats feminism *as* popular culture, not just as a means of reading popular texts that only academic elites can master. I have chosen feminists as my audience group because I consider them to be a popular audience experiencing popular culture. Reception theorists such as Fiske may argue that my audience group is insufficiently popular, because these viewers come from an elite context—the university. Fiske argues that members of the dominant culture can participate in popular culture, "but to do so they must reform their allegiances away from those that give them their social power. The businessman entertaining his colleagues in a private box at a football game is not participating in popular culture" (43). Fiske's division of audiences into dominant and popular is faulty, because many people are ardent consumers of both high and popular texts and can occupy both subordinate and dominant subject positions simultaneously. While some of my audience group used academic discourse to analyze the film, most of the primarily emotional responses were expressed in a common, popular language for discussing film. Feminists in an academic community should not be treated as necessarily outside of or in opposition to "the real world" or "the people." My audience group's discussions of the feminist politics of the film borrowed from popular feminism and reactions against feminism as much as from any academic theorizing. It should also be noted that academic and popular feminism share a rich history of fruitful exchange.

"Academic feminist," then, does not indicate a definitive articulation site, because the ideologies of the respondents were influenced not only by their lives outside the academy, but by disciplinary boundaries as well (e.g., nearly all of the sociologists responded in similar ways to the film's sexual politics). While academic feminists have wrongly been characterized as homogeneous in the popular press, this case study demonstrates that even a single university setting can harbor quite a range of discursive communities and political viewpoints. In her essay "Reading As/Like a Feminist," Sara Mills argues that feminist reception scholars need to acknowledge the existence of a wide range of feminist positions. In opposition to Judith Fetterley's notion that women are "resisting readers" of canonical masculinist texts, Mills conducted a study of women resisting female-authored texts, aiming "to question that there is a unified woman's reading position or even that there is a unified feminist reading position" ("Reading" 31). The diverse response to Jane Campion's film *The Piano* among this group of academic feminists (both female and male) underscores Mills's point and challenges the essentialist assumptions of many reception studies.

Melodrama Meets the Avant-garde

Despite my critique of the textual determinism exhibited by spectatorship theory, I do not deny that the film text can play a crucial role in suggesting to audiences a variety of spectator "positions." In the case of *The Piano*, this positioning process is complicated, however, because of the film's reliance on both high and popular cultural codes. For viewers, genre categories raise expectations about the purpose of the film and the proper audience response. Further, where a text is perceived to fall on the high/low culture continuum can have a significant impact on audience interpretation. In his essay "The Aristocracy of Culture," Bourdieu notes that the normative response to highbrow cultural forms is one of distance and critical appreciation, while popular cultural forms invoke intense participation, both emotional and bodily. The socially acceptable response of the viewer to a particular text, from the pole of distanced appreciation to that of passionate engagement and identification, is suggested both by the textual strategies and by the reception context, such as reviewing, publicity, and type of theaters showing the film.

How, then, did viewers construct their relationship to *The Piano*, a postmodern melodrama which invites both emotional engagement and critical distance simultaneously? Important to my analysis is the film's dual investment in surface and depth models for understanding both textual representation and the self—models that have often been associated with avant-garde art and popular culture respectively. Popular culture has been known for its manipulation of emotions supposedly welling up from the depths of the viewer's psyche and for its acceptance of realism and essentialist identities. In the twentieth century, critics have often defined as "high art" or "avant-garde" those texts which emphasize surfaces of textuality, employ irony, question realism, and deconstruct essential character to reveal the shifting and constructed nature of subjectivity. While I use avant-garde and popular to signify a dichotomy, my usage of the term "avant-garde" may invite contention, since it has been defined as variously as has the term postmodernism. Andreas Huyssen may object to my view of "avant-garde" and "popular" as antonyms, because he argues that the early-twentieth-century subversive "historical avantgarde" (including Dadaism and surrealism) actually tried to break down the barriers between high and popular culture, art and life, before its aesthetic values were co-opted and depoliticized by high modernism (Huyssen, *After the Great Divide* 3–7). While Huyssen's argument is historically accurate, the word "avant-garde" is most often used by literary and film critics to indicate a high cultural break with mimesis, sense, traditional narrative, and rational order. This view aligns the avant-garde with high modernism and places it in an antithetical relationship with popular culture; Barthes outlines a similar dichotomy between "writerly" and "readerly" texts in *S/Z* and *The Pleasure of the Text*. Lyotard also sees the avant-garde as a precursor to his anti-popular version of postmodernism. My usage of the term also derives from the specific context of film. As Anne Friedberg has argued, film historians often present avant-garde cinema and Hollywood melodrama as opposing traditions (*Window Shopping* 165–66).

The Piano can thus be considered postmodern because it combines both high and low cultural strategies—avant-garde and popular. This combination of high and low has been defined as a key feature of postmodern cinema, evident in Robert Altman's *The Player* and the films of the Coen brothers, for example. *The Piano*'s commentary on the process of representation, and the process of representing gendered identities in particular, borrows from avant-garde and postmodern rubrics by questioning realistic representation and essential identities. Yet it also resembles depth-model melodramas by employing "readable" character types and symbols to convey an emotionally drenched scene of heightened realism. This mixture confused reviewers, some of whom were disturbed by inconsistencies in the film's tone and narrative structure, and most of whom simply ignored the film's relationship to melodrama by trying to cast it as an unambiguously highbrow or experimental art film. Many reviewers recognized the film's romantic or Gothic qualities, and they ignored the fact that these genres have usually been considered popular; instead, they compared *The Piano* to high cultural literary texts such as *Wuthering Heights*. The press releases for the film and interviews with Campion also perpetuated this highbrow categorizing. Oddly, Campion did not place her work in a film lineage, but repeatedly cited literary influences, primarily nineteenth-century canonical novels. This literary frame of reference is somewhat curious, since the film's plot structure and devices have much more in common with twentieth-century cinematic melodramas. The plot begins with mute heroine Ada McGrath and her daughter Flora journeying to the New Zealand bush, where Ada is to be wife to Stewart, who acquired her through an arranged marriage. Once there, Ada's strong will and her passionate piano-playing attract neighbor George Baines, with whom she has an affair that causes an explosive reaction from Stewart. Stock elements of the melodramatic film genre, which can all be found in *The Piano*, include a focus on a suffering heroine and the realities of her domestic life, family conflicts, romantic triangles, swelling background music and rich landscape to accentuate the emotional content, dichotomous structures and allegory, and a pronounced emphasis on the symbolic potential of *mise en scène*.

Ada McGrath bears some similarities to heroines of melodramas and Gothics in that she is both a victim and a powerful woman. Campion, in making Ada

McGrath mute, has ironically literalized the stock trope of the silenced martyr. Mute characters abounded both in "women's pictures" of the 1940s such as *Johnny Belinda* (Doane, *Desire* 54–56), and in French theatrical melodrama, which found its roots in pantomime (Brooks 62). The fact that Ada is "sold" to a husband that she has never met also recalls female slave narratives, an early melodramatic form. This film echoes the plot of many Gothic films, such as Hitchcock's *Rebecca,* which depict the anxieties of vulnerable young wives concerning their seemingly dangerous husbands. *The Piano,* however, deviates importantly from Gothics by refusing to redeem Ada's husband Stewart as truly good, refusing to depict Ada as a powerless waif, and refusing to repress Ada's sexual desire. Despite her similarity to other female victims in melodrama, Ada also contains strong reserves of female power and self-sufficiency as do the heroines of the films *Stella Dallas* and *Mildred Pierce*. While Ada is just as headstrong and controlling as Stella Dallas, the end of *The Piano* revises the end of the 1937 film, in that Ada gets to keep her daughter, her sexuality, and her man, whereas Stella sacrifices all. The endings of melodramas and Gothics have been noted as one of their most conservative features, because bourgeois order is usually restored, and any subversive female desires and complaints let loose earlier in the plot are contained (see Mulvey, "Notes on Sirk"). As we will see, *The Piano*'s ending complicates this pattern in important ways, but it nonetheless contains recognizable elements of Hollywood romantic closure, as Ada, Baines, and Flora appear to live happily ever after in their white town house, far from the sexual and dangerous jungle.

The fairy-tale resolutions common to melodrama often depend upon a usage of dichotomous structures, allegory, easily recognized character types, and uncomplicated symbols. In this genre, gender and race are presented as essential identities that overdetermine a character's function in the plot; thus, melodrama offers a depth-model view of the self, implying that the inside equals the outside. Its reliance on legible symbols also suggests a depth-model view of representation (rather than a poststructuralist one), a belief in the power of the signifier to represent the signified (Gledhill, "The Melodramatic Field" 33). *The Piano* employs many dichotomies common to melodrama, such as male/female, primitive/civilized, angel/devil, hero/villain, victim/oppressor, and many overt symbols such as the hatchet, Flora's angel wings, hoopskirts, Ada's silence, and the piano itself. Campion, however, also twists these melodramatic structures in moves much more common to the avant-garde. *The Piano* deconstructs many of those dichotomies and obfuscates some of the symbols, thereby deviating from melodrama's usual attachment to legible meaning and simple categories. Ada's silence is perhaps the single most elusive "symbol" of the film, and the diversity of interpretations offered by my audience group makes it difficult to argue that this film invokes a popular allegory obvious to all viewers. The film also critiques melodrama's frequent essentializing of gendered and racial types (the happy-go-lucky native, the harlot, the virtuous hero) by creating characters who escape their initial typecasting. For example, George Baines evolves from voyeuristic pervert to sympathetic lover, and Flora defies categorization as either angel or devil child. Although many of melodrama's dichotomies and stereotypes are shattered in *The Piano*, some remain, possibly as a testament to the entrenchment of such cultural categories. Maori critic Leonie Pihama has leveled the charge of racism against the film's depiction of the native Maoris as simple and sexual, while some feminists have complained that the film gives new life to the old stereotype that women really love being objectified (see Gullette; hooks, "Gangsta Culture"). While *The Piano* attempts to undermine melodrama's stereotypes, it nonetheless disturbed some viewers who felt that the types were uncritically presented.

The film critiques melodrama's symbolic language and character typing in important ways, but it employs the affective strategies common to the genre wholeheartedly and uncritically. A few reviewers praised the film for its "lack of sentimentality" but ignored the fact that a manipulation of emotional response is nonetheless a primary strategy of this film, as of all melodramas. Extreme emotions of terror, disgust, passion, joy, frustration, and anger dominate Campion's palette, and are emphasized by the piano score, by close-ups of faces, by the grisly depiction of the scene in which Stewart chops off Ada's finger, and by the alternation between cold blue and warm gold tones in the lighting and film stock. The film's love story plotline, complete with a romantic ending uniting Ada, Baines and Flora, is also a crowd-pleasing melodramatic tactic. Many of my respondents commented that they were moved to tears, to anger, to revisit the film in their dreams, or to the point of clutching their companion's hand in the theater. Such somatic responses, as Bourdieu has argued, are common to the experience of viewing popular cultural texts (*Distinction* 31–34). Many critics dismiss melodrama's affective strategies as merely money-making, anti-intellectual devices designed either to mollify or thrill audiences. Stuart Klawans of *The Nation* objects to *The Piano* on the grounds that it is a "contrived, allegorized melodrama" (705) that "gives reason nothing to do" (706). Contesting Klawans's false dichotomy between emotion and reason, I argue that melodrama's emotions carry intellectual weight, and thus are connected to the realm of the political. Feminist philosopher Jaggar questions the cultural dichotomy of reason and emotion, arguing that emotions are a socially constructed, interpretive discourse, a means by which we "engage actively and even construct the world" (152–53). Our emotional capability is linked to a capacity to evaluate our social condition and thus is intricately connected to the political sphere; displeasure may lead to change, and happiness to stasis. Likewise, Thomas Elsaesser reads melodrama as an important conduit of sociopolitical mores: "the height of [melodrama's] popularity seems to coincide . . . with periods of intense social and ideological crisis" (45). Melodramas, therefore, must be recognized as offering important social commentary, as engaging with politics at the level of everyday life. It is in this sense that *The Piano* borrows most fruitfully from a melodramatic heritage; by engaging us in Ada's desires and struggles, the film uses emotion to provoke political thought. While the film both inherits and challenges some of the more conservative aspects of melodrama, its use of popular techniques of emotional engagement and identification may be the factor most crucial to its political impact. As Murray Smith argues in his cognitivist study of emotion in cinema: "character engagement need not . . . anaesthetize our will to act on social problems, as Brecht argues; rather, it may enable us to apprehend experiences other than our own, and—possibly—use this new knowledge to act in the world in a more informed way" (236).

While *The Piano*'s melodramatic, popular cultural elements have received little attention from critics and reviewers (see Sue Gillett for an exception), its avant-garde or experimental style has been much discussed. *The Piano*'s reception as high-brow *objet d'art* was furthered by Campion's reputation as arty director of the films *Sweetie* and *Angel at My Table*, and by the fact that the film was shown primarily in art-house theaters until it made a mainstream marketing bid for the Academy Award for Best Picture. In addition to the many awards that the film has won, it has become somewhat of a darling among academic film theorists, who analyze it as a feminist art film. Several critical articles in *Screen* have praised the film's deconstruction of the character types and gender roles of classical film (see Bruzzi and Gordon). The film's ironic postmodern commentary upon film theories of voyeurism and the male gaze place it in opposition to popular genres, and on the side of feminist experimental cinema. For example, in one scene which upsets gender stereotypes that usually ground melodramas, Ada curiously examines Stewart's naked body but refuses to let him touch hers. The sexually repressed Stewart is emasculated and objectified, as Ada and Campion turn the tables on the familiar scene of the woman as object, of men's gaze and of the camera's. And while Baines at first appears to be the stereotypical male voyeur, he is later feminized by acknowledging his desire for Ada's love rather than just sex, a shift that is underscored by his admission of weakness and emotional need: "I can't eat, I can't sleep." The film clearly attempts to break down the stereotypes of woman as passive object of the gaze and man as desiring subject, and also shatters the age-old equation of male desire with sex and female desire with love. In addition to reworking theoretical debates about voyeurism and gender in film, *The Piano* makes postmodern self-reflexive moves in the scenes in which Stewart peers through a camera at Ada, and in which he peeps at Ada and Baines making love. These "viewing moments" imply that Stewart is an impotent rather than an all-powerful voyeur, and thus force the audience of *The Piano* to question the illusion of control and power that viewing usually entails. By laying bare the construction of gender stereotypes and the nature of film as a voyeuristic medium, *The Piano* questions classical film strategies that offer audiences a fantasy of themselves as powerful, unitary subjects with clear gender roles.

The Piano is also avant-garde in its subtle questioning of realism, the system of representation through which classical films maintain the illusion that film is a mirror of reality, rather than a myth-making construction (see Bordwell, Staiger, and Thompson). Although most melodramas offer a depth-model view of representation by extending the project of realism and implying that the signifier equals the signified in a mimetic way, Campion's film calls attention to its construction and periodically shatters the mirror. Despite the fact that much of the film adopts realist stylistic techniques such as continuity editing and point-of-view shots, and offers "authentic" details such as period costumes, mud, greasy hair, and the severed fingertip, a few techniques borrowed from surrealism upset the illusion of depth-model realism. In order to simulate the claustrophobia that Ada experiences, the cinematographer shot many of the scenes with blue-tinted film and a telephoto lens that flattened the image and accentuated the surface of the film. Campion's own interest in film began with her work in surrealistic art circles, which could have influenced her to emphasize surface and design, and to flout the realist view of art as an extension of the human eye. *The Piano*'s cinematographer occasionally places the camera in spaces that would be literally impossible for a human eye to inhabit; when the shot emerges from inside Stewart's pocket or inside the piano, the viewer's sense of reality is challenged, albeit subtly. The most deliberate attempt to upset a realistic aesthetic is the insertion of a cartoon frame depicting Flora's father, transformed into a torch. Placed after Flora's melodramatic yarn "explaining" her father's death and her mother's silence, the cartoon underscores the fictionality of the girl's speech, but the two-dimensional insert also calls attention to the disjunction between reality and representation and disrupts the viewer's immersion in the depth of the on-screen world.

In highlighting the disparity between reality and representation, between the signified and the signifier, *The Piano* creates crucial "sublime" moments of ambiguity characteristic of high cultural postmodernist and avant-garde works. Unlike many popular cultural texts, this film makes the viewer work to find meaning, just as the male characters must work to understand Ada's voice. Just like Ada, Campion leaves a lot unsaid—for example, why is Ada silent? Who was Flora's father? Does Ada truly love Baines? Why does Ada choose life? Some of my audience group were alienated by this ambiguity because they desired the answers they are accustomed to receiving from "entertainment," while others enjoyed the interpretive challenge. This freeing ambiguity, especially in the double ending sequence, was most often cited by my respondents as the reason for the film's status as art. The film reaches for sublime moments, particularly in the final shot, that stretch the limits of representation, perhaps even to the point of silence. Ada's silence itself could be seen as sublime, since it both resists simple interpretation and highlights the paucity of language. In contrast to the melodramatic scene where Ada and Baines live happily ever after, the last shot leaves us with the sublimity of silence and death, as Ada dreams of herself drowned, at the bottom of the ocean with her piano. As we see this shot, Ada recites a stanza from the sonnet "Silence" written by Thomas Hood, a nineteenth-century poet influenced by John Keats, another master of the sublime: "There is a silence where hath been no sound/ There is a silence where no sound may be/ In the cold grave, under the deep deep sea" (see Hood, <http://www.daypoems.net/poems/600.html>). This empty silence serves as a dramatic contrast to the plenitude of melodramatic closure, which speaks in excess by wrapping it all up and leaving nothing untold. The last underwater shot of *The Piano* speaks the language of avant-garde film, whereas the previous happily-ever-after scene speaks the language of melodrama.

This coexistence of both avant-garde and melodramatic elements in *The Piano* is crucial to its impact upon audiences. Although some viewers may ignore either strand in their interpretive process, I contend that the bricolage of these high art and popular aesthetic, generic, and emotional registers has contributed to the film's power to provoke strong political responses among its viewers. While questioning the representational logic of realist classical film, *The Piano* promotes critical distance but avoids a more extreme Brechtian alienation effect by combining this distance with the emotional engagement of melodrama. This hybrid text allows viewers to think while feeling, to be soothed and disturbed at the same time, and to question familiar paradigms while still acknowledging the emotional value of traditional social formations and identities. Unlike other melodramatic texts, this postmodern melodrama upsets entrenched models of identity and of representation by allowing enough distance to promote questioning. And unlike many postmodern films, with their ironic disdain for both romance and political struggle, this postmodern melodrama insists that personal relationships matter and that the personal is political. While the film relies on the emotional identification commonly induced by melodrama, its emotional strategies provoke audiences to rethink traditional modes of understanding gender identity, and to strengthen their own feminist ideologies.

Gender Identity and "Political Identification"

Many feminist film theorists have seen identification as a trap for female viewers, a means by which melodramatic texts seduce women into accepting their place in patriarchy. Apparatus film theorists imply that viewers are passive dupes, unconsciously inserting themselves into accepted cultural identities. Because many of these psychoanalytic theories of identification were developed to explain the spectator's relationship to classical film texts that essentialize gender, they are inadequate to address postmodern texts in which identities are explicitly contested rather than assumed. As Jackie Byars has noted, Lacan's ideas are valuable as a description of the status quo, but they cannot explain ideological change ("Feminism" 98). While *The Piano* provokes intense identifications as do most melodramas, it also aims to make that process conscious so that it can be politicized. This postmodern melodrama employs identification in the service of feminist goals rather than patriarchal ones. My study of feminists identifying with this film underscores the need to consider identification as more than just an unconscious process that sutures viewers into stereotyped gender roles, but as an active and political process of understanding and constructing oneself and one's ideologies in relation to other choices. Because much of psychoanalytic identification theory reifies the gender binary, it cannot be usefully applied to a film like *The Piano*, which plays with the boundary between masculine and feminine. While Ada, Baines, and Stewart contain some characteristics of melodrama's gendered types, they also destabilize those categories. The European men of the film obviously have the familiar patriarchal power to control and manipulate women, but they are both feminized at various moments. Stewart's impotent gazing upon a woman he cannot truly possess is an ironic reversal of the usually omnipotent male gaze and Baines needs Ada to the point of being emasculated and stripped of his former menacing edge. Ada's character, as the battered wife manipulated by men and yet the willful maker of her own destiny, exhibits both feminine passivity and masculine rebellion.

Some participants in my survey were such avid consumers of melodrama that they were confused and disturbed by the fact that this film upsets melodrama's gender dichotomies and its usually uncomplicated portrait of good and evil. Some were dismayed that they were made to sympathize with Stewart's vulnerabilities, because they wanted to read him as the villain of the piece. One man said the film fell apart for him because it lacked a clear dichotomy of good versus evil: "I found Stewart a confusing character, because some elements of his character were admirable. He wasn't portrayed as enough of an ogre for me to understand what Campion and Ada were doing." These viewers' own expectations about film structure and their desire to inhabit simple identificatory positions were thwarted by *The Piano*'s deconstruction of gender. On the other hand, other viewers were keenly aware of the film's attempt to deconstruct binary gender rubrics, and this conscious recognition affected their identification with the characters. Some viewers who defined themselves as anti-essentialist recognized a kindred spirit in Ada. An anthropology graduate student who studies androgyny said this of Ada: "this woman is bucking all the gender categories that she's got. I think she'd be putting on pants if she had the chance. I'm also interested in taking apart gender as coming from some biological essence. I don't want to posit some universal category of woman." This woman strongly identified with Ada, but her connection to the character was based on a recognition of a shared fluidity or androgyny rather than a rigid identity. Although some viewers identified with Ada as androgynous, many of the female interview subjects related to her "as a woman," claiming access to either a shared feminine essence or similar life experience. One graduate student recognized in Ada's sexual experiences with Baines her own college struggles with fraternity boys, the age-old game of male aggression and female defense. Another woman identified with Ada as a survivor of sexual assault, arguing that "every woman has felt or will feel [Ada's] emotions at some points in her life." Some women felt that their gender gave them a special access to the film: "My boyfriend didn't get it. The three women I had seen it with couldn't exactly put words to it at times, but just felt like we understood what it was about." While most understood their similarity to Ada as a function of the socially constructed experience of gender, a few called upon a female essence to explain their connection not only to Ada, but to Campion as well: "this film seemed like a woman's way of telling a story; it felt very intuitive to me." The notion of female identity, either biological or socially constructed, was obviously crucial to many viewers' identification process, as apparatus theorists would predict. However, these female-to-female identifications do not result in a reinforcement of conservative gender roles as *Screen* theory implies, precisely because of Ada's own resistance to femininity. Psychologist and cultural critic Lynne Layton reminds that "the strategic identification of females with other females . . . can contest hegemonic masculinity and femininity" (62). Identification is not merely a trap for women, but a means of building empowering solidarity.

In addition, apparatus film theory cannot account for the fact that a significant portion of the female viewers defined themselves as "Ada" and "not-Ada" simultaneously; their ambivalent identification included a reaction against the vision of "woman" they encountered in the film. While Freud and his disciples occasionally discuss the ambivalent nature of identification (see *Totem and Taboo*), they see such love/hate relationships as a result of repressed psychic hostility and the violence of incorporating the other into the self. Because they treat identification as unconscious, they do not consider that such ambivalence could be a conscious political choice. Many of the viewers in my audience group were aware of the difference that their own contemporary feminism made to their experience of being a woman, and thus they saw in Ada a less radical (or occasionally even a more radical) nineteenth-century version of themselves. Most of the negative reactions to Ada were prompted by her sexual choices, her love for Baines, and her impractical silence. While one graduate student was pleased that the film "explores women's erotic desires from their own point of view," she also found Ada's pleasure in her own objectification troubling. Ultimately she reconciled her differences with Ada by standing up for the individuality of desire: "you have to allow her that, her pleasure. . . . Why shut that down because I think it should be some better scenario?" While some found Ada to be a less radical feminist than themselves, a Spanish professor was alienated by Ada's radical gesture of silence, by her refusal to engage with the "real world" as most women must. These viewers' responses, and their ambivalent reactions to Ada, were influenced by their definitions of themselves as women and by their feminist ideals.

Since being a feminist woman within patriarchy usually entails a conscious struggle over one's relationships with men, the women I interviewed often focused on Ada's relationship with Baines or Stewart as a means of interpreting the film's relationship to feminism, which then influenced their identification with Ada and the text. Not only were the male-female relationships in the film perceived as highly political, but so were the construction of male identities. While some of the female interviewees were able to empathize with the male leads, even Stewart, others simply loathed them. Most of the women who were angered by Ada's choices located the source of their irritation in her love for Baines, whom they saw as just another male oppressor. Although the film takes pains to locate Stewart and Baines's masculinities as socio-historical formations, and to suggest that they were less oppressive (to varying degrees) than other Victorian men, many viewers did not see these qualifications. For example, Stewart is very self-conscious and hesitant at first to claim his "conjugal rights" with Ada. Baines's connection to the Maori tribe obviously separates him from British patriarchal laws and practices, particularly since the Maori women seem to have greater freedom than the European women. As Baines falls in love with Ada, he is also portrayed as sensitive and feminized in important ways that qualify his connection to patriarchy. Despite potential evidence to the contrary, some of the female viewers lumped Baines and Stewart together as figures of universal oppression. Their reading of both men in the film as patriarchal oppressors influenced them to reject the love story as anti-feminist. The pattern of their identification was not so simple as that delineated by apparatus theory, which predicts that the women would either identify with Ada's feminine subject position, or would experience a "transvestite" identification with the more powerful male voyeur. These few women in fact identified with neither the female victim nor the male oppressor (in their terms). They saw themselves as "not-Ada" precisely because of Ada's love for Baines. Psychoanalytic theory often neglects to consider that women's sense of gendered identity may differ widely, in this case as a result of differing feminist ideals about the relationship between women and men. Since empathy for a character is strongly determined by favorable moral judgment of that character's actions (Zillmann, "Mechanisms" 45), these viewers could not identify with Ada because her behavior offended their feminist ideals. Rather than falling into a gender-based identification, some women used the film to actively construct themselves as different kinds of women and feminists than Ada McGrath.

Just as some women rejected an identification with Ada (and with her male suitors), so did some of the male feminists in my group. Some feminist psychoanalytic critics might argue that this lack of identification merely underscores how difficult it can be for men to identify with a culturally devalued feminine position. While this may be true, these men's political ideologies add texture to their refusal of identification. One feminist man argued that he couldn't identify with Ada because he objected to the film's aestheticization of a woman in pain. Two men complained that they found the film's politics muddled or too complicit with patriarchy, and thus they resisted an identification with Ada as an ideal feminist heroine. These refusals of identification with the female lead were much more politically radical than the response of one man who admitted identifying with Ada, but only as a representative of the "universal" experiences of "mankind" rather than womankind. While some of the male feminists disidentified with Ada, many of them crossed gender lines to identify strongly with this woman in pain. Studlar aptly points out that Mulvey and Doane have neglected "the [radical] possibilities of male identification with the female" (278). Male-to-female identification, however, can result in a facile form of connection that does nothing to challenge patriarchy. Believing that "gender is just spare parts," one equality-feminist male identified with Ada, but his identification amounted to little more than a colonization of the Other to reflect back the self-same ("mankind"). Remarkably, he saw the film as having little to do with gender difference. One could argue that this man has produced a "resistant reading" of the film, since he ignores major themes of the text; this aberrant response reminds of the fact that not all forms of resistance are necessarily progressive.

Despite this one man's universalizing, appropriative identification, many men who identified with Ada did so in an excorporative way with more radical political significance. Some of these men extended their connection to Ada to the point of feeling her pain somatically; one man noted that the finger-chopping scene nearly made him physically ill. Several of the men used their own marginalized identities as racial and sexual minorities to empathize with Ada's experiences. A man who defines himself as queer hated both men for objectifying Ada and understood Ada's frustrations with the limitations of heterosexual men ("I could romance a woman better than Stewart!"). As a gay man, he also connected with Ada's muteness and her expressive piano playing: "you could really say that about a number of groups that have been oppressed, such as homosexuals, that there's an outlet, an escape that they find in artistic expression. I myself wrote a story where not muteness but an inability to feel tactilely was kind of a metaphor for being homosexual." Drawing an analogy between gender oppression and racial oppression, one African American male student understood Ada's experiences as parallel to his own: "there will always be sexism, just like there's always racism that keeps you down at the bottom of the ocean." These examples are testaments of the potential for coalitions among subordinate groups; male members of marginalized social groups may feel more affinity for women than for white or heterosexual men.

In short, the diverse reactions of these male and female viewers to Ada McGrath raise significant questions about gender-essentialist theories of spectator identification. Despite the one universalizing humanist who de-emphasized gender, most of the male and female feminists whom I interviewed interpreted this film as being about the difference that gender makes, but their own views about gender difference varied widely and thus influenced their identification with the film's characters. Some women used their own gendered experiences to empathize with the female lead, but they often did so out of a political desire for feminist solidarity, rather than due to the mere fact of their sex. Other women disidentified with Ada, not because they are self-alienated or desire to occupy the male position of power in a film, but because their ideologies prevented them from identifying with a character they deemed unfeminist. Some men disidentified with Ada for the same feminist reasons, not because they were threatened by femininity. And finally, several men crossed gender lines to identify with Ada, but in an excorporative and empathetic rather than an appropriative way. Although gender often played a central role in the viewers' identification with the characters, this process was much more conscious, active, and complex than psychoanalytic theory would have it. How the viewers read the text in relation to recognized feminist narratives and ways of understanding gender was more important to their identifications and disidentifications than feminist film theorists allow.

The Feminist Politics of Genre

Identifying along gender lines was complicated for these viewers because of the redefinition of gender roles at our cultural moment, and identifying with the text or the characters as "feminist" was also made difficult due to the multiplicity of feminist discourses in the 1990s. The variety of feminist and non-feminist plots that audiences saw in the film can also be linked to its mixture of avant-garde and melodramatic narrative strategies. For example, several in my viewing group noted that experimental or art-house films often close with the death of the heroine, an end which can be viewed as either feminist or misogynist, while melodramas often end with a happy marriage, a destiny that feminism has long tried to de-romanticize. These high-art and popular endings are both evoked by *The Piano*, thereby forcing the viewer to consider which emplotment, or neither, appeals to his or her feminist political sensibilities. The film's plot elements speak to many opposing versions of feminism at once, and particularly to the individual who is herself struggling to reconcile different feminist viewpoints. Furthermore, the process of reading a politics into the film is made more difficult because neither an avant-garde nor a melodramatic aesthetic necessarily implies a consistent and singular political metanarrative. Although some of my viewers read the avant-garde or anti-essentialist elements of the film as categorically subversive and deemed the melodramatic plot elements anti-feminist, that simple dichotomous reading was rejected by many other viewers with differing notions of feminism.

Despite this confusion of codes, two key elements of the film appealed specifically to postmodern feminists influenced by poststructuralist theory: the film's deconstruction of gender identity and its suggestion that women are power-desiring sexual subjects rather than innocent victims. Postmodern feminists such as Donna Haraway hope to dismantle the binary gender system and construct a "post-gender world" ("Cyborg Manifesto" 150). Arguing that "the standpoints of the subjugated are not 'innocent' positions" ("Situated Knowledges" 191), Haraway concludes that women are always implicated in the quest for power and cannot rightly claim innocence or a privileged victim status. Standing against essentialism, she further argues that "there is nothing about being 'female' that naturally binds women. There is not even such a state as 'being' female, itself a highly complex category constructed in . . . social practices" ("Cyborg" 155). Postmodern feminists with sympathy for Haraway's ideas read Ada McGrath as a heroine fighting against her culture's categorization of "woman," rejecting the status of victim, and grasping for all the power she can get. They see her as a complicit yet powerful agent in her own right, not as a representative of essential "Womanhood." Essentialist feminists, on the other hand, were more attracted by the melodramatic elements of the film. Psychoanalytic feminism, like melodrama, embraces a depth-model view of the self, evident in the concepts of repression and the unconscious. Difference feminists invested in notions of essential "womanhood" and adherents of standpoint theory, who believe that women have a shared and unique perspective as victims of patriarchal oppression, have used sentimental rhetoric to evoke pity for oppressed women and to idealize femininity. The so-called "victim feminists," such as anti-pornography lawyer Catherine MacKinnon, emphasize gender as *the* defining aspect of a person's life, and this worldview is invoked by melodramas that prescribe characters' destinies and functions according to their gender. While poststructuralist feminists aim to move beyond gender as a meaningful category, essentialist feminists remind us that this may not be possible in a patriarchal world, or even desirable, because women have gained much politically by uniting as a special interest group. Some feminists in my group read Ada McGrath's strange muteness and her intense piano-playing as figures for the precious difference of the "feminine voice." It was not surprising that viewers in my group who are sympathetic to essentialist or difference feminism responded most strongly to *The Piano*'s melodramatic explorations of gender difference and of the victimization of women by men.

Postmodernist feminists often responded politically to the avant-garde elements of *The Piano* and essentialist feminists to the melodramatic strategies. However, it would be a misrepresentation to draw such a simple response pattern because individuals' responses to texts rarely follow a rigid ideology. Many respondents expressed several opposing beliefs when asked to describe their feminist ideals and were sometimes conscious of the contradictions. In many cases, I have avoided using specific identity-nouns (i.e., "poststructuralist feminist") to refer to particular respondents because their feminist autobiographical narratives borrowed from so many different discourses. It is important to avoid reifying and fixing identities that are actually quite fluid. Nonetheless, I have employed terms like "difference feminist" in several cases within this chapter: 1) when referring to an individual respondent who used such an identity term to define herself, 2) when referring to groups of respondents who both employed this particular feminist discourse and responded to the film in similar ways, and 3) when discussing an individual whose feminist narrative focused on this discourse exclusively, even if she did not use the term itself. My use of the noun form for a particular feminist is not an attempt to fix identities, but to refer to the predominance of a particular discourse in an individual's interview narrative or response pattern. In sum, the response patterns of the viewers were thus strongly affected by *The Piano*'s invocation of different feminist positions. Some viewers reacted with anger or confusion because the film seemed conflicted, appealing to some of their beliefs while challenging others. Others appreciated the hybridity because it reflected their own identity crises as feminists struggling with competing ideologies. The respondents in my group who were the biggest fans of *The Piano* have adapted a practical kind of "strategic essentialism" in their daily lives, working with insights from both postmodernists and essentialists to empower women, and the film's hybrid feminism struck a chord with them. The rest of the chapter examines audience responses to four issues that were hotspots for feminist interpretation: silence and voice, cinematography and the gaze, heterosexual desire and romance, and the postmodern ending of the film which puts all the feminist themes in play.

Silence, Voice, and Representation

Ada McGrath's silence, and her attempts to speak through her piano, have been at the center of feminist debates about the film. Her muteness has been variously interpreted as either feminist or non-feminist, radical or conservative, and as a sign of either strength or powerlessness. Since the gesture of silence offers an implicit commentary on theories of language and representation, it functions differently in melodramas and avant-garde texts because of their different investments in the power of representation. In fact, silent characters have frequently appeared in both genres. How, then, do muteness and Ada's alternative musical voice function in this hybrid text, and how did the viewers assign a feminist politics to it? Mute heroines have abounded in melodramatic theater and film, and Peter Brooks has read melodramatic silence as an excuse to explore an alternative language of gesture. Silence, he argues, does not indicate an abandoning of meaning, but rather allows an alternative means of communication, "the language of presence and immediacy, the primal language" of gesture, which conveys emotions that the spoken word cannot (67). Jackie Byars notes that melodrama "exploits excessive uses of representational conventions to express that which cannot (yet) be said, that which language alone is incapable of expressing" (*All That Hollywood* 13). The melodramatic project usually entails a belief in a buried essence that can be expressed through non-verbal means of communication, through signs, which "attempt to give material existence to the repressed" (Byars, *All That Hollywood* 17). Thus Ada's silence should be recognized as a classic trope of melodrama, as her piano and her signing allow her to speak that which cannot be said in words—particularly her sexual desire. Although Ada is silent, she has other outlets such as gesture, writing, and music that allow her to communicate meaning and deep feeling. *The Piano*'s treatment of silence is typical of melodramatic films because the film respects meaning itself and suggests that Ada does indeed have something important to "say" that is buried deep within her.

Poststructuralist critics, on the other hand, may read this substitution of a musical voice for a literal one as an endless deferral, exemplifying the impossibility of reaching the signified, of creating meaning in a one-to-one correspondence. Lyotard has valued the sublime as a postmodern gesture toward the unrepresentable, beyond language and even meaning itself. Thus, Ada's silence and her music could be seen as examples of the postmodern sublime at the limits of representation. In their review in *American Anthropologist*, Patricia Sharpe and Frances Mascia-Lees argue that the film comments upon poststructuralist ideas about writing and speech, since it is "suspicious of the spoken word" and aware of the "inadequacies of language" (765, 767). Ada's sublime silence is celebrated in the last shot of her underwater dream, and this ending was inexplicable to many viewers, almost beyond meaning. Ada's subtle gestures throughout the film are not as easy to read as in a typical stylized melodrama full of exaggerated facial expressions; one graduate student remarked that "we never cross the threshold with Ada," we never quite access her meaning, which may make some people wonder if her actions "mean" anything in the conventional sense. In his reading of Ada's piano playing, film psychologist Ed Tan concurs: "the viewers may also wonder about a particular significance that her playing has for her, one that apparently completely escapes them. It seems that there is more to Ada than we can grasp" (Tan, *Emotion* 174). The film offers the avant-garde suggestion that meaning is not so transparent, nor so easily transmitted, as melodrama and realism would have it. The trope of silence, therefore, has roots in both postmodernism and a popular melodramatic aesthetic, and takes on a different valence in each context. The mixture of these two worldviews in *The Piano* enabled some viewers to construct a negotiated reading of Ada's silence, weighing its many meanings against each other. For example, if one pays attention to the film's melodramatic use of silence, one would not simply equate Ada's silence with the postmodern sublime as described by Lyotard, who values it for imparting "no knowledge about reality," for being beyond representation (78). *The Piano*'s exploration of the sublime nature of silence seems to coexist with a realistic commitment to signifying and to the serious political import of expression, particularly for women who have long been a silenced group. Despite her attempts to thwart communication through her willful muteness, Ada is greatly invested in her piano as a means of expression and a deeper form of communication, one that will force her listeners, such as Flora's father and Baines, to work hard to hear her meaning. Ada's struggle with representation—her dilemma over whether to speak legibly or to question the value of communication with her silence—is parallel to the film's conflict over whether to make interpretation easy or difficult for the audience, to make sense (popular culture) or to question sense (avant-garde). The film's treatment of representation is avant-garde in its desire to stretch representation to the limit, perhaps even of silence, and popular in its acknowledgment of the emotional importance of meaning and communication.

Not only is silence an abstract commentary upon representation, but it also comments upon the power of the word and of the speaker, which clearly relates to gender and the socio-political. The issue of voice is central to Ada's relation to patriarchy. An important context for many of my audience group was the work of feminist theorists Hélène Cixous, Julia Kristeva, and Luce Irigaray, who argue that language is phallocentric and thus silences women, and that women should search for a new female voice, perhaps one more attuned to the female body and its rhythms. Since Kristeva argues that women are socially "estranged from language" ("Interview" 166), she might interpret Ada's piano playing as a return to the "semiotic chora," a rhythmic base beneath language that she describes as pre-Oedipal, musical, "indifferent to language, enigmatic, and feminine" (*Revolution* 29). Ada McGrath's silence, and particularly the final shot in which she dreams of her silent, drowned self, could be seen as an example of Kristeva's vision of women who "find refuge in the valorization of a silent underwater body . . . [and] reject everything loaded with meaning" ("Interview" 166). In opposition to the French feminists, who either applaud silence or champion a different female voice, practical-minded equality-feminists counter that speaking conventional language is the only way to get access to power, and they deny that language is necessarily phallocentric. Among my audience group, one could observe three poles of response relevant to the melodramatic and avant-garde takes on silence and representation: 1) a poststructuralist feminist view of language, applauding Ada's silence because it confounds a masculine desire for women to be readable and easy to interpret, for them to make sense; 2) a "melodramatic" feminist view, applauding Ada's alternative musical voice as a separate, female language, full of meaning and outside of patriarchy; and 3) an equality feminist view that rejects the previous two in favor of a "realist" aesthetic, arguing that language and speech are practical, transparent and gender-neutral conduits of meaning. To this third group, Ada's muteness is tantamount to insanity, or to a relinquishing of all power. This anti-silence standpoint was taken by all the sociologists of my group, who are annoyed by feminists' obsessive focus on language and direct their feminist impulses towards combating more tangible forms of oppression. On the other hand, the literary critics and anthropologists in the group were more apt to praise a rejection of linguistic communication as a feminist gesture, in part because they are more familiar with French feminist theory and poststructuralism.

Those who felt that Ada's silence was purposive usually saw it as a powerful feminist gesture, but they emphasized either her silence or her alternative voice. Difference feminists tended to stress the positive qualities of Ada's "female voice" of music and gesture, while postmodern feminists were most attracted by her silence, which one respondent called a "rejection of the whole patriarchal means of communication." An English graduate student, who studies nineteenth-century women novelists' subversive uses of language, wished that the film had gone even further into exploring an "independent women's other language." Many pointed to her music as a beautiful expression of an independent female self that preserved her strangeness and difference from the other women of the town, who spoke only the silly gossip that patriarchy deems appropriate for women. On the other hand, postmodern feminists were concerned not with Ada's female voice, but with the power that silence could offer women. One self-defined postmodern feminist called Ada's silence a "statement of power, amazing self-defining power to resist patriarchy" and to "wig out her husband." An English graduate student interested in poststructuralist theory was impressed by the ironic power of her muteness: "her silence is a subversive enactment of what society already says women should be anyway. I'm supposed to be silent, so I'm silent. It's not merely a metaphorical stand-in for women's silence, but a kind of willful or subversive compliance." While some talked about Ada's voice in melodramatic ways, as a sign of difference or a search for a female system of meaning, postmodern feminists enjoyed the sublime nature of Ada's silence and its power to disrupt phallic speech.

Although many felt that Ada's silence was an effective weapon against patriarchy, others read it negatively as a sign of weakness or an inability to integrate or function normally. An undergraduate with some sympathy for Ada's independent muteness nonetheless noted that she felt implicated by Ada's choice: "I think there's a real desire on the part of the viewer for Ada not to be able to exist in silence, because what does that say about us and our language?" Many others reacted more strongly, defending "our language." A male professor of sociology called her silence a "psychiatric disorder," and his reading was echoed by most of the social scientists. A self-defined equality feminist complained that "it was really the old idea of hysterical muteness. The hysteria actually reinforces the cultural paradigm of women as weaker." Some of these more practical feminists directly rejected a French feminist reading of Ada's muteness as an ideal feminist gesture. An English graduate student argued: "I react against a French feminist view of phallocentric language, the idea that Ada should reject language because it's male language. Even the most gynocentric cultures use language. Now she's found someone who is actually willing to listen to her, so her speech is a good development." Ada's movement from silence into speech at the end of the film also elicited a variety of responses, from anger to celebration. This narrative shift provoked some viewers to consider both the positive and negative effects of both silence and speech. With this ambiguous treatment of speech and silence, the film mediates between a popular and avant-garde view of representation and communication. While some viewers appreciated the resulting mediation between these two extremes, others were annoyed by the mediation and felt it resulted in a confused politics. A woman who sympathizes most with Marxist feminism argued that "her silence is definitely coded as resistance, not complicity, and that's why I don't like the fact that she's trying to speak at the end. The critique gets lost because she changes her mind." A graduate student (Donna) remarked that "nobody needed her to speak. I don't like that black veil that she wears at the end. It's almost as if she's been shrouded again." Yet Donna feels that although Ada's feminist liberation was "muted" and qualified, Ada's return to speech might be necessary so that she can wage a form of protest that does not require so much personal risk.

Many others also tried to construct a negotiated reading of the multiple meanings of silence and speech. Even an anthropology graduate student who describes herself as radical saw Ada's first attempts to speak as a necessary development: "the fact that she doesn't speak indicates a kind of power that comes from being on the bottom . . . but it also makes her incredibly dependent on her daughter. I don't see it as a relinquishing of power that she desires to speak at the end, but as a maturing process." A women's studies student also liked her subversive silence, but recognized its limitations: "it's precisely these subversive tactics that might become destructive. Speaking is a good thing. I see her speaking could also be construed as writing herself back into traditional forms of discourse, but I still felt that it was liberating." These viewers who responded positively to the film's ambiguous stance on the politics of silence were already ambivalent about feminist theories of language. They are feminists who have radical political desires, but who try to temper them with practical concerns. They are angry about a masculine control of language and about the limitations of language for women, but they nevertheless still want to be heard and are willing to work within the system rather than reject it for a "purer" form of subversion. Ada McGrath's oxymoronic "silent voice" echoed these feminists' own ambivalent voices and enabled them to identify with her. As such, the film's hybrid aesthetic—its evocation of both melodramatic and poststructuralist views about language and silence—offered a feminist politics of compromise that appealed to many viewers. While the ambiguity sometimes led to confusion and anger, it not only offered something for everyone but also encouraged a negotiation between limiting extremes.

The Politics of Cinematography and the Gaze

While voice and speech have been central concerns of feminists, the "gaze" has been an even more important concept for feminist film theory about spectator identification. Rather than giving us an uncomplicated "intended spectator position," *The Piano* seems to play with common identification techniques of classic melodramas, at times adopting them uncritically and at other times challenging them. At different moments in the film, we are given point-of-view shots as if looking through Ada's eyes (e.g., our first view through her fingers in the opening shot, her peak behind the curtain to discover Baines's nude body, and her struggle to free herself underwater). At many other points, however, we gaze at her along with Baines and Stewart. The questions I set out to explore were these: Does the film's cinematography affect audience members (both male and female) to identify with Ada's look or with that of the male voyeur? Are female spectators forced into a masochistic position by identifying with Ada as an object of the gaze, or do they resist this objectification as Ada does at key moments in the film? Did the film's experiments with the gaze result in a different form of audience identification than in typical melodramas? Did it encourage the viewers in my group to resist the psychoanalytic dichotomy of male/active/voyeur and female/passive/looked-at, or did it merely replicate these gendered polarities? The audience response to the film's treatment of looking was even more complicated and varied than their readings of Ada's silence. Because the text itself sets up many characters' point-of-view shots and many neutrally positioned shots, audience members in my study disagreed about which characters had the power of the look, and they did not necessarily identify with each character whose point-of-view shots were presented. The striking thing was that even though Ada is objectified by the other characters' looks, most of the viewers nonetheless identified with her, rather than with other lookers in the film. Furthermore, for many in my group, the process of identifying with Ada was not simply masochistic as Mulvey or Doane might predict, because many viewers resisted reading Ada as a victim stripped of subjectivity (Mulvey, "Afterthoughts;" Doane, *Desire* 32–33). I contend that the film does encourage the viewer to look *at* Ada, but not necessarily in the voyeuristic, colonizing, and phallic way that Mulvey claims is inevitable. Traditional scopic cinematic techniques are critiqued here, and looking bears a different relationship to identification and to gender in this film than in typical melodramas.

In a few scenes more typical of avant-garde feminist films than melodrama, *The Piano* directly attempts to upset the traditional cinematic relationship between voyeurism and masculine power, as outlined by Laura Mulvey. As discussed earlier, several scenes in which Stewart gazes upon Ada—through the lens of a camera as he takes their wedding portrait, and through the floorboards of Baines's hut as Ada and Baines are having sex—suggest that it is Stewart, rather than the female, who is the powerless figure because his look cannot control his wife. As Stella Bruzzi argues, Stewart is "emasculated rather than empowered by his possession of (only) the look" (261), and most male and female viewers therefore reject an identification with him. Many of my audience group remarked that it is Ada's look that controls Stewart, as her silent stare prevents him from raping her when she is ill in bed nursing her amputated finger. One woman compared Ada's glare to "Medusa's evil eye." Most of my viewers thus connected strongly to Ada as a person with at least some power to control by her look. They also talked about another reversal—that the male figure becomes a sexual object for an implicitly female viewer, which is rare in mainstream films. One woman remarked: "even though originally she was the object of Baines's gaze, he becomes at least as much an object of the viewer's gaze, particularly when he is naked, dusting the piano." Campion shows that both men and women are simultaneously sexual subjects as well as objects of desire (with vision serving as a metaphor for desire), and thus these roles are not gender-bound. Baines's dual position as both voyeur and naked spectacle makes visible the fact that he both wants Ada and needs to be wanted by her. In an even more curious moment, Ada explores her newfound sexual subjectivity by gazing at and kissing her own image in a mirror; this masturbatory moment ironically collapses the distinction between subject and object of the desiring look, leaving the male out of the chain of vision altogether.

Despite these moments which turn the tables on classic film relationships between gender and viewing, throughout most of the film the viewer gazes upon Ada, as do Stewart and Baines. We even see Ada's fetishized leg and the hole in her stocking explicitly from Baines's point of view as he peers under her dress. Many viewers and critics were disturbed because they interpreted the film as participating in the objectification of women. In *Screen*, critic Suzy Gordon proposes that "*The Piano* achieves a fundamentally masochistic form of looking" (202) for the identifying feminist viewer, because the viewer has to experience the violence against Ada and her willing acceptance of object status in order to manipulate Baines. In a scathing review in the *Boston Globe*, Margaret Morganroth Gullette expressed anger at the film for making her identify masochistically with a "female loser," while male viewers, she argued, are identifying with Baines's voyeuristic look and feeling "masterful" (59). Although Gullette's assumptions about male spectator identification were not played out among my sample of male feminists, a few women in my group who are tired of representations of female victims echoed Gullette's disgust at the position in which they felt placed. An undergraduate said, "I remember thinking that I was surprised that a woman wrote it. I don't think it's a good message as far as women's control over their own lives. She's definitely an object of the male gaze through the whole thing." This student's work as a counselor at a rape crisis center, and thus her sensitivity to issues of victimization, might have influenced her to see the film as just another text enabling the male gaze rather than critiquing it, particularly in the voyeuristic scenes in Baines's home. Because she did not see any resistance to that appropriating male look and felt Ada was reduced to an object, she had difficulty identifying with her and experienced the film as just another instance of misogynist popular culture. Doane might read this woman's response as a positive self-preservation strategy for the female viewer to avoid over-identification with the on-screen, degraded female object found in most melodramas (*Desire* 32–33).

But despite these women who felt manipulated by the film's use of the gaze, the majority of my audience group gladly identified with Ada because they saw her as an active subject fighting valiantly against oppression, rather than as a violated object or a victim. Most felt empathy for Ada and did not experience this solidarity as masochism because they believed that the film liberated her. Anti-essentialist feminists and those interested in feminist avant-garde film strategies were more likely to see Ada as resisting the male gaze, and to credit Jane Campion with upsetting these melodramatic gender dichotomies. Those viewers who used the rhetoric of equality feminism were sometimes annoyed because they felt that the film merely reified women's status as visual object, and they did not see any directorial critique of that process. Whether or not a viewer experienced an identification with Ada as empowering or masochistic depended on interpreting Ada as either a postmodern feminist role model who defies gender stereotypes by assuming the power of the look, or a sad example of woman's "to-be-looked-at-ness" (to borrow Mulvey's term).

One male viewer (Marc) in my group felt that the film's presentation of Ada as an image to be looked at presented an even larger problem than the one of masochism—the problem of not being able to identify with her at all. Focusing more specifically on the gaze of the camera rather than the male characters' voyeurism, Marc argued that the cinematography leaves the viewer emotionally alienated from Ada. In his reading, *The Piano* is not a melodrama but is rather an avant-garde film that emphasizes the beauty of surfaces, and thus it seduces the gaze of the viewer (perhaps implicitly male in his formulation) by turning Ada into a fetishized object of beauty, an aestheticized body in pain. He contended that *The Piano*'s avant-garde aesthetic puts distance between the audience and the heroine, and therefore gets in the way of its potentially subversive gender politics: "[Its feminist statements] that should be political, that should hit us at an ideological level, are finally subordinated to how beautifully they are staged, how beautiful she looks while in pain. . . . It does seem to me that it is putting itself in a tradition of some of the worst misogynist films, and authors like Robbe-Grillet, who are so concerned with the surface and with play . . . and [critics] ignore the fact that every one of his novels is full of pages of bloody, horrific deaths of women." Informed by his own Marxist feminist ideology and his concerns about the politics of the avant-garde, Marc's response was idiosyncratic rather than representative of this audience group. My ethnographic study challenges Marc's belief that the film's concern with the beauty of its cinematography, or its gaze upon Ada's beauty, necessarily alienates or distances audiences, objectifies Ada, or results in misogynist politics. It is clear that Marc's reading of the film is motivated by his Marxist and masculine preference for a violent revolutionary "politics with teeth," as he put it. His commentary is also based on interpreting the film as an avant-garde text, rather than as a melodrama or a hybrid form. As such, he echoes the concerns of many leftists, such as Fredric Jameson, who read postmodern and avant-garde culture as apolitical or conservative for eschewing concepts that have been crucial to political movements, such as teleological narratives and emotional commitment to a cause. The implication is that an overemphasis on formalist aesthetics alienates audiences and results in the neglect of social and political analysis that had once been a powerful motivator for the production of art. Marc's interpretation ignores the important role that beautiful aesthetics, and that gazing upon other women, have always played in popular culture aimed at women, and thus he undervalues both their political import and their role in *enabling*, rather than preventing, identification with the heroine. Here, perhaps, is one instance in which the gender of the viewer—in conjunction with his political orientation—did play a significant role in affecting interpretation.

In contrast's to Marc's experience of alienation, the sight of Ada and the lush representation of her world played a crucial role in creating emotional identification among my survey group, which led many to see the film as feminist or female-centered in its aesthetic. Because we cannot hear what Ada thinks, it is doubly important to see what she sees, so the film's almost fetishistic attention to the detail and mood of her surroundings is crucial to experiencing her emotions. Furthermore, the minute detail that melodramas lavish upon all the particulars of *mise en scène* contributes to the genre's appeal for female audiences, since the surface aesthetics of fashion, decorating, and makeup have long been an emotional part of many women's lives. The beauty and intricacy of *The Piano*'s surface in fact created a "deep" emotional connection—intimacy rather than distance—for many of the people that I interviewed. As one female viewer remarked: "I was struck by all those blues and grays, and I just felt kind of blue and gray along with it. It's just such a beautifully made film, and it was poignant to me. I tend to really get caught up in movies." Many of the participants recalled being haunted by particularly beautiful images, such as the last frame of Ada's body floating like a bell above her piano, and such images play no small part in *The Piano*'s political power as a text. My point is that this film's construction of beautifully constructed tableaus for the audience's viewing pleasure did not necessarily trap them in a rigid position and politics, nor did it reduce Ada to the status of fetishized object in their minds. It is important to remember that it is Ada's face rather than her body that the camera directs our attention to most frequently. With her face as the focus, the act of gazing upon Ada created a response of empathy, rather than alienation or colonizing control, among viewers of both genders. Especially since she is mute, one viewer remarked that Ada's "face is so important as an expressive force." Looking at her is crucial to the process of "hearing" her meaning. Several particularly focused on her facial expression after her finger has been cut off, and one man remembered the empathetic moment vividly: "I could barely watch. The fact that her face was emotionless, that she just kept a straight face but then she was so pale and the red blood—it was really moving."

A cluster of concepts in film criticism help to explain this male viewer's identification with a victimized female subject on display. When a female figure dominates the frame throughout a film, Barbara Creed argues that the space is gendered female, and that this technique serves as an alternative means of constructing a female point of view and of facilitating identification with the heroine (134). In *Loving with a Vengeance*, Tania Modleski describes a similar phenomenon among female viewers of soap opera, and suggests that the scopic economy of soaps is dominated by empathy. Modleski argues that "soap opera stimulates women's desire for connectedness through the constant, claustrophobic use of close-up shots" (99). Similarly, cognitive film critics claim that an expressive reaction shot can be more effective than a point-of-view shot in fostering identification and empathy (see Gaut; Plantinga; Murray Smith; Tan). Although the gaze of the camera is often either neutral or directed at Ada, the resulting text nonetheless offers a female point of view and encourages viewers to identify with her as a subject. Non-visual "focalization" techniques (see Andringa, Tan, van Horssen, and Jacobs), such as Ada's voiceover and the plot's emphasis on both her suffering and triumph, allow viewers to sympathize with Ada's subjective experiences. As Murray Smith astutely points out, the psychoanalytical concept of identification or "suture" is "based on the conflation of sight and subjectivity" (157). The fact that these close-ups created sympathy for Ada among both women *and* men (albeit feminist men), rather than a desire for mastery over the female object, serves as an important qualification of Mulvey's reading of cinematic narrative pleasure as derived from an objectifying masculine gaze.

Some film theorists who distrust sentimentality and affective forms may argue that these moments of pathos work against female agency (see, e.g., Doane), but I contend that the sympathy that audiences feel when viewing Ada's story is crucial to the film's feminist impact. Doane argues that "pathos always connotes a loss or fading of individual subjectivity," and that it produces an masochistic overidentification with a female character which results in a collapse of subject/object; this collapse prevents the female spectator from ever achieving a "well-defined subjectivity" (*Desire* 177). In my view, Doane's theory exhibits a problematic emphasis on the "rigidity" of identity, neglecting to consider that a more fluid connection between self and other could enable feminist solidarity, a kind of identity through relation with others. The fact that *The Piano* enables identification of male viewers with Ada also aligns it with the aim of some feminists to engage male sympathy for women's concerns. Rejecting melodrama as degraded, Doane finds more feminist possibilities in avant-garde texts that disrupt identification and the gaze and offer distance from the image (*Femmes Fatales* 197–98). However, as the interviewee Marc has suggested, a distanced avant-garde aesthetic can often be politically anemic. Gaines has voiced a similar complaint that feminist avant-garde film has alienated female viewers by "annihilating the pleasure of identification" ("Women" 81). Silverman also argues that feminist film critics have overglorified the Brechtian "alienation effect," and she denies "that only a cinema which thwarts identification can be truly transformative" (*Threshold* 85). Since sympathy and anger are at the root of most political drives for change, affect and identification can be crucial to the political effectivity of a text. Doane's contention that pathos causes a collapse of the viewer and the image did not hold true in my interview group, most of whom were able to identify with Ada yet also to disagree with her actions and choices. Their sympathetic gaze did not eradicate their subjective difference from the on-screen woman.

In summary, my study of viewer responses to the film's complicated treatment of looking and subjectivity revealed several things that challenge psychoanalytic gaze theory. First of all, the majority of the male viewers did not respond to the film's solicitation of their gaze any differently than did the women, and the most common response was to identify strongly with Ada, even when she was the object of the camera's or a male character's gaze. Despite one viewer's reading of the film as an avant-garde text that alienates audiences by creating superficial tableaus of

Ada's body, nearly everyone else was able to identify emotionally with the heroine as in other female-oriented melodramas. Those feminists who saw little difference between *The Piano* and more misogynist popular culture experienced that identification as masochistic, while others felt liberated by Ada's challenge to the male gaze and Campion's avant-garde disruption of the traditional functions of cinematic gazing. While the film's identificatory strategies were quite successful, my group interpreted the politics of that identification process as either feminist or non-feminist depending on their own ideology, which influenced them to see Ada as either subject or object, or perhaps both. They were also influenced by their preferences for either melodrama or avant-garde film, and by their determinations of where *The Piano* fit aesthetically and generically. As I have been arguing, the film doesn't exactly fit either polarity, because it allows melodramatic, emotional identification but alters that process by granting Ada and the female viewer at least a few moments of powerful looking and a more fully realized subjecthood than popular culture usually grants to women. For most viewers in my group, the combination resulted in a feminist experience of the relationship between looking, power, and subjectivity that was emotionally felt as well as intellectually perceived.

Sexual Agent or Sexual Object?

Audience disagreement about Ada's silence and how she is positioned by the gaze also fed into heated controversy about the film's treatment of female sexuality. This debate was fueled by contemporaneous feminist controversies about pornography, sexual harassment, domestic violence, date rape, and "victim feminism" versus "power feminism." Citing Ada's silence and her "to-be-looked-at-ness" as fuel for their interpretation, some viewers in my group compared Ada to a victimized object in porn films or domestic violence scenarios, while others saw her subverting the male privileges of speech and the look in order to become a sexual agent. Barbara Johnson argues that *The Piano*'s ambiguity about female sexuality echoes an age-old canonical literary preoccupation with the "undecidability between female pleasure and female violation" (152). To the contrary, one could attribute this film's "undecidability" and the diverse responses it engendered to the moment of its articulation within a 1990s feminist discursive context. The viewers' readings of Ada's sexuality were strongly influenced by the media-inflamed debate about the categories of "victim feminism" and "power feminism," an argument about whether feminism should focus on women as victims of patriarchy or as complicit but powerful agents in their own right. Furthermore, while Johnson takes a negative attitude toward this undecidability, arguing that the film conflates pleasure with violation, I see the textual ambiguity as crucial to the film's political power, to its ability to move viewers to articulate and strengthen their own feminist identities in response.

The categories of victim and power feminism are slippery at best and have been interpreted variously (see Maglin and Perry). My audience group identified victim feminism with anti-pornography activist MacKinnon, Take Back the Night rallies, date rape educators, and other groups who seek female solidarity and emphasize women's continued oppression under patriarchy. Power feminism, defined in opposition to victim feminism, was originally coined by Naomi Wolf in her best-seller *Fire with Fire* (1994) and was later associated with Camille Paglia and Katie Roiphe. Roiphe's book *The Morning After* (1993) launched a critique of the new "puritanism" in the anti-pornography and date rape awareness movements on college campuses. These power feminists, sometimes called "postfeminists," contend that women have a tremendous amount of power at an individual level, which they should use for their own social betterment. When they extend this argument to the field of sexuality, their thesis (and particularly Roiphe's) might be summed up by the phrase "Just Do It and Enjoy It." In the early 1990s, Paglia believed that current feminism's "public proponents are in a reactionary phase of hysterical moralism and prudery" and she hoped for "a new kind of feminism, one that stresses personal responsibility and is open to art and sex in all their dark, unconsoling mysteries" (vii). Power feminism shares a few basic premises with "pro-sex" social constructionism and postmodern feminism, although the tension between popular and academic feminists has obscured their similarities. These groups agree that women are not innocent victims but are embroiled in the values of capitalism and patriarchy, that working within the system may be more effective than radical revolt from a supposedly untainted female space, and that sexuality cannot be essentialized or made "politically correct." A pro-sex feminist influenced by poststructuralist theory, Linda Williams attacks anti-porn activist Andrea Dworkin and applauds some forms of S/M porn for underscoring the "inevitability of power in pleasure" (225). The 1990s catchword "power" is not the sole province of popular power feminists, since it has also been a central term in postmodern discourse influenced by Foucault. The crucial difference between these two uses of the term is that postmodernists emphasize the systemic nature of power operating upon people, while power feminism locates it within the individual.

Many participants in this audience group employed the rhetoric of empowerment to describe their readings of *The Piano*, but their interest in celebrating female sexual power did not completely take the place of concerns about victimization and patriarchy. When I asked them whether they liked Paglia or MacKinnon, many of those interviewed expressed sympathy for both points of view, but their responses to the film suggest that power feminism and postmodern feminism are the more dominant discourses in their lives. *The Piano*'s treatment of the power or victimhood of Ada bears some similarities to classic melodrama, in which women are sometimes represented as abject and sometimes as powerful. In melodramas, however, female power (especially any sexual power) most often gets contained by the conservative endings of the films. Those viewers who identified with "victim feminists" viewed Ada and *The Piano* as participants in this melodramatic tradition. But the fact that this film focuses more explicitly upon female sexual desire and doesn't fully domesticate that power differentiates it from typical melodramas. This challenge to the sexual roles prescribed by Hollywood cinema allowed many viewers to read the film as feminist in a postmodern sense. The majority of my audience group tended to emphasize empowerment over victimization in their responses to the film, and read Ada McGrath as a sexually liberated, postmodern feminist heroine, rather than a poignant example of the need for domestic violence education or anti-pornography activism. Despite the predominance of pro-sex feminism among the group, many of them were made uncomfortable, at least temporarily, by Baines and Ada's sexual relationship. The early scenes in which Baines proposes an exchange—the piano for the chance to touch Ada's body—made many feminist viewers queasy, since it appeared to be a familiar instance of objectification and prostitution. Ada seems to be uncomfortable in those early scenes, suffering stoically for the sake of her piano as Baines orders her to lift her skirt higher. One sociology graduate student voiced an interpretation representative of the views of rape-crisis feminists and followers of MacKinnon: "some people call it a seduction, but I would use the word rape for it. I'm not saying she wasn't aroused, but that it was exploitation, not a liberating thing. I look at it not as a forced rape, but an emotional rape." Her comment echoes that of reviewer Gullette of *The Boston Globe*, who "felt sullied by *The Piano*, muted, mutilated, threatened by rape." Gullette argues that "men who identify with Baines are going through a soft-porn experience," while female audiences are forced to re-experience the victimization of women in a masochistic mode. One problem with Gullette's review is that she makes assumptions about how gender determines audience responses, much like the apparatus film theorists. While some women in my interview group shared her viewpoint, it was challenged by many others. Male as well as female viewers in my study were disturbed by the bartering scenes, but a larger group (thirteen people) experienced them as both erotic and disturbing, often simultaneously. Most importantly, ten feminists that I interviewed found the sexual power play to be purely erotic and radically feminist.

In opposition to those who read Ada as a powerless victim, several viewers argued that she accepted the bargain freely and exerted her power in setting the terms—five keys for letting Baines fondle her neck and arms, ten keys for lying down nude. An anthropology professor contended that "she is the one who calls the shots as far as her bartering with Baines is concerned. I don't see that 'arrangement' as demeaning to her, for it seems to be something she chooses." Gayle Rubin and others have used arguments like this one to defend female sex-workers, who may gain power and/or pleasure from selling their bodies (Rubin 33–34). An undergraduate that I interviewed concurred that Ada does exert some bargaining power, but concluded instead that "it's so minimal compared to the male power over her that her resistance seems just sad and ineffectual." Still others recognized that Ada exerted free will, but were nonetheless disturbed that she made this particular choice, because "it plays into stereotypes that we have been fighting for so long, of women using their bodies to get what they want, that being their ultimate piece of property that they can disperse at will." For some people, then, the fact that Ada was not truly powerless redeemed the scenes, making it more difficult to view them as rape, but others still resisted calling Ada's power liberatory or feminist. Although the initial bartering sequence usually struck people as either a critique of or an apology for prostitution, most noted that the film soon shifted, complicating that simple plot of a woman as sexual object controlled by men. The shift occurs, of course, when Ada begins to enjoy the sexual game and eventually falls in love with Baines. The MacKinnon sympathizers found this shift the most difficult to take, and some concluded that the film was anti-feminist for reinforcing the myth that "women really do want to be raped, and that when they say no, they really do mean yes." Eight of the thirty-one people in my group saw *The Piano* as a retrograde rape fantasy, akin to Gothics and romance novels, and therefore "politically not right." These respondents did not see any positive qualities in Baines that might justify Ada's love for him. As the *Globe* reviewer Gullette exclaimed, "She may fall in love right on time, by his emotional timetable. But why should we? How can she and we forgive him?" (59). The majority of my interview group, however, did forgive him, or felt that there was nothing to forgive in the first place. While those who read the film as a fable about sexual liberation held diverse feminist positions, the eight who interpreted the film as perpetuating female victimization shared a similar feminist orientation. Most of them either volunteered for the rape crisis center on campus, sympathized with lesbian separatism, admired MacKinnon's work, or were sociologists studying victimized female populations such as battered wives or incest survivors. While this group ultimately hopes that women can be freed of victim status, their interests often necessitate some essentializing of the categories of "woman" and "man" as victim vs. oppressor, which influenced them to read Ada as a woman betraying her gender and the feminist cause by loving Baines.

"Equality feminists" in the group took a different view, focusing on the equalization of power between Ada and Baines. They felt that the film became more erotic and less disturbing once the balance of power is ensured, when Ada takes more control and Baines is somewhat emasculated, like Rochester at the end of *Jane Eyre*. Once Baines returns the piano, he no longer controls Ada, and his new vulnerability is revealed by this stereotypically feminine admission: "I don't eat, I don't sleep. . . . I want you to care for me, but you can't." In her study *The Romance Revolution*, Carol Thurston points out a similar plot development in recent, sexually explicit romance novels that works to equalize men and women—the male hero now must grovel and give ample evidence of his feminine masochism before the woman can find him sexy and worthy of love (25). The intense emotional pain that Baines suffers places him and Ada on more equal terms, and it is crucial to Ada's decision to act on her desire for him. One male undergraduate felt comfortable with the sexual politics when he realized that "Ada was willing to do it. . . . Their relationship seemed more on equal terms." A reviewer from *New York* magazine defended *The Piano* against MacKinnonites: "this is a feminist version of heterosexuality that also clearly rejects conventional feminist sexual politics. If you believe someone like Catharine MacKinnon, women always receive, so to speak, the short end of the stick, since the power resides in the man. Not so, says Campion. The power resides in equals" ("Piano Foreplay"). Equality feminists were most likely to read the film as a feminist fable implying that love and sex are best when both partners have equal power.

Rather than desiring a sharing of power, other viewers who embrace power feminism applauded the scenes in the film where Ada fondles Stewart's nude body but refuses to let him return her touch. One was pleased that "Ada's definitely in control, dominant and toying around with dominant forces of sexuality," while another put it more bluntly: "She was acting as a modern male, using him as a sexual toy." Graham Fuller of *Interview* magazine enjoyed the film for offering "a female usurpation of masculine Byronic will. This Eve, Ada, is almost an Adam." This group's pleasure at Ada's display of masculine power put them in the same discursive field with Paglia and Roiphe, who have been derided by difference feminists for their integrationist suggestion that women should act like men in order to get ahead. Mulvey might argue that Ada is just a transvestite assuming the male role of active voyeur, and that this should not be conceived as a feminist move ("Afterthoughts"). Doane might also disagree with these respondents, because she thinks that "it can never be enough simply to reverse sexual roles" (*Desire* 177). The power feminists in my group, however, feel that this reversal *is* enough, at least for now. And although most respondents saw Ada as a powerful woman, those with anti-essentialist and postmodern feminist ideas read the sexual politics very differently—instead of emphasizing either equality or female usurpation of male roles, these viewers saw in the film a Foucaultian message about the relationship between power and desire. For them, the film's most radical statement is that sex is inherently about power, a power that can never be equalized because it is a fluid dynamic, shifting from moment to moment. One self-defined anti-essentialist concurs that "sex is a really interesting situation of reciprocity, but never of equality. It's both mutual and not, because it's asymmetrical between a man and a woman. It could be mutual but not equal." Accepting that sexual desire is often fueled by such a power imbalance, these Foucault-influenced feminists reject the traditional feminist desire for equality in the bedroom, and instead seek to expose the fact that women desire sexual power as much as men do, and that they sometimes find a submissive role to be erotic as well.

The film emphasizes equality as essential to love, but it also suggests that relinquishing power can be important to sexuality. The narrative implies that Baines's initial objectification of Ada awakens her by enabling her to think of herself in sexual terms, which in turn leads her to become a sexual subject. It is precisely this suggestion—that being seen as an object can be exciting for a woman—that many feminist critics such as MacKinnon either neglect to consider or dismiss as "false consciousness," but that one-third of my interview respondents recognized. As one argued, "as Baines runs his finger along her arm and neck, her chest rises and falls, and although she may be scared, I find it more likely that she is aroused." Unlike those feminists fighting against pornography, these postmodern feminists believe that women's sexual desires cannot be essentialized, and that finding objectification sexy is not necessarily anti-feminist. As one English graduate student put it: "it's ironic that her pleasure is brought about by this prostitution scenario, but it is her pleasure and you have to allow her that. You can't judge other people's sexual desire according to politically correct standards. Women's sexuality has been so controlled for so long.

Then what the heck, if it turns her on, it turns her on." Ada's contractual strip-tease for Baines might be compared to sadomasochistic practices that Linda Williams argues are actually reciprocal agreements in which the submissive, masochistic party exerts a fair amount of power and agency in pursuing pleasure (212). While it is implied that Ada at first sees their sexual bargain as merely a desire-free economic exchange—her body for the piano—this simple relationship shifts to allow desire on Ada's part. Thus Ada seems to be both object and subject of desire at the same time, and the film ends up emphasizing "oscillating positions over strict sexual identities" (Linda Williams 226). Some respondents nonetheless tried to read the film's sexual politics in terms of rigid gender and sexual identities, and were confused or angered by the oscillation. With its suggestion that power is inevitable in all sexual relations and that this power imbalance could result in female pleasure, *The Piano* was understood by some feminists to be speaking the language of postmodern feminism or even power feminism and standing against Dworkin's equation of heterosexual sex with rape.

Ample evidence exists of the strong connections between the respondents' feminist ideology and their interpretation of the film's sexual politics, but it was also notable that more than a third (thirteen) of the group experienced the sex scenes as *both* erotic and disturbing at the same time, possibly because their own feminism is a mixture of different ideological positions. One woman whose entry into feminism was through a "touchy-feely" difference-based support group, and who was strongly disturbed that Ada's "resistance turned into desire for Baines," nevertheless was pleased that "the movie does not revel in her victimhood at all." Her response did not seem to fit a prescribed script written by either Roiphe or MacKinnon, and many others echoed her ambivalence about the victim/power debate: "the reality of women's lives is that they fluctuate between total victim and total self-creator, with most falling in between." Even those viewers who read the film as a fable about a woman's individual empowerment also noted that the film critiqued the ways in which patriarchy has historically oppressed women economically and sexually, by forcing them into arranged marriages, by denying them ownership of their property and their bodies, and by justifying male violence as a form of conjugal "rights." The film appeals to some viewers precisely because it resists the dichotomy between women-as-victim and woman-as-empowered, poles which they feel do not adequately represent their complex life experiences. They applauded the film's critique of some essentialist conceptions of female sexuality, yet were also sensitive to Campion's attention to the circumstances that unite all women who live under patriarchal conditions. In a sense, these viewers were responding as well to the textual hybridity of the film; by mixing melodramatic and feminist avant-garde strategies for representing women, the filmic codes combined anti-essentialist and essentialist conceptions of sexuality and gender, and this synthesis or conjunction resonated with their everyday lives.

One of the tensions present in the film that resonated powerfully with my audience group was the often difficult negotiation between feminist ideals and a desire for love and marriage. Like many other feminists texts since Betty Friedan's *The Feminine Mystique*, *The Piano* critiques marriage by comparing Ada's love affair with Baines to her violent relationship with Stewart, implying that the marriage is actually the truly prostituting relationship. Despite this critique of power relations in marriage, the film also relies heavily on a sentimental investment in the romance between Ada and Baines, and the majority of my audience group enjoyed this melodramatic plotline and rooted for them to stay together. Several self-proclaimed romantics felt that Ada and Baines's love wiped away all the sexually disturbing aspects of their earlier interactions. One expressed this view, albeit with embarrassment: "But he loved her, and that's what made it good, that they were both in love. . . . Is that cheesy?" For many of these romantics, sexuality is inextricable from the discourse of love; what turned them on was the love affair, not necessarily the sex. However, some women in the group were resistant to Ada's love for Baines precisely *because* of the sexual power-play; this group tended to be more skeptical about marriage and heterosexual romance, arguing that it hinders feminist goals by seducing women into following cultural roles prescribed by patriarchy and reinforced by melodramatic texts. These viewers (almost all female) thus declared the film's happy ending segment to be anti-feminist, while others loved the romance and felt that it was wholly compatible with their feminist ideals. By drawing attention to the existence of an understudied group—academic feminists who love romance—my case study speaks to Radway's call for more research on romance consumption among highly-educated professional women (*Reading the Romance* 50).

What is at stake in *The Piano*'s treatment of romance, clearly, is the familiar liberal feminist concern about how to reconcile one's intellectual theories or professional interests with one's sexual and/or romantic desires, in this case heterosexual desires. A new backdrop to this discussion was the advent of a "postfeminist" generation influenced by power feminism as well as postmodern feminism. The term postfeminist has been used by writers such as Tania Modleski as a synonym for an anti-feminist backlash fostered by men (see Modleski's *Feminism without Women)*, but in the popular press it is often used neutrally or positively, and connected with power feminism or postmodern anti-essentialist feminism (see Patricia Mann). In my survey of the term's usage in three hundred magazine and newspaper articles on the Lexis/Nexis database, "postfeminist" is most often associated with a return to femininity, with "politically incorrect" sexual desire, with female sexual power, and with a traditional desire for kids and family as well as careers. Heterosexual postfeminist women see themselves as equals to men and accept the empowering benefits of feminism, but they also reject feminism's overemphasis on success in the workplace and its purported connection with militant lesbianism (an image fostered by anti-feminist media personalities such as Rush Limbaugh); they instead want to flaunt their femininity, have kids, and love men without worrying about political correctness, power dynamics or sexual objectification. A lot of the undergraduate women I interviewed sympathize with this popular reaction and are somewhat ambivalent about identifying themselves as feminist because they "like men" and do not feel particularly oppressed by them. *The Piano*'s melodramatic love plot, and particularly the happy ending scene, strongly appealed to their desire for an end to the "battle of the sexes." The ending of the film, however, deserves more careful attention, since its multi-part, hybrid structure complicated audience responses and affected their interpretation of its feminist or possibly "post-feminist" meanings.

Multiple Endings for Multiple Feminisms

The Piano offers not one but three ending sequences, each appealing to different audience tastes for either avant-garde or popular plots. This ending sequence also attempts to resolve or address all the feminist-related themes under discussion here—silence, speech, sexuality, romance, empowerment, victimization, resistance to patriarchy, subjectivity and self-determination. The first "ending" depicts Ada leaving the island with Baines, nearly drowning herself, and choosing life; the second is the sentimental, sun-lit shot of Ada and Baines's newly established home, where she has begun to speak and now teaches piano lessons; and the third presents Ada's dream image of herself dead, at the bottom of the ocean with her piano. The three-part structure causes difficulties for viewer interpretation, since it evokes both the traditional melodramatic happy ending and the dark, often ambiguous endings of many avant-garde films. It ends up doing both, and therefore neither, offering a strange hybrid ending that challenges audience expectations by offering closure and then suspending it. This multipart ending allows viewers to privilege their own preferred ending and makes the process of interpretation even more politicized and personal. For the most part, my audience group grappled with the mixed messages of the three endings and constructed a reading that synthesized them. This symbiotic interpretation parallels the hybrid identity that many feminists have constructed for themselves out of the various discourses of gender present in contemporary culture—an identity that allows them to indulge their heterosexual love fantasies yet to strive for their feminist ideals, to deconstruct gender yet to function within their gender role every day. Most of my audience group were pleased or at least satisfied with the compromise feminist vision that the endings offered (if read as a whole), while more radical feminists rejected the melodramatic romance ending and used the film as a launching pad for their own concerns about the bourgeois "watering down" of feminism. Regardless of their responses, the film enabled these viewers to shape and strengthen their own political identification as feminist and provoked them to argue publicly about what feminism is and why it matters.

The film's endings adjudicate between melodramatic closure and postmodern openness and juxtapose the sentimental with the sublime, but it was tempting for viewers to read the melodramatic scene as "the" ending of the film. However, a significant number of my group tried to connect all three endings together in a signifying string and to think about how each new scene changed or qualified the previous segments. While many argue that the film could have ended effectively as Ada rose out of the ocean, having chosen life, I contend that the last two shots profoundly affect the feminist meaning of the film. When we are transported from this emotionally wrenching drowning sequence to a brightly lit shot of Ada reestablishing a domestic life with Baines while Flora turns cartwheels in the yard, we are encouraged to indulge in the comfort of this sentimental closure. We know that Ada is safe in a more civilized town, that Flora is carefree, that Ada can play the piano again via a prosthetic finger, that she is in love, that she is trying to speak—in short, we are transported to the familiar ground of Hollywood domesticity and bourgeois normalcy that usually closes out melodramatic texts, which often wrest a happy ending out of the most dire of circumstances. But Campion does not let us rest there, and follows up with a coda that destabilizes the preceding endings. The first-person voice-over tells us that this last shot is a recurrent dream of Ada's that serves as her "strange lullaby"—that she went down with her piano and remains silent "in the cold grave, under the deep deep sea." This coda may have been a compromise on the part of Campion, whose first drafts of the screenplay ended with Ada's death by drowning. Although Ada does choose life in the final version of the script, she still dreams of death, almost mourning the loss of her former silent self. The fact that we are left with a visual image of a drowned Ada unsettles the sentimental closure of the previous ending, making us wonder whether that domestic bliss is wholly fulfilling for her. The audience is suspended along with Ada's body underwater; we cannot know definitively what this last shot means because it evokes the sublime, as opposed to the sentimental. By including Thomas Hood's sonnet about the sublimity of silence ("there is a silence where hath been no sound/ There is a silence where no sound may be"), the coda makes us wonder if silence has more power than speech. The previous sentimental ending suggested that verbal communication is an improvement over Ada's frustrated muteness, but now we are not so sure. The tension between the two endings—one sentimental, the other sublime—attempts to dissuade the viewer from simply enjoying one ending and ignoring the other. It urges you to consider both in conjunction, and it leaves you with questions rather than answers.

This ambiguity disturbed a few viewers, however, who "selected" one ending as the real or most meaningful one. The interview subjects' sense of the film's high or low cultural status and their own taste preferences affected their expectations about how it should end. One woman appreciated the "Cinderella ending like we like in the United States, that you go off and live happily ever after." Many of those who desired the happy ending, even against their feminist "better" judgment, simply repressed the sublime underwater shot from their memories; as one person noted, "I didn't remember the last shot. I thought the happy ending was trite, trying to reach mainstream audiences. But since I forgot the last ending, maybe I wanted the happy ending that I thought was so trite." Many viewers like this one could not overcome their distaste for the clichéd melodramatic closure, and felt that an avant-garde film ought to have ended in death. An English graduate student admitted that "we have this idea that art can't have happy endings." Several of the students of literature that I interviewed, no doubt influenced by postmodern artists' rejection of such tidy endings, desire openness instead of closure and criticized Campion's sentimental ending for catering to a "pathological need for resolution of every issue." Most of those I interviewed, however, noticed that the film's ending was trying to both open and close—to offer a resolution, but a limited one, and to combine a comforting romance with the disturbance of the sublime. Many tried to work out a complex interpretation that wove the endings together, as one undergraduate did: "I had a 'warm fuzzy' in the scene where he fashioned her a new fingertip. . . . I think that's why it was important to cut to the scene of her floating above the piano. It makes sure that I didn't forget what had just happened prior to the happy ending." A graduate student in literature liked the "postmodern ambiguity" of the double ending, arguing that "the last scene . . . qualifies the liberation which she does achieve." While this film could be seen as doubly coded for different high and low cultural audiences, it is clear that the majority of my audience group was attracted by the mixture of cultural codes, possibly because this mixture spoke to their identities as intellectuals who are also avid consumers of popular culture. The viewers' responses to the endings' high and low cultural elements were generally tied up with their feminist ideals—those who prefer avant-garde culture were usually those with a more radical feminist agenda, protesting against bourgeois patriarchy in all of its manifestations, while those viewers who allow themselves to enjoy the romance of melodrama were more amenable to a liberal feminist agenda in which they could retain the "feminine" and work alongside men to make change.

Two events in the ending sequence separated my audience group strongly into radical and liberal positions—Ada's suicide attempt and her decision to settle down with Baines—and these two plots of death vs. romance/marriage can easily be connected to avant-garde and melodramatic traditions. Like the death vs. marriage subplots, Ada's choice between silence and speech also seemed to divide viewers into radical and practical feminist camps, as discussed earlier. Liberal feminists liked the sentimental ending because they felt that George was worth speaking to precisely because he listened to and understood Ada. While some viewers may think she has lost power and some of her self-determination by speaking, many thought she has gained the wisdom to see that outright revolt may lead to alienation and even annihilation. She decides to learn the master's language, but she will make it speak new and different words because she will remain the "town freak." A few viewers connected Ada's compromise with one that they think feminism is strongly in need of—a means to attract more mainstream women into the fold, to prevent them from fashioning themselves as "postfeminist" and abandoning the feminist work that still desperately needs to be done. Even though Ada is still perceived as a freak at the end of the film, she is certainly less freakish and more socially integrated than she had been while silent, and this change appealed to many viewers with more mainstream feminist desires.

As Ada abandons a more radical choice of silence, she similarly rejects suicide as the ultimate feminist protest. Those viewers with a more pessimistic view of the possibility for change felt that following through with her suicide attempt would have been a stronger feminist condemnation of patriarchy, as in the film *Thelma and Louise* and Kate Chopin's novel *The Awakening.* One self-proclaimed "radical" was disappointed that Ada chose to live under patriarchy, arguing that "at least *Thelma and Louise* offered a clear feminist critique—there is no place for a woman in this environment except death." The Marxist graduate student who prefers his politics "with teeth" wished that the film has ended with Ada's drowning—"that at least would have been a bleak, harrowing ending." It is important to note, however, that these feminists desire more radical feminist politics from representations than they are willing to pursue in their own personal lives—none of them was suicidal, and they were all successful students and professionals, some happily married as well. By pointing this out I do not mean to criticize these viewers for the disjunction between their lives and their demands of texts, since radical feminist representations serve as an important counter-balance to the plethora of misogynist texts in our culture. This desire for representations more radical than one's own politics is clearly a widespread phenomenon, as evidenced by the enormous popularity of *Thelma and Louise,* a film which celebrates feminist suicide, among women who do not define themselves as feminist at all. *The Piano*'s sentimental ending scene strives for a more realistic note than *Thelma and Louise*, because it tries to refamiliarize Ada's situation, to take it out of the realm of fantasy, and to make audiences recognize in the representation a similarity to their own lives, in which compromises are far more frequent than revolt.

Some participants in the audience group argued that suicide is not necessarily radical or even feminist. As Bruzzi points out, "to die in the mode of a tragic heroine would have been to succumb to another masculine tradition" (266). One male viewer in my group was glad the film stood in opposition to male writers like "Poe, who believed that the most romantic and poetic subject in the world is the death of a beautiful woman." In an astute review, Graham Fuller of *Interview* remarked that "the watery grave she contemplates is a tantalizing Gothic option, akin to Edgar Allan Poe's Annabel Lee 'in her sepulcher there by the sea,'" but Fuller ultimately applauds Ada's refusal of the fate that misogynist (and some feminist) writers have reserved for their heroines. Many thus interpreted Ada's decision to rise to the surface as a more progressive feminist message than any death wish. One viewer remarked of the moment when Ada's will chooses life: "it was basically her only conscious choice in the whole movie; she took charge of her life then." More than two-thirds of my audience group felt that "choosing life" was one of the more important feminist statements of the film. Although the options of suicide or life divided responses, many viewers felt that the coda or last ending, in which Ada dreams of herself dead, offered an important mediation between these two poles. The coda suggests that Ada has achieved a hybrid position—she accepts life under patriarchal conditions but fantasizes about the peace of death as the ultimate freedom. One student remarked that the coda "restored my faith that she didn't get completely changed; she still has that silent, morbid side to her." Even a self-proclaimed radical feminist, who had strongly desired the suicide ending, was moved by this suggestion of a sort of "death-in-life" and read it as subversive, although in a more muted way. Campion's decision to end the film with this dream of death, rather than Ada's actual death, seems to have succeeded in appealing to a much wider feminist audience than either of the endings alone might have done.

The coda was perceived positively by most feminists, but the previous "happily-ever-after" shot produced significant controversy in the press and among audiences. Ada's choice to live, of course, is also a choice to make a life with Baines, and some perceived this arrangement as a loss for Ada, a reinscription into bourgeois patriarchy. African American feminist writer bell hooks was the most outspoken critic of Ada's decision to live with Baines. Hooks argued that the film's ending is misogynist, akin to gangsta rap: "[Ada] lets go her longing to display passion through artistic expression. A nuclear family now, Baines, Ada, and Flora resettle and live happily ever after. Suddenly, patriarchal order is restored. Ada becomes a modest wife. . . . Baines is in charge" ("Gangsta" 120). Furthermore, she believes that the film "advances the sexist assumption that heterosexual women will give up artistic practice to find 'true love'" ("Gangsta" 121). Several among my audience group agreed with hooks. An anthropology professor found it problematic that Ada gets "tamed and domesticated," while a student similarly mourned what she saw as the loss of Ada's art: "she's not going to be the same person or have the same music, now that she's taken the boat back to society." Many of these viewers argued that a life with Baines would put her "back to the same oppressive situation that's not qualitatively different than what she had before." One man felt the happy ending tries too hard to "redeem Baines as the better choice," as somehow outside of patriarchy, when actually the two men are both really "stand-ins for a patriarchal order, which made all of Ada's problems possible in the first place."

In contrast to those participants in the survey who criticized the film's redemption of Baines as Mr. Right, many viewers felt that Ada's decision to live with Baines should not be seen as a capitulation to patriarchy. Many argued that choosing a more sensitive man, who may occasionally lapse back into macho habits, is in fact what most feminist heterosexual women do in their own lives. Furthermore, Kathy Maio of *Ms.* magazine emphasizes the radical nature of Ada's choice in its nineteenth-century context: "by choosing whom to love, Ada brings down the wrath of patriarchy." Since opting out of the marriage market altogether is nearly impossible for a Victorian woman with no means of financial sustenance, her choice of George could be seen as a subversive one, since he is decidedly unconventional and is sensitive to her sexual desires and artistic passion, unlike her husband Stewart. Beyond applauding Ada's choice of Baines, many felt that romantic bliss should not be seen as incompatible with feminism, as one woman said: "I don't see falling in love or finding happiness as falling into the hands of patriarchy." Most of these pro-romance viewers define themselves as liberal feminists because they see joining society and getting married as a positive thing. Even one feminist with affinity for radical separatist theory acknowledged a split between her theory and her everyday desires: "if you are a feminist, you aren't supposed to want the heroine to get married, but in real life, sometimes you do want to get married." Campion's film can be read as a critique of the popular "backlash" view of feminists as frigid, selfish, career-minded zealots who don't need anyone, least of all men. This film also questions hooks's implication that art is a more worthwhile pursuit for a feminist than love.

As I have been arguing, the film tries to adjudicate between two plotlines traditionally associated with female characters—self-righteous death or marriage—and this compromise offers important political messages for our contemporary moment. Nancy Miller was among the first of feminist literary critics to note that women's fiction has repeated the plots deemed plausible for women—either love or be an independent self, but not both. Discussing George Eliot's *The Mill on the Floss* as a prototypical text, Miller argues that "Maggie Tulliver, too, would be herself and love, but the price for that unscriptable wish proves again to be the deferral of conventional erotic longings, what Maggie calls 'earthly happiness'" (353). I would argue that *The Piano* attempts to allow Ada that feminist "unscriptable wish" to be herself *and* love, but the film also recognizes that love and marriage can entail some muting of self-definition, although not necessarily a loss of self. Ada is happy in the end, but she also dreams of her former glorious stand of silence. While some experienced the romance plot as a loss for Ada, many others recognized its importance against a backdrop of either/or plots for women. One graduate student preferred Campion's film to the ending of another famous text about an adulteress, *The Scarlet Letter*, because "Ada doesn't have to choose between living on the outskirts of town in this liminal position, or being totally boringly integrated. She's allowed to have a whole family, she's allowed to have her lover, unlike Hester Prynne."

The final shot of the film also serves to remind us that Ada's choice of a monogamous coupling with Baines was not made without some regret that keeps resurfacing in her dreams. Ada does not simply become co-opted by patriarchy, because she creates a personal space in which she continues to question her relationship to men and to life. As she says of her death dream: "it is a weird lullaby and so it is; it is *mine*." The use of the word "mine" echoes the earlier scene in which she claimed the piano as her own, despite the lack of women's property rights, and this lexical repetition suggests that Ada has not given up her desire for self-determination. Although the previous melodramatic ending had more staying power for many viewers, the coda offered to some a poignant moment of withdrawal from the romance script. *The Piano*'s treatment of romance gains an added significance if it is read against a backdrop of contemporary feminist concerns. The myth that feminists are man-haters still disturbs the heterosexual women in my audience group, most of whom desire to interact with and love men and to succeed in the world without feeling oppressed all the time. Many of the male feminists I interviewed also felt beleaguered by some feminists' equation of all men with patriarchy, and desired peace with women. Most of the audience responses underscored the tension between feminism and a sentimental desire for the genders to coexist happily, and the film plays precisely upon this ambivalence. Some critics were angry at the film's ending for watering down its message by attempting to "have it both ways," to offer a feminist tale of a powerful, sexually desiring woman resisting patriarchy but also to appease those melodramatic tastes for a romantic happy ending where the girl gets the guy. The film certainly attempts to have it both ways, but so do many of the people that I know. Feminists *do* read romance novels and watch soap operas, but not always for the purpose of critiquing their ideology. As one graduate student put it, "I don't feel like it's selling out if Ada and Baines do get married at the end. One of my projects as a feminist is that you can be married, somewhat normalized, and still have even a radical feminist agenda. I want to be a practical feminist and still live in my world with my house and my husband, and the ending [of the film] is just a relief." *The Piano* has power as a cultural text precisely because it allows many possibilities to be in play at the same time, without cancelling each other out, and thus recognizes the multiplicity of women's (and men's) desires. Its power is amplified by its ability to provoke so many strong responses, in so many different directions. This film is political in a very basic sense in that it moves people to feel passionately and to think critically about their ideal feminist world.

Some may argue that *The Piano*'s compromise politics are nothing new and may dismiss the film as just another liberal feminist text. My response would be that liberal feminism, or at least its attempt to reach a wider, more diverse audience, needs to be revalued as an emotionally potent weapon against both an antifeminist backlash and the apathy and waning of affect that accompanies postmodern sensibilities. Furthermore, *The Piano* cannot simply be explained by the vague and outdated political designation "liberal feminist," because its particular combination of ideologies situate it in relation to newer feminist discourses present in the early 1990s, particularly the popularity of postmodern feminism, power feminism, and post-feminism. While the film returns to some stable narratives of old, with its romance thread and its invocation of gender difference, it also juxtaposes them with new discourses of anti-essentialism and politically incorrect sexuality. The result is a hybrid text whose politics can be called neither radical nor liberal, because it involves a reconsideration of both positions.

The film's particular mixture of the aesthetic strategies of avant-garde film and popular melodrama could be seen as a textual reflection of the concatenation of different worldviews and identities present in contemporary culture. *The Piano*'s textual hybridity works to brings these identity conflicts to the surface, so that audiences are able to become conscious of them and react emotionally and intellectually to the versions of gender and feminist identity presented there. Not only did this hybrid feminist text reflect current discursive conflicts, but it also spoke to and appealed most directly to a kind of female viewer who is hybrid herself—one with sympathy for both victim and power feminists, who uses gender essentialist concepts but also hopes to move beyond them, who desires romance but fights against patriarchy, who is wary of objectification yet can also be turned on by it, who desires to be both feminine and feminist. In this vein, Susan Bordo hopes that a combination of postmodern anti-essentialism with a continued attention to gender difference will offer a feminist theory and practice most in tune with the realities of our lives, in which "our deepest desire may be to 'transcend gender dualities'. . . . But like it or not, in our present culture, our activities are coded as 'male' or 'female' and will function as such within the prevailing system of gender-power relations" (Bordo 152). By depicting such a realistic struggle between surface and depth constructions of gender, *The Piano* suggests the value of political compromises in an era where feminism is losing popular support. The film's compromise vision soothes while still upsetting, invoking familiar paradigms and simultaneously challenging viewers to rethink them. Viewing *The Piano* is a political experience, because it implicates each viewer in the postmodern struggle between competing melodramatic and poststructuralist versions of gender and feminist identity and offers a precarious balance that both comforts and destabilizes, just like real life.

Chapter Four

Northern Exposure and Postmodern Utopian Communities

Once one of the most popular programs on television and winner of an Emmy for Best Drama in 1991–92, *Northern Exposure* was unusually highbrow television fare, offering viewers weekly philosophical ruminations about cultural pluralism, democracy, gender and sexuality, and the meaning of artistic production. Many television critics have commented that *Exposure*'s demise after six seasons (1990–95) was less surprising than the fact that this intellectual show ever commanded such a large following. Ranked in the Nielsen top-15 for three seasons, the program spawned several fanclubs, including an Internet newsgroup (alt.tv.northern-exp). While "quality" television programs aimed at affluent and educated consumers (shows such as *St. Elsewhere*, *Hill Street Blues*, and *thirtysomething*) had found a niche on the tube in the '80s, few of those shows were as committed to postmodern aesthetics and theoretical concerns as was *Northern Exposure* (see Feuer, Kerr, and Vahimagi; Betsy Williams). Rather than extolling *Northern Exposure* as a rare example of "high art" within a culturally debased medium, this chapter explores how the program juxtaposed seemingly incompatible strategies of high and mass culture. Although the program often employed postmodern self-reflexivity and ironic intertextuality, it also adopted sentimental and romantic strategies common to popular culture—a strong investment in "heart and soul," in populist values, and in utopian visions of harmonious communities. The ambiguous positioning of this text requires a reconsideration of existing frameworks for analyzing television and its audiences.

Analyzing this hybrid program allows me to uncover blind spots in several critical traditions. Television critics tend to focus on the pleasures and politics of distinct genres (such as the soap opera, sitcom, sci-fi drama, and talk show) rather than investigating the more ambiguous politics of hybrid forms and texts such as *Exposure*. Cultural studies television critics in particular have slighted highbrow texts, preferring to analyze mass-produced lowbrow genres and their consumption by viewers with low cultural capital (see Hobson; Newcomb; Radway, *Reading the*

Romance). In his book *Understanding Popular Culture*, Fiske asserts that "popular culture is the culture of the subordinate and the disempowered" (5). Since the early Birmingham School's efforts to recover working class culture and history, cultural studies scholars have been committed to investigating mass-produced culture as an instrument of power and hegemony, and to uncovering resistant subcultures among disempowered groups (see Cary Nelson, Treichler, and Grossberg; Hebdige, *Subculture*). Although this perspective is crucial to cultural studies work in the field of television, an exclusive focus on lowbrow texts and disempowered audiences underestimates the diversity of class groups and taste cultures to which television appeals. Even more problematic is the fact that the majority of postmodern theorists view television as irrelevant to the field of postmodernism. Lyotard, for example, equates postmodernism with an avant-garde rejection of realism and the "solace of good forms" offered by mass culture (81). In *The Politics of Postmodernism*, Hutcheon focuses on high-cultural literature and art films, and dismisses television as "tangential" to postmodernism: "most television, in its unproblematized reliance on realist narrative and transparent representational conventions, is pure commodified complicity, without the critique needed to define the postmodern paradox" (10) of "complicitous critique" (2). I will be arguing, counter to Hutcheon, that the writers of *Northern Exposure* offer precisely that—a form of complicitous critique. The existence of programs like *Northern Exposure* challenges Jameson's claim that affective popular texts are merely "residual" products of realism or melodrama, outside of the "forcefield" of postmodernism (*Postmodernism* 6). In contrast to Jameson, who ignores television as a throwback to historically anterior aesthetic practices, Baudrillard focuses on the postmodern qualities of the medium as a whole—its flow and fragmentation, and its creation of a "hyperreal," image-saturated space. Influenced by Baudrillard, many cultural critics emphasize the "medium over the message" (Seiter, Borchers, Kreutzner, and Warth 9), and thus rarely treat individual television programs as postmodern texts in their own right (see Joyrich for an exception). This lack of attention to the narrative and aesthetic strategies of particular television texts is a central problem in television research. Jackie Stacey notes that "television studies have tended to privilege the context over the text" (*Star* 35) and have been dominated by audience research in the fields of communications and cultural studies; most of this work ignores the text's role in setting up interpretive possibilities.

Important questions about the processes of consumption are raised by *Exposure*'s textual bricolage of high art and popular strategies and themes, from postmodernist aesthetics to sentimental romance plots. To examine how viewers negotiate these competing discourses, I conducted a study with members of the Internet newsgroup fanclub alt.tv.northern-exp, which includes several hundred fans in the U.S., Australia, and Europe. My research consisted of reading about 1,000 newsgroup posts during 1994–95 (and intermittently after the show's cancellation), and analyzing the responses of forty-four newsgroup readers who completed my detailed questionnaire. Since this sample is clearly limited to viewers with Internet access, and to fans ardent enough to fill out a questionnaire, this study does not make totalizing claims about the *Northern Exposure* audience. Instead, I offer a localized case study of audience response, recognizing that reception histories are always partial and contingent, but may nonetheless open up new lines of inquiry for media scholars.

If one accepts the dominant arguments about aesthetic taste in cultural theory, one would assume that this hybrid television program is doubly or multiply coded for different taste cultures—for the librarians as well as the soap opera fans—and that each group might be ignoring major strands of the program. But my survey indicated that these individual fans belong to several purportedly distinct taste cultures at once. This finding challenges Bourdieu's schematic connections between taste and class, and his reduction of individuals to a single aesthetic disposition or mode of identification with texts (critical distance vs. engagement). My group's taste "identities" were hybrid (TV-junkie librarians), and their response to the program was a complex combination of critical appreciation and intensely emotional engagement. While I found that my group was skewed towards the upper-middle class in terms of education (56% had gone beyond a B.A.), and thus fit the marketing demographics for "quality" television, they were not merely attracted to the show for its arty aesthetics and thought-provoking writing, but also for its ability to make them feel as well as think. This case study of alt.tv.northern-exp sheds light on a group whose existence is often ignored by audience researchers—well-educated, elite viewers who are nonetheless devoted to popular culture and accept many of its sentimental values.

Not only did my audience research suggest the need to rethink a class-stratified theory of taste cultures, but it also challenged the common understanding of identification as self-recognition. The majority of this audience group did not identify primarily with those characters who shared their social positions. The identification process was also influenced by the fact that gender, religious, and racial difference are major themes on *Northern Exposure*. The text's treatment of these issues vacillates between an assertion of group difference common to melodramatic popular texts and a postmodern deconstruction of essentialist identities. This program's ambivalent treatment of subjectivity encouraged viewers to respect difference, but not to reify it. Although the program often focuses on narratives about identity, it is even more intensely concerned with the issue of community, of uniting disparate individuals into a harmonious democratic unit. While political theorists have lamented the lack of utopian desire and communitarian feeling in postmodern societies, *Northern Exposure* offers a utopian vision of a postmodern society rooted in pluralism. Like many American popular texts, the program is intensely invested in the traditional value of community, of uniting disparate individuals into a harmonious democratic unit. But while mass culture often relies on static identities of race, ethnicity, class, and region as the grounding for communal belonging, *Northern Exposure* deconstructs essentialist identities without dismissing the sentimental pleasures of solidarity. *Northern Exposure*'s idealization of a diverse multicultural community encompasses both the emotional comfort of humanist and Enlightenment utopian myths as well as a rigorous critique of the universalizing tendencies of communitarian philosophies. By uniting a sentimental, humanist faith in community with a postmodern commitment to celebrating "difference," the program attracted liberal and politically radical viewers with a vision of democracy that rejects the nihilistic strands of poststructuralism. *Northern Exposure*'s neo-liberal political vision is what attracted many of these viewers to the text. Instead of identifying with this popular text primarily because they recognized their own identities on display (as many critics of mass culture would have us believe), they in fact identified much more consciously with its progressive utopian politics and postmodern pluralist ideology. Their identification process was not only consciously ideological, but also thoroughly sentimental. One viewer experienced "warm fuzzy feelings inside" as she contemplated the liberal political message of this postmodern utopian community. My study of this television program and its fans complicates the usual equation of postmodern high culture with subversion and sentimental popular culture with the status quo. In fact, this television text aided viewers in constructing themselves as liberal or even leftist political subjects, thereby disrupting the Marxist critical assumption that television interpellates viewers into conservative subject positions.

Production and Consumption Contexts for the Television Medium

Although I am grouping this television text along with films, a novel, and a musical as examples of "sentimental postmodernism," I want to underscore the difference that the medium of television has made in my investigation of *Northern Exposure* and its viewers. First of all, this study differs from those on *The Piano* and *Kiss of the Spider Woman* both in its survey methodology and in the type of audience group analyzed. Because television texts, unlike most novels and films, encourage the creation of fanclubs, I focused on an already existing fan group that could be called a "subculture," since its members influence each other's interpretations. While my other audience groups were united solely by locality and in most cases did not know each other, participants of this Internet "newsgroup" represent an on-line community whose members meet regularly in virtual space although they live in many different states and foreign countries (including England, Croatia, Finland, and Australia). The geographic dispersal of the newsgroup members made it necessary to solicit their responses by questionnaire, rather than by personal interview.

In the construction of my questionnaire document (see Appendix C), I attempted to heed the warnings about empiricism raised by proponents of more qualitative, ethnographic research methods. The general argument against quantitative sociological research is that multiple-choice questionnaires do not tell the whole story; they constrict the respondents by setting up leading questions and a limited range of terms and answers, they ignore viewing context, and they reduce responses to numbers, ignoring the complexity of each individual and each viewing situation (Ang, "Wanted: Audiences," *Desperately Seeking the Audience*). To address some of these criticisms, I combined qualitative and quantitative analysis and employed both multiple-choice and open-ended questions. In response to the concern that multiple-choice surveys reveal more about the researcher's language than that of the respondents, I wrote the questionnaire using phrases and vocabulary culled from the newsgroup postings over the course of a full year. The few multiple-choice questions that I constructed were based on sliding scales and ranking systems rather than the controlling direction to choose a single answer. Multiple-choice questions were also followed by broader ones about a similar theme, asking the respondents to answer at length in their own words. Discrepancies between my constructed choices and the respondents' own explanations usefully underscored the way that cultural discourses affect interpretation. Sociologist Eva Illouz defends the questionnaire on the grounds that the discourses it reveals are a main channel of access to hidden states: "rather than giving us insight into meaning in context and action, it gives us insight . . . into discourse about meanings" (21). My questionnaire was constructed to access discursive structures and taste preferences, just as most ethnographers use interviews. My analysis not only foregrounds patterns of response along social group axes, which is the predominant goal of quantitative sociological audience research, but also uncovers disruptions to patterns and acknowledges contradictions within individual responses, as in qualitative, ethnographic analyses.

The most frequent objection to using questionnaires has been that it does not give a researcher any access to how the text is consumed, usually in the home (Morley, *Television*). But since this fan culture exists outside the home on the Internet, and its members rarely meet in person, observing viewers in their domestic arrangement would have been beside the point. Instead, I met members of the fanclub through the disembodied words of on-line posts and email exchanges, just as they meet each other. However, the survey did address viewing contexts by asking questions about their attitudes toward television, their cultural tastes, which parts of the whole series (six seasons) they had watched, whether their viewing was casual or intensely involved, and whether they treated it as an ephemeral text or one to be taped and treasured. I also asked about their participation in the newsgroup, to determine if they were peripheral or central members of this fan subculture. All of these contextual issues were directly or indirectly related to a discussion of taste cultures and identification. The wider context of the television medium and its specific conditions of production, in comparison to film and literature, also has salient effects upon viewer identification and interpretation. No television program has a single author, and authors of individual episodes must work in tandem with network producers. Shifts in the program content may be directly affected by the network's marketing strategies or fears. This diffused control makes it more difficult to attribute a politics to a whole television program, since single episodes may subtly contradict the messages of other episodes, and a program's themes or aesthetics may change over time due to market concerns. This diachronic factor is the most challenging aspect of studying television texts, for one has to decide what constitutes the text: is it the whole series, particular seasons, or individual episodes?

I treat the *Northern Exposure* "text" as the sum of its parts, by focusing on a few key episodes, referring to textual moments from all six seasons, and noting the shifts in focus, politics, and aesthetics that have occurred over time (the fanclub was also acutely sensitive to these shifts, with many newsgroup posts lamenting such changes in the program's politics and aesthetics in the latter seasons). My analysis moves back and forth from the part to the whole, acknowledging that any sense of the whole is filtered through an individual viewer's perspective, including my own. Since each one of my audience members had seen different episodes out of a total of 110, I could not ask them to interpret the same episode; instead they were prompted to "explain" their three favorite episodes and one they had seen recently, since the show was in its final season and also airing in syndication. The fact that each viewer was responding to a different set of texts might seem to compromise any generalizations one could make about reception. Yet it would be impossible to study audience response to serialized forms, or any television series for that matter, without accepting the fluid parameters of the text as a basic and unavoidable principle. Furthermore, my analysis focused precisely on the ways in which the viewers constructed totalizing narratives out of their partial knowledge of specific episodes; what parts they emphasized, and how they negotiated the contradictions, revealed a great deal about their priorities and tastes.

In addition to the mosaic nature of television texts, the diachronic factor—their daily or weekly appearance over a period of years—influences and often intensifies audience identification with TV shows and their characters. Jane Feuer has pointed out crucial differences in the viewing conditions for television and film that affect their "metapsychology." Whereas the public and silent viewing of film leads to immobilized immersion akin to a dream state, television invites interaction and erases the boundary between the on-screen world and the home (Feuer, "Narrative Form" 104). While television commercials disrupt immersion, interfering with the psychic fantasy that one experiences watching film, a viewer's identification with TV characters is enhanced by weekly or daily encounters, as they are woven into the fabric of one's private routines and experiences. *Northern Exposure* was on the air for more than eight years (six on CBS, and then in syndication on the Arts & Entertainment channel), and most of the fans grieved deeply after the CBS cancellation. One respondent summed up the group sentiment when he wrote, "I felt as if I had lost touch with an old friend that I would never hear from again." In contrast, film viewing might be described as a "one-night stand," a two-hour interaction even if viewed repeatedly, versus 110 different exposures of *Northern Exposure*. The diachronic factor influences fans to discuss television characters as if they are real people, perhaps more so than they do with cinematic or literary characters. Among my Internet group, a prominent mode of audience response is one that Liebes has categorized as the "Real," "in which characters and situations [from television] are incorporated uncritically into viewers' lives and vice versa" (179). As Liebes notes, individual viewers may experience this type of referential engagement along with more distanced or critical modes of involvement, which Liebes characterizes as "Ideological" and "Aesthetic"; those modes of response were also prevalent in my group. The intense engagement in the "Real" mode, however, was nearly universal among these fans. I contend that this phenomenon is not only common to the reception of popular culture, but more particularly of serial televisual forms.

The intense engagement associated with television sometimes engenders a defensive reaction among culturally literate viewers who fear being perceived as dupes glued to the tube. Ellen Seiter has noted that television watching, unlike watching films or reading books, "can be a touchy subject, precisely because of its association with a lack of education, with idleness and unemployment, and its identification as an 'addiction' of women and children" ("Making Distinctions" 388). Given that the majority of this audience group had earned college degrees, I wondered if some members might be harboring elitist biases against television that could influence their responses to this show, so I asked them to compare *Northern Exposure* to other TV shows and to list all the programs that they watch regularly. While a few denigrated TV as a whole for offering merely "ratings-generated entertainment" rather than "art," all saw *Northern Exposure* as superior to and more original than other television programs because it encourages active and thoughtful viewing. The newsgroup members accentuated their critical activity by posting evaluative analyses of episodes, potential scripts they had written, and critiques of the show's development. A self-proclaimed "diehard elitist" in the fanclub remarked on the irony of his investment in a piece of pop culture: "I put a higher value on my *Northern Exposure* video library than all the movies I've ever seen or books I've ever read put together. Whoda thunk it?" The debased nature of the television medium was thus an important backdrop to the pride that this man and others have in being fans of *Northern Exposure*. Their elitist response to the television medium, however, did not prevent them from indulging in sentimental responses and rhetoric, nor did it preclude an investment in the program's populist themes.

The Critical Dialectic of Popular Postmodernism

The fact that this program attracted viewers with both elite and popular tastes is no accident, given the writers' deliberate mixture of both popular and postmodern modes of address. In order to talk about the postmodern qualities of this television narrative, it must first be acknowledged that television bears a different relationship to the cultural trajectory of realism-modernism-postmodernism in literature and art history. As Jane Feuer has pointed out, since television was often deemed the "great other of [high cultural] modernism," "postmodern television is almost an oxymoron, because there was no modernist television" (Feuer, *Seeing* 6). Modernist aesthetic discourse arose for the first time in '80s television shows such as *thirtysomething*, but these programs were also keenly aware of their own commodification, which the presence of commercials makes plain. Having skipped over a high modernist phase in which the "goals of art and commerce are opposed ideologically" (Feuer, *Seeing* 95), network television employs avant-garde aesthetics with a postmodern twist, accepting complicity with the commercial imperative to appeal to popular desires and pocketbooks. For example, despite the high-art discourse that *Northern Exposure* invokes, it also spawned a successful commercial market of books, videos, CDs and memorabilia. The studio went so far as to auction off the set after the show's cancellation, literally transforming performance art—the piano that artist-character Chris catapulted in one episode—into a commodity.

As a brief look at the program's plot concept should suggest, *Northern Exposure* evinces a high-art sensibility while remaining cognizant of the constraints of its mass-media form. *Northern Exposure* focuses on the interactions between Dr. Joel Fleischman, a Jewish Brooklynite, and the inhabitants of the frontier town of Cicely, Alaska, who have paid his medical school tuition in exchange for five years of his services. Conflicts ensue between East and West, male and female, city and country, and rationalism and spiritualism, but the town manages to unify its very different individuals in the spirit of cultural pluralism. The other main characters include Maggie O'Connell, a feminist "bush pilot" and Joel's sparring partner/love interest; Ed Chigliak, a Native American teenager who dreams of becoming the next Steven Spielberg; Maurice Minnifield, a bigoted millionaire and former-astronaut with a sensitive side; Holling Vincoeur, rugged 60-something outdoorsman and owner of the local pub; his teenage girlfriend/wife Shelly Tambo-Vincoeur, a former beauty queen; Ruth-Anne Miller, the no-nonsense elderly owner of the grocery store; Marilyn Whirlwind, Joel's Native American taciturn receptionist, who serves as a quiet oracle; and Chris Stevens, the radio station's disc jockey and an ex-con who became an artist, preacher, and eclectic intellectual. This is not exactly a "cookie-cutter" ensemble cast, and nothing is television-typical about the writers' ruminations on such themes as performance art, the subjective nature of truth, the played-out possibilities of the frontier, the value of literature, the nature of democracy, and the wisdom of Native American and Jewish spirituality.

At first glance the show appears to be unambiguously aimed at an elite, well-educated audience. The creators of *Northern Exposure*, Joshua Brand and John Falsey, were veterans of the MTM television studio that pioneered "quality programming" (Feuer, *Seeing* 3), and they had previously created *St. Elsewhere* in this vein. The creators' status as *auteurs* paved the way for reviewers to confer a similarly high status on their new program. Boasting that the show was not conceived for a "mass audience" (Kenneth Clark 3), Brand and Falsey drew upon their academic training for many of *Northern Exposure*'s literary references (Brand has an M.A. in English from Columbia and Falsey earned an M.F.A. from the Iowa Writer's Workshop). In *Seeing through the Eighties*, Feuer notes that *St. Elsewhere* tried "to interpellate an elite subject" (101) with its use of "modernist art discourse" (62), and the same could be said of *Exposure*, which targets college-educated viewers by frequently alluding to luminaries of intellectual and literary history such as Jung, Freud, T.S. Eliot, Kierkegaard, Kant, Nietzsche, Proust, Homer, and Dante. However, *Northern Exposure* differs from the yuppie-oriented *St. Elsewhere* by aiming for a more inclusionary, populist style of address. Accompanying the high-cultural allusions are numerous references to popular icons such as Mr. Rogers, Vanna White, Winnie the Pooh, Nancy Drew, Jimi Hendrix, Oprah, and Monty Python. Despite the creators' assertion that the show was not directed at the masses, they took care to create a premise and structure that evoked many popular mass-market formulas and genres. Echoing the formulaic structure of popular film screenplays and television dramas, the program's three intertwining plot lines usually converge at forty minutes past the hour and are neatly resolved at the end. Episodes often end on a note of harmony, in which lovers or friends are reconciled or communities unite in celebration. The show's central focus—a New York Jewish doctor in Alaska—recalls the familiar fish-out-of-water plot from *Green Acres* and *The Beverly Hillbillies*, combined with a nod to the medical drama. Maggie and Joel's frustrated, opposites-attract romance is clearly a television and film cliché, patterned on such pairs as Sam and Diane of *Cheers* or Hepburn and Bogart in *The African Queen* (Thompson 162). Even the frequent dream sequences and fantasy elements can be traced to soap operas and "magicoms" such as *Bewitched* and *I Dream of Jeannie*.

Betsy Williams has called *Northern Exposure* "narrowly targeted [at the affluent and educated middle class] but polyvocal" in its attempt to offer narrative elements that will attract a larger number and wider variety of consumers (152). Jim Collins contends that many programs in the early '90s sought to compete with cable by widening their net to reach "coalition audiences" ("Television" 342). While Williams assumes that this polyvocal combination of narrative strategies succeeded in attracting a wider audience, I contend that it appeals in particular to a newly emerging middle-class postmodern consumer, one with a taste for both high and low. The popular references noted above signal a deeper connection to the ideologies of mass-produced culture than some of this audience group would like to acknowledge, although others admitted an attraction to precisely those elements. A self-proclaimed "snob" argued that "if *Northern Exposure* had been one of those shows that mixes high quality elements with cornball material for the masses, resulting in an amiable compromise, I probably would never have bothered with it. By some divine fluke, *Northern Exposure* managed to combine all the right elements and to show one masterpiece after another." This chapter interrogates the effect of the mixture more closely, arguing that there is indeed a sort of amiable compromise at work, but one that has progressive rather than conservative politics. *Exposure* employs many cultural strategies and sensibilities that would seem to be at odds, such as sentimentality and irony, melodramatic and postmodern aesthetics, and essentialist and anti-essentialist models of subjectivity. This juxtaposition of seemingly contradictory codes operates at the level of thematics, aesthetics, and the relationship constructed between text and viewer.

Northern Exposure has been both heralded and criticized by reviewers for its "quirkiness," a vague term that gestures towards its adoption of postmodern strategies and themes. Dubbing the program the "granddaddy of CBS High quirk," a *New York Times* reviewer defines the term: "It's a smarter than average show that demands the fullest attention of its audience because it proceeds in a nonlinear manner, and it wouldn't hurt if you've attended an accredited university, either, come to think of it, since they make use of a lot of gratuitous literary references. . . . there might be an angry midget in it, too, someplace" (MacGregor 34). Addressing itself to a viewer versed in literary and cultural theory, *Northern Exposure* invokes one of the most characteristic strategies of modernist and postmodern art—a self-reflexive commentary on its own medium and the process of meaning production. Jim Collins argues that postmodern televisual self-reflexivity "does not revolve around the problems of self-expression experienced by the anguished creative artist so ubiquitous in modernism" but instead focuses on the ways television circulates and is valued or devalued in our culture ("Television" 335). One episode of *Northern Exposure*, in which Shelly becomes addicted to her satellite dish, comments ironically on the stupefying properties of television. After a spending spree on the Home Shopping channel, Shelly finally kicks the habit and turns off her tube, rejecting the global village for her own locality. At that moment the viewer's screen also cuts to black, implying ironically that *Northern Exposure* itself might be sucking us into the marketplace and drawing us too far away from our own local worlds. This plotline simultaneously admits the show's complicity with commercialism while also offering a critique of the technologies of postmodern capitalism. Although Linda Hutcheon dismisses television, here is a perfect example of her theory of postmodernism as "complicitous critique."

Besides reflecting on the mediation of television, *Northern Exposure*'s scripts more ambitiously address contemporary literary theories concerning the production of meaning through narrative. For example, the ironic episode "The Graduate" revolves around Chris's M.A. oral exam in English literature, in which he defends his deconstructionist thesis before an examiner invested in what Walter Benjamin calls the "aura" of classic works of art. Troubled by Barthes's poststructuralist essay "The Death of the Author," Chris dreams of a trench warfare sequence in which Shakespeare is slaughtered while uttering the last words of Dickens's *A Tale of Two Cities*. The knowing viewer is invited to laugh at this literal translation of one of the key tenets of deconstructionist theory. By killing the most revered author in Western literature, the show's writers also self-reflexively spoof the self-importance of writers while simultaneously aligning themselves with cutting-edge literary theory. *Northern Exposure*'s meta-fictional commentary is enabled by its postmodern layering of intertextual allusions, often voiced by the character of Chris Stevens. As a radio DJ, Chris acts as a kind of narrator or Greek chorus speaking both to Cicely and to the wider television audience. While many television programs refer to popular television and film icons, very few allude to T.S. Eliot in the same breath as *Leave It to Beaver* and therefore require such wide-ranging cultural literacy of their viewers. One of the fanclub's favorite episodes, in which Chris flings a piano as performance art, perfectly illustrates the program's intertextual spirit and its relationship to postmodern parody. Entitled "Burning down the House" after the song by the postmodern band Talking Heads, the episode begins with a visit from Maggie's mother, who informs Maggie that she is divorcing her father and accidentally burns down Maggie's house, a symbol of the nuclear family. In a veiled reference to the *Wizard of Oz* (Taylor and Upchurch 83), the only things that survive the blaze unscorched are the green (not red) pumps belonging to Maggie's mother, a figurative wicked witch. Meanwhile, Chris has decided to create, in the vein of a religious sacrifice, a piece of performance art using a giant catapult, but is distressed to learn that his idea of flinging a cow has already been carried out in the film *Monty Python and the Holy Grail*, itself a spoof of the Arthurian legends. This plotline offers a postmodern critique of the modernist belief in the pursuit of pure originality, anatomized in Harold Bloom's *The Anxiety of Influence*. At first Chris cries in modernist angst that "repetition is the death of art," but he eventually finds an outlet for his creativity via recycling, as did Andy Warhol. Chris decides to reenact Monty Python's fling but with a twist—he flings a piece of Maggie's charred piano instead, thus paying homage to the past while helping Maggie to move on. While the soundtrack to the fling reaches back into the past with the traditional waltz "The Blue Danube," the cinematography includes graphic match cuts that recall the opening sequence of Kubrick's futuristic avant-garde film *2001: A Space Odyssey* (Crawford 21). Tradition is thus merged with the "shock of the new" in a postmodern fusion. This episode self-reflexively addresses the production of art in a postmodern world, with Chris's postmodern performance art serving as a mirror for the recycling of past culture that the writers themselves enact with their wide-ranging allusions.

By calling attention to the cultural plots that we have inherited, the series both critiques and respects those traditions. Hutcheon calls this ambivalence a constitutive feature of postmodern parody which "uses the re-appropriated forms of the past to speak to a society from within the values and history of that society, while still questioning it" (*Politics* 12). Critics such as Betsy Williams and Iain Crawford have noted that *Exposure* reveres its historical antecedents, but they argue that its intertextuality lacks the critical edge of postmodern parody, because it works "precisely *not* to question, disrupt and destabilize. . . [but] to find answers, restore order" (Crawford 15). While Crawford's analysis rightly highlights the program's sympathy with past traditions, he underestimates the importance of the distance created by irony, which allows viewers the space to reevaluate the past. Nostalgia and ironic distance operate in tension here, as the program mediates dialectically between a popular and an avant-garde sensibility. Crawford also ignores the program's repeated questioning of the traditional representational strategy of realism. While many of the plotlines focus on the quotidian problems of small-town life as in realist fiction, the writers disrupt that aesthetic by drawing upon the whimsy of Latin American "magic realism." The program urges us to entertain the possibility that Maggie might indeed be cursed, because five of her boyfriends have died from bizarre accidents, the most recent a victim of a satellite crashing to earth. Challenging a viewer's notion of reality as grounded in the empirical world, several episodes explored Ed's sleep-flying, Rick's reincarnation as a dog, and Maggie's romance with Arthur the bear/man. While Native American mysticism often informs their questioning of rationalist thinking, the writers also cite postmodern fiction writers as their inspirational models. In an episode called "Mister Sandman" in which the aurora borealis causes the townspeople to swap dreams, Chris Stevens breaks the frame and acknowledges that the plot was stolen from Gabriel García Marquez's *One Hundred Years of Solitude*.

The dream-swapping episode also exemplifies the program's attempt to question rigid identities and endorse a more fluid postmodern sense of subjectivity; if dreams are no longer imprisoned in a single psyche, the boundary between self and other is blurred. In that episode, gay B&B owners Ron and Erick experience the foot-fetish dreams of the homophobic Maurice, and the swap enables Maurice to accept his own non-normative sexual desires and extend a peace offering to the gay couple. The writers frequently use the character of Maurice to deconstruct rigid identities because he embodies seemingly incompatible types at once. This homophobic, macho astronaut and former marine is also an aesthete and a sentimental fan of opera and show tunes, causing Ron and Erick to mistake him for "one of us." An additional irony is that his first name recalls E.M. Forster's novel about gay sexuality. Nearly all of *Northern Exposure* 's characters present viewers with ironic incongruities. The mythic "Bigfoot" character on the program was gradually revealed to be an amalgam of gourmet chef, backwoods hermit, former-POW, urbane misanthrope, and doting husband, whose wife is a prescription-dependent hypochondriac who nonetheless professes to be a Christian Scientist. By naming this incongruous couple Adam and Eve, the writers make plain their desire to shatter archetypes often found in melodrama and other low-cultural television forms. Although *Northern Exposure* aims to disrupt and destabilize popular norms by employing self-reflexivity, magic realism, and poststructuralist theory, one can also trace its strong connections to romantic, sentimental, and humanist beliefs and ideologies. While some episodes extol the fluidity of identity in a poststructuralist vein, others seek to celebrate gender difference in an essentialist fashion. Native American and feminine difference is extolled in the episode "Survival of the Species," in which Maggie finds Indian women's artifacts buried in her yard. Fending off an aggressive attempt by the men of the town to use the archeological dig for their own profit, she ends up rallying other women to rebury the artifacts and prevent them from being tainted by "white male greed." Another sentimental treatment of "difference feminism" appears in the episode about Shelly's baby shower, which asserts that women's maternal urges are biological. The female guests at the shower reject Chris's attempt to "become a woman" in spirit after being inspired by Simone de Beauvoir's constructionist dictum that "a woman is made, not born."

While the show is only occasionally essentialist in its presentation of gender identity, its writers regularly espouse a belief in the interior depths of the "soul." With its respectful and moving treatment of many spiritual traditions (Judaism, Catholicism, Native American myths, and Asiatic religions), *Northern Exposure* offers a heightened moral register similar to the genre of melodrama, which "refuse[s] to allow that the world has been completely drained of transcendence" (Brooks 22). One of the main conflicts of the program is the one between Joel's "faith" in the rational powers of medicine and science and a more irrational, emotional, and intuitive religious faith espoused by the Native Americans, who eventually move Joel to spiritualize his own practice of Judaism beyond a more limited sense of Jewishness as a cultural or racial identity. The moment when Joel breaks his Yom Kippur fast while eating an orange alone on a mountaintop is a perfect example of the romantic sense of the sublime as a transcendent experience. At the end of the last season, this once urbane and cynical New Yorker retreats to a primitive Tlingit village, practicing native healing arts and living a monk-like existence that recalls Thoreau on Walden Pond. On *Northern Exposure*, the heart and soul win out over an Enlightenment faith in the mind, but this strike against Enlightenment rationalism is not made solely from a postmodern philosophical perspective, but also from melodramatic and romantic worldviews rooted in metaphysical truths. The program's faith in God is also accompanied by a romantic idealization of the pastoral. In one episode, the townspeople rally against cutting down an ancient tree because of the Native American belief that all living beings have souls (and Chris throws in a reference to Heidegger's sense of "Being" as another form of essence to be respected). In addition to this "tree hugging" episode, the program's romantic, ecological organicism even extends to embracing dust mites which feed on human skin as evidence that we are all part of a giant, pulsating ecosystem. A common theme of the program, harkening back to the Romantic poets, is the sublimity of the Alaskan wilderness, which offers a refuge from the industrialized city and from the hubris and disconnectedness of city dwellers represented by Joel.

This central dichotomy between the eastern city and the frontier town of Cicely, Alaska places the program in a long lineage of melodramatic film and television westerns. This television western harks back to the era of humanist, mythic frontier narratives that predate Sam Peckinpah's ultraviolent *Wild Bunch* (1969). On *Northern Exposure*, there is goodness in all Cicelians, even bigoted capitalists such as Maurice Minnifield, and as one newsgroup member noted, "violence is rarely a part of Cicelian life, unlike [other postmodern programs] *Twin Peaks* and *Picket Fences*." Whereas cynical postmodern texts expose the pettiness and violence of humanity, *Northern Exposure* ennobles the human condition in a romantic mode. The program also weds a romantic investment in the individual with the popular American idealization of democracy and small-town community life. Although the show's characters are free spirits who have escaped the shackles of their original communities, they have forged a utopian multicultural community in the frontier town of Cicely, Alaska, a bastion of pluralism and tolerance. Almost every episode offers an example of the communitarian spirit, as we witness feasts, dances, dinner parties, town meetings, and camaraderie at the Brick pub. Many episodes end on a note of communal harmony, as when the townspeople gather to "experience" many of Chris's sculptures. My questionnaire respondents cited the sense of community as one of their favorite aspects of the program, and one said that the show made him feel "excited, happy and secure" like a kid going to his grandparents' house for Christmas. In many ways, *Exposure* shares the life-affirming warmth of *The Waltons* and *Little House on the Prairie*, both set in simpler, idyllic rural communities of the past. *Northern Exposure* also connects its popular mythology of community harmony to another sentimental myth of popular culture—that of the monogamous, loving couple as the bedrock of society. Although the writers mocked romantic television dialogue in the first and second-season interactions of Joel and Maggie, romantic heterosexual relationships increasingly became a focus of the program.

Pairings between Shelly and Holling, Ruth-Anne and Walt, Joel and Maggie, and later Chris and Maggie were sentimentalized in the last few seasons. One episode from season five closed with a muted shot of Holling caressing his pregnant wife's belly, and another ended with Maggie's discovery that Joel fit comfortably in her new chair, both literally and figuratively. We even learn that the town was founded by a romantic monogamous couple, albeit a lesbian one (Cicely and Roslyn). The final montage of the series' finale offered shots of all the residents happily coupled up, and some newsgroup members complained about this seemingly conservative closure in a show that often strove to defy convention. I would argue that *Northern Exposure* is both conventional and transgressive at once, just like the figure of the lesbian "married" couple (the town's founders).

As in Hollywood melodramas, *Northern Exposure*'s poignant happy endings usually resolve any tensions raised during the hour, and this kind of narrative closure is often regarded as ideologically conservative. The program clearly satisfied a desire for sentimentality and comforting resolutions among some of its newsgroup fans, who often posted messages about their feelings of joy, contentment, and optimism. As one respondent put it, "I feel a peaceful sense of the world being integrated and holding together." In her article "Narrative Form in American Network Television," Feuer has argued that the neat closure of sitcoms is an inherently conservative structure, while melodramatic serials allow disintegration and an ambiguous non-resolution of problems that she deems a progressive strategy. Tania Modleski, in *Loving with a Vengeance*, has also praised the open-endedness of soap operas for being a truer reflection of the real lives of women. *Northern Exposure*'s neat endings are similar to those of situation comedy or film melodrama, but the program also allows antagonism to resurface and be reexamined in subsequent episodes (like a serial) in a way that destabilizes facile order. Employing the popular forms of both the serial and the series may result in a kind of ideological balancing act in *Exposure*, yet it seems problematic to correlate form so tidily with ideology. Just as not all popular texts are retrograde, neither does sentimental closure always serve a conservative function. For example, I will be arguing later in the chapter that the program's happy endings offer utopian visions of harmony that may have subversive potential.

As I have been suggesting, *Northern Exposure* is a rigorously hybrid fictional universe with allegiances to postmodern forms and sensibilities as well as to melodrama, humanism, and transcendental romanticism. More importantly, these opposing discourses operate in dialectical tension, opening up a space for questioning both poles. While modernists like James Joyce quoted popular culture ironically from a detached position above it, the writers of *Northern Exposure* often employ popular sensibilities to question the excesses of high theory and experimental aesthetics. For example, the episode "Fish Story" offers a meta-critique of realistic television plots by including a "magic realism" storyline in which Joel (as Jonah) finds himself conversing with his rabbi in the belly of a large fish. In the same episode, however, the writers simultaneously question Chris's self-reflexive emphasis on the artistic "process over the product." Turning a deaf ear to Chris's modernist diatribes, Holling finds joy in painting landscapes with a kitschy paint-by-numbers kit, and the writers thus defend the value of mimetic aesthetic traditions. In "The Graduate" episode about Chris's M.A. orals, Chris finally renounces his thesis, which deconstructed the popular nineteenth-century poem "Casey at the Bat," and chooses instead to enact the poem and pay homage to the experiential value of literature as traditional humanists do. In Chris's reenactment, it is the deconstructionist examiner who "strikes out" because he has lost an appreciation for literature. Despite the fact that this episode appears to champion popular reading practices at the expense of deconstruction, it nonetheless uses intertextual parody (via the ironic "death of the author" dream) in order to make its point, thus supporting postmodern aesthetic sensibilities while simultaneously questioning them in the diegesis. *Northern Exposure* employs the critical edge of postmodernist parody to distinguish itself from lowbrow televisual forms, but it also endorses popular values to question the excesses of postmodern culture and high theory.

Blurring the Boundaries of Taste

I have been arguing thus far that *Northern Exposure* both affirms and critiques popular ideologies and mass-cultural strategies. Now I will turn to my study of the Internet newsgroup to suggest that their responses to this "high-pop" program raise provocative questions about sociological categories of aesthetic taste. Examining the testimony of over 1,000 newsgroup posts and the questionnaires answered by forty-four members of the group, I set out to test two assumptions: a) women might be more strongly attracted to the show's romantic elements, and b) that people of a higher class bracket with the most formal education would watch the show for its intertextuality or postmodern aesthetics rather than for its populist, melodramatic, and humanist values. Neither of these assumptions turned out to be unequivocally true. My analysis of this subculture suggests that the boundaries between taste cultures (or aesthetic disposition) may be more permeable than Bourdieu's influential sociological theories allow. This study contributes to a growing body of scholarship on taste fragmentation in postmodern media societies.

One particular effect of *Northern Exposure*'s mixture of highbrow and lowbrow strategies is that it promotes viewer involvement at several different levels simultaneously. In her theoretical categorization of viewer involvement in television, Liebes argues that lowbrow culture fosters "referential" engagement while high culture provokes "constructional" forms of viewing. Liebes defines referential or "Real" engagement as a process "in which characters and situations [from television] are incorporated uncritically into viewers' lives," and viewers do not reflect on the fictionality of the texts (179). Two constructional modes of involvement are the Ideological and the Aesthetic, which indicate a critically distanced viewpoint and sophisticated understanding of the writers' political, artistic, and meta-critical goals (179). In "Television and Postmodernism," Jim Collins has argued that groundbreaking postmodern shows such as *Twin Peaks* and *Northern Exposure* have encouraged an oscillation on the part of the viewer between the emotional, referential involvement of popular culture and the ironic detachment promoted by the avant-garde. Collins proposes that the television medium's bricolage of signs and styles, and the rapid changes in viewing posture made possible by surfing through cable channels, have helped to break down boundaries within individual texts, leading to the development that "viewing perspectives are no longer mutually exclusive, but set in perpetual alternation" ("Television" 348). A new juxtaposition of modes of viewing that were once rigidly separated is also a byproduct of postmodern culture's relaxing of the boundaries between high and low.

My study of alt.tv.northern-exp corroborates Collins's speculations. *Northern Exposure*'s oscillation between high and popular cultural strategies was a crucial reason that many of the newsgroup members became fans of the show. When one fan dubbed the program a "magical realism soap opera" and a thinking person's weepie, little controversy was sparked. The fans' attachment to a mixture of equal parts became even clearer in the last season, when they loudly complained that the program seemed to be "plummeting from its High Mountain" and lapsing into a clichéd melodrama or soap opera, a sort of "*thirtysomething* lite." Many were particularly saddened that Chris was no longer being employed as a narrator of the intellectual themes of the program, and thus the intertextual references to philosophers, writers, and artists were considerably lessened. One man summed up the general newsgroup sentiment about the final season when he wrote (with an implied sigh), "back to reading books." This program is worthy of study precisely because it succeeded, for most of its run, in breaking down the perceived cultural dichotomy between books and television, between elite readers of postmodern fiction and lowbrow TV-junkies.

The results of my study contribute to recent work in sociology that questions the universal applicability of Pierre Bourdieu's theories of "taste cultures" and cultural capital (see Gans; John R. Hall). In his book *Distinction: A Social Critique of the Judgement of Taste,* Bourdieu argues that a person's cultural taste or "aesthetic disposition" is largely determined by the class "habitus" in which that subject has been inculcated. Bourdieu nuances reductionist Marxist theory by situating aesthetics in a complex network of social stratification, and by moving beyond economics to consider cultural capital as a form of power that legitimates social hierarchies (*Distinction* 7). However, Bourdieu makes a fundamentally class-based argument when he claims that "aesthetics can only be, except in certain cases, a dimension of the ethics (or, better, the ethos) of class" (Bourdieu and Darbel 27). While he draws important attention to the connections between aesthetic taste and power, I contend that his analysis tends to dichotomize too rigidly, by suggesting that highbrow and lowbrow aesthetic dispositions are mutually exclusive due to the entrenched social and economic order in France. What he neglects to consider is that either texts or viewers could exhibit a "high aesthetic" disposition towards critical detachment and contemplation, while also displaying a popular aesthetic disposition towards emotional participation and sensory pleasure in realism, legibility, and moralism (Bourdieu, "Aristocracy"). Perhaps because his theories are based upon a country more firmly rooted in class hierarchies than the United States, Bourdieu's theory of class-stratified taste cannot fully explain the responses of the fans of *Northern Exposure* that I surveyed. If one were to apply Bourdieu's theory to my audience sample, one would expect that people of a higher class bracket with the most formal education would watch the show for its intertextuality or postmodern aesthetics rather than for its populist, melodramatic, and humanist values. In fact, the majority of the group members appeared to have no preference for either the high or low cultural aspects of the program, and were involved in the program on the levels of the Real, Ideological, and Aesthetic (in Liebes's terms) in relatively equal degrees. Most of my questionnaire respondents were upper-middle class (33 out of 44) and well educated (88% had earned a B.A.), but they were much less critical of mass culture than their demographics would suggest. Only a small percentage of the group (18%) watched the show solely for its high art references and tropes and described their engagement mainly in terms of Aesthetic or Ideological involvement, while 14% were attracted mainly by the popular elements common to melodramas, and responded to the text primarily at the referential level of the "Real" rather than to its ideology or aesthetics. The majority (68%) cited a balanced mixture of high and low themes or strategies, and both constructional and referential types of response. Clearly, the existence of deconstructionist irony did not undermine the audience's emotional investments in identity and humanism, as Jameson would have us believe (*Postmodernism* 12–15). One fan whose own tastes are more highbrow aptly described the hybrid forms of investment that he observed on the newsgroup: "fans are very conscious of the writers and whether or not they do a good job with a particular script or character development. But in the next paragraph of a post, almost as if in the same breath, a fan will talk about a character as if he/she was real, and as if the story was real life unfolding. To be that conscious of the hands of the puppet master and also able to suspend disbelief, and all so quickly, is surprising to me."

Among the smaller percentage of fans that did fall into distinct highbrow or lowbrow taste categories, there was some correlation between their class status and their taste preferences. All eight viewers who expressed predominantly highbrow tastes and disdained the sentimental aspects of the show were upper-middle class (professional-managerial) and had earned advanced degrees or were graduate/professional students. The high status indicated by many of their actual and prospective professions (professors, doctors, ministers, consultants, and lawyers), and the influence of their academic training in critical and textual analysis, might have led to their elitist cultural tastes and their rationalist reactions against sentimentality and romance. For example, an Episcopalian priest who is well schooled in philosophy was annoyed by the newsgroup's "investment in the romantic/erotic relationships" of the characters, and found this form of "Real" involvement to be "a bit immature." However, since the majority of the forty-four respondents also were middle-class and had gone to graduate school, it is difficult to conclude that educational level (Bourdieu's "academic capital") or a general middle-class income ("economic capital") are the primary causes of anti-popular tastes. A more significant difference is that their occupations were of a slightly higher intellectual status than the rest of the group. Among these fans, the accumulation of "cultural capital," or cognitive skills in deciphering cultural artifacts, appears to have at least some impact upon taste. As Bourdieu admits, cultural capital is not reducible to economic capital, although both are forms of power available to the privileged. Wealth and status do not necessarily result in highbrow taste, but my study does support Bourdieu's contention that a *lack* of cultural capital often corresponds to lowbrow taste. The six "lowbrow" viewers in my group expressed interest only in the program's humanist values and its sentimental and romantic content, treating it much like a soap opera. They discussed the characters as if they were real (e.g., "the cast are my friends"), related the program to their own lives (e.g., "Shelly is just like me when I was her age"), and rarely commented upon its ideology or aesthetic construction, except to praise the comforting happy endings. Five of these six viewers were lower-middle class, and only one had received a B.A. Since four of them were undergraduates (the only undergraduates in the survey) at non-prestigious universities, they had not yet acquired a significant amount of cultural capital. The other television programs that they watched were markedly different from those listed by the highbrow group, and included *The Jerry Springer Show, America's Funniest Home Videos, Home Improvement*, *Married with Children,* and many different soap operas. In addition to their lack of cultural capital, five of these six lowbrow viewers were female, which suggests that their tastes for melodrama and soap opera could also have been shaped by gender prescriptions.

To complicate Bourdieu's equation between a lack of advanced education and lowbrow taste, I should emphasize that four out of the ten lower-middle-class people in the survey were in fact attracted to the intellectual elements of the program, as was the only working-class member of the group, who noted that he enjoyed the irony and postmodern themes. This finding resonates with sociologist Herbert Gans's identification of a growing "cultural convergence" in contemporary America (*Popular Culture*, rev. ed., 10). Gans suggests that the recent expansion of "upper-middle culture" (e.g., *Northern Exposure*) can be partly attributed to its consumption by "the better educated or culturally more adventurous parts of the lower-middle class public" (Gans, rev. ed., 150). Given the fact that "upper-middle cultural" programs like *Northern Exposure* and the ironic, sophisticated sitcom *Frasier* have garnered top-15 Nielsen ratings, one can logically assume that some of their fans must come from the lower-middle class, which Gans identifies as America's dominant "taste public." It is difficult to ascertain, however, just what motivated the "upward straddling" (Gans, 1974 ed., 109) of the lower-middle-class fans in my survey group who praised the intellectual aspects of *Northern Exposure*. Were they simply status-seekers (as Bourdieu has defined the *petite bourgeoisie*) who pretended to like irony and parody because of its high-cultural status? While this is certainly a possibility, their responses indicated a knowledgeable familiarity with these intellectual discourses that reflects an ongoing popularization of formerly elite aesthetic sensibilities. Furthermore, it is important to note that some of these fans did not live in class-segregated environments. For example, one lower-middle-class woman was once married to a professional, and the one working-class man (who did not finish high school) shared an apartment with college graduates. Since he watches television and consumes other kinds of culture with them, he is part of their taste community. While I would deny Daniel Bell's neo-conservative argument that cultural choices are no longer determined by class position, it seems evident that a loosening of taste boundaries is underway, at least among the ranks of the American lower-middle and upper-middle classes.

I find it significant that the majority (68%) of these *Northern Exposure* viewers expressed allegiance not to a distinct camp, but to many taste communities at once. These highly educated cultural elites did not conform to the expectation that their tastes would be predominantly highbrow, favoring critical distance and intellectual appreciation. For example, one fan who is a doctoral student in physics at Stanford professes elitist tastes ("most TV is stupid, really stupid") and responds to the program in a constructional "Aesthetic" way, by appreciating allegory and metaphor and transcribing insightful bits of dialogue to think about more critically. On the other hand, he is also intensely emotional about the program's communitarian values and desires sentimental closure, enjoying the way that *Northern Exposure* makes everything "come out OK in the end." One 72-year-old female textbook editor with an M.S. in educational philosophy had similarly hybrid tastes. While her educational background would predict that she watches "lots of PBS," she also tunes in to *All My Children* and *General Hospital*, and was a fan of the original *Star Trek*. Although she finds Chris's intellectual monologues and the moments of magical realism to be highlights of the program, she is also emotionally drawn by the romance plots and the spiritual themes. She commented that she loved Chris for his "lack of cynicism despite his knowledge," and this phrase aptly describes the larger audience that this program attracts—people whose critical edge does not negate sentimental attachments, and whose education does not alienate them from popular pleasures. These findings resonate with new sociological studies of the growing fluidity of taste boundaries. While Gans agrees with Bourdieu that "cultural choices are still affected by class" (Gans, rev. ed., 9), he also notes an increasing incidence of "cultural straddling" which can be both "downward" (slumming for the purposes of catharsis or relief) and "upward," for status climbing or self-improvement (Gans, 1974 ed., 109). Similarly, other sociological studies have described upper-middle class professionals as "omnivores," whose disposable income allows them to consume a wide range of cultures in a quest for knowledge (Peterson and Simkus 169), or as "postmodern" consumers, whose "appreciation of high cultural forms of art such as opera and classical music exists cheek by jowl with an interest in disco dancing or stock car racing" (Savage, Barlow, Dickens, and Fielding 108). Many of these sociologists argue that such shifts in taste are primarily the result of economic changes in the structure of post-industrial capitalism. While it is entirely plausible that this shift has economic roots, more attention needs to be paid to the role that popular culture, and particularly television, plays in fostering an eclecticism of taste.

Some scholars, including Bourdieu, regard television as an instrument of oppression. In contrast, one could argue that it has also served as a democratizing force, eroding cultural boundaries that were once entrenched. In his lectures on television journalism, Bourdieu argues that television "poses . . . a threat to political life and to democracy itself" (*On Television* 10). Implicit in his focus on news and political talk shows is the belief that fictional television programs have nothing to do with politics, or with the promotion of democracy. Since Bourdieu equates television in the 1990s with the talk show, "exploiting and pandering" to the tastes of the lower-class public (*On Television* 48), he ignores the significant development of high-pop programs that Collins sees as groundbreaking. Although I largely agree with Bourdieu's critique of the depoliticizing aims of news programs and political talk shows, he underestimates the potentially democratizing effects of cable television, which has made culture and information of all kinds, from opera to Senate proceedings, available to all classes. In contrast to Bourdieu, Jencks has argued that the explosion of choices in our postmodern media culture has led to a "fragmentation of taste cultures" (*What Is Post-Modernism?* 49) that enables audiences to develop a "taste for pluralism itself, and for the juxtapositions it entails" (55). In this pluralized media landscape, professing a taste for popular culture no longer stains one as lower class or uncultured; rather it is a sign of "hipness" that has even infiltrated the ivory towers of the academy, where professors of popular culture are now routinely granted tenure. The academic popularity of cultural studies may have further reduced the intellectual disdain for popular taste and lessened the belief in television's downward pull. Further, I found it telling that although the respondents knew that their questionnaires would be read by an academic, they made surprisingly few attempts to impress me with their knowledge of high culture or to denigrate the practice of watching television, a defensive strategy that Seiter has observed among viewers from lower-class backgrounds ("Making Distinctions"). Perhaps my respondents freely admitted a taste for the popular because I had also asked them to list their educational degrees, which served as proof of their cultural capital. Having already acquired status through education, they did not need to rehearse their knowledge to prove their status. Unlike the middlebrow readers that Radway describes as class-climbers eschewing mass culture in the hopes of improving themselves, these mixed-taste fans of *Northern Exposure* do not fear contamination by the "bad taste" associated with the working or lower-middle classes (*A Feeling for Books*). It seems significant that the only person who admitted any shame about his engagement in popular culture and *Northern Exposure* was not American, but a Finnish student who tried to repress his emotions after he "found out how stupid it is to be so keen on something that comes out of TV." This reception study suggests that at least some of the cultural elite in America are in fact "keen on TV" and no longer embarrassed to admit it. In the contemporary United States, class may now bear less relationship to taste cultures than it did in the France described by Bourdieu, or the mid-twentieth-century United States that Radway has studied.

The Finnish man's shame about being emotionally invested in a television text could be linked not only to class concerns but also to a fear of the feminizing effects of mass culture. Seiter has examined "denigration of women as an ego-defense" ("Making" 396) in an interview she conducted with two male soap opera fans. Because these men associate passive television viewing with women, they worked extremely hard to assert that their own viewing of soap operas is intelligent and active. Since not only television viewing in general but also the particular genre of melodrama has long been associated with women, one might expect some of the men in this fan group to be critical of the melodramatic elements of *Northern Exposure* and to gender them feminine. However, I found surprisingly little negative reaction among the male respondents to the emotional, romantic aspects of the program and encountered almost no language linking anti-sentimentality to masculinity. Ironically, the one person on the newsgroup who complained about an episode in which Ed cries over losing his girlfriend was in fact a woman. After bemoaning that "this once fine show has fallen from its High Mountain down into a blubbering soap opera," she complained that Ed "couldn't swallow hard like a brave instead of crying on big strong Maurice's shoulder." Her sexist newsgroup post was immediately challenged by many men who asserted that "real men do cry as well as eat quiche." Most of the male survey respondents cited the show's ability to move them emotionally as crucial to their viewing pleasure. None of these fans disdained melodrama because of its associations with femininity.

It might be tempting to attribute this non-sexist response solely to gains won by feminism; however, a more conservative explanation might be the fact that *Northern Exposure* masks its connection to "feminine" melodrama by including elements that strongly appeal to masculine tastes. Cicely, Alaska could never be mistaken for the glamorous locales of melodramatic films and programs aimed at women. *Exposure*'s setting on the rugged Alaskan frontier, and its focus on traditional "men's men" such as Maurice and Holling, helped to make the program the most popular series among male baby boomers in its first two seasons (Taylor 27). CBS even added more commercials geared to men in its third season (Stuart Miller 23). Lynne Joyrich has noted a hypermasculine quality in many otherwise melodramatic programs, which "attempt to evade TV's 'unmanly' connotations" and create "spectator distance by . . . obsessively re-marking the masculinity of their thematics" (79). Although only *some* of *Exposure*'s thematics are marked as masculine, and the program oscillates between spectator distance and intense connection, there appear to be enough "manly" qualities to keep male viewers tuned in. *Northern Exposure* offers an emotional viewing experience that men find unthreatening, but the program has been even more popular with women. In the middle of the third season, as the program was reaching the height of its popularity, it drew an average of 23 million total viewers, of which 8 million were women aged 18–49, and 6.1 million were men of the same age group (Stuart Miller 23). This female to male ratio (57% to 43%) nearly matches the ratio of my audience group—59% women and 41% men. Although the overall pattern of the responses may have been affected because of the larger number of women in this study, the tastes of the women involved appeared to be more diverse than those of the men. Women made up the majority of both the lowbrow (5 out of 6) and the highbrow groups (5 out of 8). While the lowbrow (mostly undergraduate) women focused on the program's emotional elements and the Joel/Maggie romance, there were just as many women with predominantly elitist tastes. In fact, the women as a whole group were more educated than the men (60% of the women had done graduate work as opposed to 50% of the men). These details suggest that *Northern Exposure* may appeal to women across a wide range of class groups or taste communities but to a narrower slice of male viewers.

Furthermore, my hypothesis that the women as a whole would be more attracted by the romantic, sentimental elements than would the men did not hold true, despite the five women who read the program as a soap opera. When I asked everyone to rank their ten favorite elements of the show, the women and the men placed equal emphasis on Maggie and Joel's romance (fourth place) and the program's sentimental treatment of community (third and second). In addition, 60% of both gender groups said they preferred the romantic to the anti-romantic episodes in which the couples do not end up in harmony. In this study, gender differences in taste turned out to be minimal, except for the greater diversity among the female participants, stretching to both highbrow and lowbrow extremes. Their questionnaires revealed two important patterns of response that upset gender stereotypes: the tastes of the female fans were not ruled by their emotions any more than the men's were, and the male fans of *Northern Exposure* appear to be less hostile to "feminine" melodrama and sentimentality than one might expect. It was also significant that the majority of these highly educated viewers were more intensely engaged in the program's popular elements than their class and academic backgrounds would suggest. "High-pop" television programs like *Northern Exposure* speak directly to this newly emerging postmodern consumer with a taste for both high and mass culture. Within a postmodern consumer society, class and gender may have less power to predict tastes than many scholars assume.

Subjects in Flux

In addition to challenging critical assumptions concerning taste, my study of *Northern Exposure* fans also examines the contested relationship between identities of viewers and the process of identifying with on-screen characters. Group difference is clearly a central concern of the program, whose characters include Native Americans, Jews, gays and lesbians, Catholics, whites, blacks, and men and women of all ages and class backgrounds. Was *Northern Exposure* successful merely because its characters resembled a rainbow coalition, and therefore all viewers could recognize themselves somewhere in the program? This simplistic assumption is immediately put into question by the fact that *Northern Exposure* directly addressed concurrent debates about identity politics and multiculturalism and encouraged its viewers to think critically about identifying oneself according to received categories of gender, race, ethnicity, and sexuality. By invoking both the melodramatic construction of identity as unitary, essential, and deep, and a postmodern treatment of identity as culturally constructed and shifting, *Northern Exposure* perfectly exemplifies Hutcheon's observation that "the postmodern involves a paradoxical installing as well as subverting of conventions—including conventions of the representation of the subject" (*Politics* 13–14). I set out to explore what effect this dual treatment of identity had upon viewers. Did the viewers identify primarily with the characters most like themselves, as some psychoanalytic theorists contend, or did the program's deconstruction of traditional identity categories complicate their identification process? Moreover, how did the viewers respond to the program's political narratives about identity that fostered feminism, religious tolerance, and cultural pluralism?

Given the program's multicultural cast of characters, many plotlines respect and celebrate group differences, as in the episode concerning the buried Indian women's artifacts. However, a poststructuralist critique of identity politics can be glimpsed just as frequently. The episode "Crime and Punishment," in which Chris faces trial for violating parole many years earlier, explicitly questions a belief in the stability of identity. Chris's defense, based on the idea that he is a "new man," invokes a broader interpretation of the self as mutable rather than fixed. He ends the episode on his radio show by musing "who are we?"—a question that resonates throughout the series—and suggests that maybe the answer must always be elusive. Usually this dual treatment of the subject—simultaneously deconstructing and respecting identities—occurs within each episode, and the differing representations speak to and reflect upon one another. A few episodes, however, offered a more essentialist treatment of the subject, installing rather than subverting conventional differences, and this was more likely to happen when *gender* identities were the specific focus. *Northern Exposure* both shares and rejects our culture's continued attachment to stereotypical gender divisions. The great majority of the survey group believe that *Northern Exposure* expresses a feminist sensibility; however, their responses revealed the diversity of feminist discourse and highlighted the writers' conflicted treatment of gender identity. The episode detailing the founding of the town by two lesbians—who turn the male-dominated, violent saloon into a *salon* and rhapsodize about female difference as non-materialist, spiritual, and pacifist—caused one female fan to argue that *Northern Exposure* is a "powerfully *feminine* series, one in which success is based less on competition and power, and more on the interrelatedness of people." Another saw a powerful feminist message in "Survival of the Species," in which the women rebury the Indian artifacts, "claiming their own feminine, cultural inheritance as their own." While some aspects of the program clearly speak to "difference feminist" viewers, at some moments this celebration of female difference veers into stereotype. The episode about Shelly's baby shower ended with a sentimental montage of female animals caring for their young—a not-so-subtle suggestion that mothering is a natural female instinct, and thus that Maggie's aversion to babies is an unnatural whim rather than a rational life-choice.

A few episodes in the final season presented gender stereotypes so uncritically that a few fans called them anti-feminist; in "Horns," contaminated drinking water causes the men and women to exhibit seemingly gender-aberrant behavior (men crying and women demanding sex all the time), until the "correct" behaviors are restored in the end. Throughout the series, the writers occasionally presented

Maggie's feminist outbursts as hypocritical and irrational. In one ironic scene, while complaining that men objectify women, Maggie simultaneously contributes to the problem by obsessing about her own appearance. The show's treatment of feminism was sometimes respectful and sometimes mocking, and the viewers with more developed feminist sensibilities took a more critical and distanced view when the text's ideologies didn't match their own. Complaining that the program's treatment of romance usually "made a woman dependent on a man," one male feminist argued that "*Northern Exposure* wanted to be feminist, but could not quite make it." It's also interesting that the two most critical viewers, who argued that the show "fell short of giving women or feminism a fair portrayal," were both men, thus underscoring the possibility of fluid identifications that cross gender lines and are based on ideological affinity rather than essential identity. At the same time that *Northern Exposure* offers both difference-feminist narratives and anti-feminist ones, it more frequently overturns stereotypes and presents gender as culturally constructed. The writers promote androgyny and question gender identity by underscoring each male character's stereotypically feminine qualities and each woman's masculine ones. Since the majority of the survey group defined a feminist text as one that fosters equality and offers non-stereotypical roles for women (and men), they applauded the program's anti-essentialist strategies. As one feminist man remarked: "all the characters differ in some ways from mainstream expectations of gender roles. Even Maurice, the most traditional male, can cook and likes show tunes." A few examples of this "androgyny effect" are Joel's general state of hysteria and his natural ability to knit baby booties, rugged Holling's admission that he dislikes watching sports, Maggie's mechanical skills and her bravery in flying planes, and "little-old-lady" Ruth-Anne's shrewd, unsentimental business sense. Ed is virtually genderless, and Chris (the artist/minister who is also an ex-con and a "ladies' man") embodies both yin and yang. Because the program deconstructs stereotypes of masculinity as well as femininity, several respondents called the program "humanist" because it promotes equality for all rather than favoring women over men, which they believed to be the goal of feminism. By invoking anti-feminism, difference-based feminism, equality feminism, and the postmodern feminist dream of a world beyond gender, *Northern Exposure* speaks to a wide range of viewpoints. While the program's feminist politics may seem merely conflicted or confused, I would argue that this tension, as in *The Piano*, leads to a more pluralist understanding of gender identity that registers with a viewer's experience of encountering these multiple views of gender and feminism in daily life. *Exposure* allows sentimental connections and identifications on the basis of gender, yet also urges viewers to step back and be critical of the limitations that can result from those identities.

Northern Exposure's varied representations of gender complicated the identification process for these viewers, thereby undermining the psychoanalytic assumption that gender identity largely determines how and with whom people identify. I asked the respondents to explain why they were attracted to their two "favorite characters," and I intentionally avoided the word "identification" to see if they would use that concept to explain their preferences without prompting. More than half of them did use the term, and ten out of the total forty-four identified with characters on the basis of shared gender. Sometimes the gender connection was subtle (identifying with Joel's rationalism as a "man of science" or with Maggie's "need to be loved") and other times more blatant ("from my male perspective, I identified more with the male characters"). However, their identifications with characters of the same sex sometimes had the effect of challenging rather than solidifying gender identity, because of the androgyny of many of the characters. For example, one young man identified with a male character, but on the basis of his feminized position: "Ed's character appeals to me because I can identify with his position of being subservient to just about everyone else on the program." Ed's age and class status, which position him as powerless, mattered more to this viewer than the authority conferred by masculinity. Many women likened themselves to Maggie and Ruth-Anne because they were strong and independent, traditionally masculine characteristics. One man's statement even redefined the ideal man as androgynous: "if I could be any character it would be Chris—both Yin and Yang, a fighter and a philosopher/healer. A complete man." While gender was sometimes cited as the reason for strong identification, it is clear that both the audience and the text stretch and subvert traditional definitions of masculinity and femininity. In fact, while ten people cited shared gender as the basis for their identifications, even more (eleven) claimed to identify with characters of the other sex on the basis of shared personality traits, such as Maggie's stubbornness, Joel's "reluctant tolerance," or Chris's introspection. One man both desired and identified with Maggie, which challenges the psychoanalytic dyad of desire/identification. This strikes me as an important freeing up of gender polarities that hamper heterosexual relationships. In general, however, the men in the group were less likely to choose female characters as their favorites than the female fans were to choose male characters. This pattern might be influenced by many factors: that feminism has allowed women more access to "masculine" behavior, that women have always been more "bisexual" according to feminist theorists such as Cixous (see "Sorties" 85), or that feminine characteristics are still less valued than masculine ones in our aggressive capitalist culture. Mulvey might argue that these women are merely experiencing a "transvestite" identification with male power that does nothing to challenge patriarchy. Her theory of transvestite identification is inapplicable here, because both the viewers and the program express feminist sensibilities and deconstruct gender stereotypes. Those women who identified with a sensitive feminist artist (Chris) could hardly be called victims of "false consciousness." The male viewers, on the other hand, exhibited less fluid identifications. Even though only a few men expressed an identification with Maggie or Ruth-Anne (and none with the hyperfeminine Shelly), many male viewers identified with the more *androgynous* male characters Ed and Chris. Although seeing themselves in a former beauty queen (Shelly) is out of the realm of possibility for them, the fact that these men liken themselves to a sensitive artist and subservient teenager may still represent liberatory change. In her study of slasher horror films, Carol Clover discusses the progressive consequences of male fans identifying with androgynous characters, in this case tomboy victim/heroines. She argues that such gender displacement may encourage viewers to conceive of gender as an ambiguous "permeable membrane" (46) rather than a fixed entity, and the same could be said of *Northern Exposure*.

As with gender, *Northern Exposure* occasionally depicts race and ethnicity as essential identities, but usually presents them as culturally constructed and therefore mutable subject positions. Although Native American traditions are generally revered on the program, the fact that all the minor Native American characters are similarly wise, peaceful, earth-worshiping, and non-materialistic recalls the noble savage stereotype. The only fully individualized Indian character is Ed, but the writers tempt the viewer to attribute Ed's difference from the other Native Americans, primarily his infatuation with the "white culture" of film, to the fact that he is of mixed race (his mother is white). Despite these few intimations that Native American identity is determined by biological racial difference, *Northern Exposure* often suggests that this identity is cultural and can therefore be shared not only by the racially mixed Ed, who becomes a shaman for the tribe, but by some whites as well. The flexible nature of racial identity is asserted in the "Thanksgiving" episode, which focuses on the local Indian tradition of throwing tomatoes at whites to express residual anger at losing their homeland. Most of the white Cicelians cheerfully accept these unorthodox "seasons greetings," but Joel protests that his Jewish heritage marks him as a victim of oppression and therefore a "person of color." The Native American Marilyn at first doubts Joel's argument, but when the state of Alaska decides that he has to serve as the town doctor for an extra year due to inflation, Marilyn accepts Joel as an "honorary Indian," not because of his religion or race but because he is a powerless indentured servant. When the Native Americans ask Joel to march in their parade because he "isn't white anymore," the writers endorse an expansive concept of racial identity as a situational affinity or as a metaphor for an oppressed or marginalized position.

Joel's self-identification as an "other," and his belief that Jewishness is a racial as well as a religious identity, are treated with sensitivity by the show's writers. The episode in which he searches through Alaskan phone books to find other Jews, and ends up calling a man in Israel who shares his name, poignantly affirms the emotional benefits of a politics of recognition, of uniting with others who share your particular sense of difference. On the other hand, the program also reminds us that not all Jews are alike. When Joel's temporary replacement Dave (another Jew) lacks any stereotypical markers of his supposed Jewishness, Joel's views about ethnicity are called into question. The writers also imply that Joel's intense identification with others of his "tribe" can result in xenophobia. "Kaddish for Uncle Manny" focuses on the difficult search for a minion of ten Jews (rare in rural Alaska) to recite the traditional mourning prayer for Joel's uncle, and the whole town seems to overlook non-Jews as possible participants. In "Fish Story" Joel worries about letting Maggie help him prepare Seder for Passover. But at the end of both episodes, Joel embraces his local community as "honorary Jews" who can share his religious practices. The religious (and possibly racial) identity of Jewishness is relaxed by the writers, who suggest that fluid alliances might be better than traditional identity politics. A final testament to the show's aim of loosening rigid boundaries between self and other is Joel's miraculous transformation in the last season from a once uptight and hyper-rational Jewish New Yorker to a virtual Native American, living an ascetic existence in a rural village and embracing holistic healing and tribal spirituality.

Even more powerful than Joel's sudden transformation is the writers' more realistic depiction of Maurice's vacillation between bigotry and tolerance. Although he is sometimes homophobic and racist, Maurice's integrity and repressed sensitivity allow him to forge a reluctant friendship with the gay couple Ron and Erick, and also to accept a North Korean woman as his daughter-in-law despite his own identity as a Korean War veteran and enemy of her people. Astounded that the African American Bernard (Chris's half-brother) doesn't "sound black," Maurice and the prejudiced viewer learn that speech patterns are cultural rather than a result of "superior racial breeding." The program's sympathetic treatment of Maurice's conflict between self and other has the potential to move similar viewers towards tolerance and even respect for marginalized people. The text's attempt to foster empathy for various others seems to have resonated with these viewers, for they expressed the capacity to identify with many characters who differ from themselves in race, religion, age, politics, and gender. As one respondent put it, "each character is unique, and I can relate to certain aspects of each one." For this group, identification was aspectual and multiple rather than whole and singular. Exhibiting a fluid identification process, one woman noted: "Although I was raised Methodist and am now agnostic/atheistic, I liked the Jewish aspect of the show. I've dated Jews and hold as much or more respect for Judaism as I hold for Christianity." She also chose two Native Americans (Marilyn and Ed) as her favorite characters. One Asian-American, Catholic woman who shares few social identities with Joel nonetheless found that "Joel and I are similar in some ways. I find myself nodding in agreement when he's talking." Most of the people with majority identities (white, Christian) and even some of the minorities (such as this Asian-American woman) experienced a cross-over identification with characters seemingly different from themselves. Most of the people from dominant groups were able to empathize with minorities, recognizing elements of sameness as well as difference. I read this as a positive development rather than a disheartening sign of appropriation, as does Doris Sommer. It is also significant that a few of the minorities in the group *did not* identify primarily with their counterparts on screen, yet I hesitate to interpret this phenomenon simply as an example of conservative assimilationism. A Jewish person in my survey group at first appeared to echo Joel's narrow identity politics and his belief that he is "non-white," since she wrote in "Russian/Eastern European Jewish" rather than checking "white" as her racial identity. She also admitted to looking in phone books for other Jews when she travels, just as Joel does. However, she was drawn not to Joel but to the characters of Ruth-Anne and Maurice. Despite her feminist liberal beliefs, she found Maurice endearing because "he was sincere about his dislike for other lifestyles."

Even though she expressed a strongly defined ethnic identity, her fluid identification pattern indicated that she was able to avoid the essentialism and separatism that Joel and Maurice sometimes espouse.

The minority viewers were more likely than the viewers from the white, Protestant, heterosexual mainstream to identify with characters of their own race or culture, possibly because such positive identificatory possibilities are rarer for minority viewers of mainstream media. Minorities who posted on the newsgroup tended to value the program primarily because it speaks to their constituency; one Native American man wrote that he watches the show "because I actually learn things about my own cultural heritage from it." A Jewish man poignantly lamented that "much of the show's soul dissolved when Joel left. No more Seders, no more klezmorim, no more rabbi-in-a-dream. It's a loss to Cicely, to *Northern Exposure*, and to me." A Catholic woman in my survey group shared Shelly's feelings of confusion about baptism and confession and admired the way the program explored "the inherent contradictions which Catholics must face." In *Outweek* magazine, Scott Sherman expressed the pleasure that the gay community found in the program's positive representation of gays and lesbians and encouraged the writers "to bring back the gay couple as ongoing characters" (22). *Northern Exposure* allows an affirmation of group identities that many marginalized people found liberating, while simultaneously encouraging those in the majority (and minority) to rethink a narrow sense of identity that could prevent cross-cultural communication and understanding. Melodramas have often been accused of provoking emotional identification merely to shore up existing, conservatively defined identities; to the contrary, this television program provokes sentimental engagement in the service of a more radical breakdown of social boundaries and hierarchies. Although it allows a politics of recognition for marginalized viewers, the program's ambitions are much more complex because it aims to address viewers from both dominant and subordinate social groups. While many sentimental texts speak primarily to dominant groups and treat the marginalized other as an object of pity, *Northern Exposure* instead promotes a sympathetic audience identification with various social others that avoids condescending overtones. This program also works to engage a minority or leftist viewer's sympathy for misunderstood dominant groups (represented by Maurice) rather than demonizing them as prejudiced oppressors. Typical mass-market melodramas have treated the other as an exotic amusement or a threat which must be contained or expunged (e.g., blacks in *Birth of a Nation* and Native Americans in westerns), or they have more recently tried to domesticate and reduce difference (*The Cosby Show*). *Northern Exposure* instead fosters metonymic alliances between self and other, between dominant and subordinate identities, without either erasing or reifying difference.

One of the main narrative goals of the program is the union of self and other in a multicultural community, a focus wholly in tune with the ethos of the early 1990s Clinton era. The show's emotional evocation of an idyllic community composed of very different individuals had a powerful effect on the members of my audience group. As one person remarked of the show: "Real life issues of race, gender, and religion are worked out within the context of ultimate (and seemingly unattainable) community. I feel a profoundly sad realization that this sort of unity of varied individuals does not exist in my world, and the longing for such a community in my own life brings tears to my eyes." Rather than identifying with the characters on the basis of specific identities, these viewers identified primarily with the *political ideology* of *Northern Exposure*—its multiculturalism and liberal democratic spirit. While most theories of identification propose that engaging with characters is an emotional, unconscious process and that responding to the ideology involves a conscious intellectual distance, I found that these viewers were both intellectually stimulated and emotionally engaged by the left-leaning ideology. For example, in response to the episode about the founding of the town by lesbians, one of the more leftist members of the group said: "I almost cried for joy when Roslyn went off to fight the Fascists in Spain." Comments like these reveal that intellect and emotion are not so easy to separate in the process of identification, and that the most successful political narratives are those that construct "mattering maps" to engage audiences affectively as well as intellectually (Grossberg, *We Gotta* 82). Grossberg points out that modernism fostered a disjunction between affect and ideology that has intensified today, causing people to question their "ability to invest in the meanings—and meaningfulness—of the world" ("Postmodernity" 290). By attempting to construct an affective politics, *Northern Exposure* aims to heal this problematic rift between affect and ideology.

It is also highly significant that these questionnaire respondents were markedly homogeneous in terms of political affiliation: only five out of forty-four people identified themselves as Republicans or conservatives, and of those five, four were women with some feminist sensibilities. Even these few Republicans were respectful of difference and viewed the program as moderate or even progressive. As a whole, the thirty-nine left-oriented viewers were more liberal than they were radical (only a few expressed anti-capitalist sentiments or dissatisfaction with Clinton's moderate politics). *Northern Exposure* offers not only a confirmation of their political views but a more thoroughly idealistic vision of them; Clinton's "bridge to the twenty-first century" is nowhere near as radically utopian as the one envisioned by *Exposure*. A conscious ideological affinity strongly influenced these viewers' identification with the text, a possibility which psychoanalytic theory largely ignores. Because *Northern Exposure*'s liberal politics seems to have been one of the most important factors in drawing viewers to the program, its attempt to mobilize affect in the service of a utopian, communitarian ideology warrants further investigation.

Popular Postmodernism and Progressive Utopian Communities

Some have proclaimed the death of utopian thinking in postmodern cultures; however, contemporary social movements such as feminism, anti-racism, and human rights activism have refused to give up on the progressive impulse to imagine an ideal world. Amidst this debate about the possibility of utopia in postmodern culture came *Northern Exposure*, hailed for its dream of a peaceful multicultural community. Iain Crawford suggests that the program's "belief in human goodness and fellowship" makes it a "fitting analog to the new mythos of Clintonian change in America, a perfect response to the call never to stop thinking and hoping about tomorrow" (21). Rather than deeming it "of the moment," pessimistic postmodernists might argue that *Northern Exposure* 's utopia is merely a throwback to a modernist sensibility, or a repackaging of liberal humanism (as Crawford's reference to Clinton implies). In opposition to this skeptical view, I propose that *Exposure* offers a potent alternative to nihilism by depicting a utopian society grounded in the principle of difference, a version of Mouffe's "radical, plural democracy" that unites a modernist faith in progress with a postmodern critique of homogeneity.

Northern Exposure 's utopianism might seem nostalgic or insufficiently critical in the eyes of some postmodern and Marxist philosophers. The traditional model of utopia as a blueprint for a rational society, espoused by Sir Thomas More and Jeremy Bentham, rested on the principles of a "common good" and universally accepted Truth. Drawing upon Enlightenment and humanist philosophies, traditional utopian philosophers believed in the innate goodness of human beings and thought the exercise of reason could lead to the perfection of human society. Utopianists were driven by a faith in the unlimited possibility of reform and progress, before such concepts were debunked by the postmodern critique of the Enlightenment. In "After Utopia," Baudrillard describes the contemporary United States as an "anti-utopia of unreason, value neutralism, and indifference" (217). Less cynical than Baudrillard, Jameson asserts that mass culture implicitly contains the "utopian or transcendent potential" to be "negative and critical of the social order from which, as a product and a commodity, it springs" ("Reification and Utopia" 29). Yet in Jameson's lexicon, utopia is generally equated with class critique and resistance to capitalism; thus his utopian concept of postmodern "cognitive mapping" invests resistant power in texts which lay bare the economic structure of commodity capitalism as it exists to contain us (see *Postmodernism*). Jameson would most likely find *Northern Exposure* to be complicit with capitalist ideology, and thus a nostalgic throwback to the bourgeois liberalism of Enlightenment utopias. In contrast to Jameson's equation of utopianism with Marxism, Huyssen argues that postmodern culture's "obsessions with memory and history . . . are not regressive or simply escapist. . . .They occupy a utopian position vis-à-vis a chic and cynical postmodern nihilism on the one hand and a neo-conservative worldview on the other that desires what cannot be had: stable histories, a stable canon, a stable reality" ("Memories" 101). Huyssen's recuperation of postmodern utopian thinking resonates with my reading of *Northern Exposure* as a mythic neo-liberal text that aims to revivify faith in democracy. Rather than simply a "strategy of legitimation" that supports the status quo (Jameson, "Reification" 29), the program's mythic utopian narratives deconstruct the problematic universalism of communitarian ideologies and reflect on the pathologies of postmodern society.

Northern Exposure explicitly evokes such utopian ideology in its "flashback" episode detailing the origin of this Alaskan town as an egalitarian community founded by two lesbians, Cicely and Roslyn, who turned this formerly violent, Old West saloon town into a pacifist modernist *salon*. By far the favorite episode of this fanclub, "Cicely" served as an ur-text for the values of the series. As one fan wrote to the newsgroup, this "pioneering community combines considerable individual freedom with . . . a set of values shared by all," values such as artistic creativity, sexual freedom, egalitarianism, spirituality, feminism, harmony with nature, and a deep respect for all humans. Two of the episode's plotlines, in which a beggar gains self-esteem by learning to read and a prostitute is transformed by love, preview the humanism of the contemporary Cicelian society, where even an ex-con such as Chris can become a minister and community leader. Clearly the program participates in the mythology of America as a land of freedom, equality, and opportunity. Because the fans claim that they lack such a harmonious and humane community in their own lives, they became intensely involved in and sentimental about this utopic television society. One respondent compared Cicely to the idyllic Camelot, "a place that is our best dreams realized and then externalized and shared." Rather than viewing this as a nostalgic regression, I view the program's attempt to revivify faith in community and democracy as a critical intervention in a postmodern society plagued by fragmentation, dislocation, violence, and meaninglessness. While humanism as a philosophy has been criticized by poststructuralist thinkers for its complacency, false optimism, erasure of difference, and conservative political tendencies, the multicultural humanism of *Northern Exposure* takes on a more subversive tone in our violent postindustrial society, in which a lack of autonomy causes individuals to abnegate civic responsibility. Cicely's frequent town meetings, held to arbitrate disputes and enact necessary reforms, offer a return to a government "of the people, by the people, and for the people" rather than an uncontrollable behemoth, an omnipotent "Big Brother." One quotation from the "Cicely" episode flies in the face of Foucault's argument about the postmodern diffusion of power and the absence of individual autonomy in our panoptic society: "One person can have a profound effect on another. And two people can change a whole town. They can change the world." While this statement may seem naive and nostalgic, this creed aims to reinvest power in the individual and to breathe new life into democratic ideals.

While these basic democratic-utopian goals are lauded by the show's writers, they simultaneously criticize the means by which Enlightenment philosophers hoped to achieve these goals—through unwavering faith in Reason. Joel and Maurice, exemplars of masculinist rationalism, are often treated as whipping boys who must learn that reason cannot explain all the happenings of the world, nor solve all of its problems. In *The Transparent Society*, Gianni Vattimo points out that after World War II and the failure of Soviet communism, dystopias took the place of the utopias of modernity, because of the "discovery that the rationalization of the world turns against reason and its ends of perfection and emancipation" (78), instead leading to fascism and genocide. On *Northern Exposure*, Joel is forced to make the discovery that his medical knowledge cannot save a dying old woman and that life cannot always be rationally "optimized." He and Maurice are often confounded by the magical events that occur in the town, and the writers usually support the Native Americans' mystical explanations of the phenomena. The program's critique of the Enlightenment is made from a poststructuralist perspective as well as an earlier transcendentalist one, which first posed emotion, intuition and spirituality as alternatives to the cult of Reason. The newly founded town of Cicely is a decidedly anti-rationalist utopia, in which the town's namesake Cicely performs mystical dances to evoke the spirit of Gaia. Although Cicely's spiritualism is valued, this episode also lampoons her modernist literary tastes and reverence for "the new." In some ways, *Northern Exposure*'s utopian project could be seen as a descendent of modernity's master narratives of progress, but this flashback episode also subtly ironizes and critiques this modernist community. While the fledgling town embodies a modernist rejection of tradition, a belief in evolutionary progress, the "manifest destiny" narrative of civilizing the frontier, and a mythologizing of individual power, the writers also mock and demystify the products of high modernist literature. In this flashback, the supposed "genius" Franz Kafka finds his way to Cicely, and is portrayed as a nervous and rather ordinary thinker who gets all his ideas for "The Metamorphosis" and *The Castle* from a woman. Under the influence of his teacher Cicely, Ned writes a minimalist poem nonsensically titled "Between Antigone" that contains lines such as "blue jays on a log, agog." This mockery of the word-salad style of another lesbian modernist—Stein in *Tender Buttons*—deflates the strongly sentimental presentation of Cicely by suggesting that her modernist literary values are somewhat ridiculous. *Northern Exposure*'s sentimental humanist utopia combines the modernist hope for political reform with a tempering spoof of modernist aesthetic experiments. Vattimo suggests that the only possible postmodern utopia is one of "inventory, nostalgia, revival," but one that also entails some ironic distance from the past (86). *Northern Exposure*'s treatment of the town's mythic origins is a case in point, since its return to the past is productive of new meanings that are also contingent upon past histories.

One way in which the 1990s Cicely marks its distance from the original utopian Cicely is in its recognition of the power of capitalism, even on the frontier. The once pure pastoral space of Alaska is now home to computers and the Sharper Image catalog. Although the program still invokes the frontier spirit, particularly through the characters of Holling and Maurice (Holling once wrestled with a bear and Maurice tamed the wilds of outer space), this formerly virgin frontier landscape of Alaska is now "contaminated" by commercialism. One humorously ironic subplot of the episode "Fish Story" suggests that the frontier has been nearly played out, even though the transplanted inhabitants still hope that Alaska will renew and purify them. In the spirit of the Beats, Ruth-Anne decides to flee the burden of her responsibilities as manager of the grocery store by journeying "on the road" with a biker gang, the Diablos. After renouncing her commercial world, she is disappointed to learn that the Diablos are actually middle-aged yuppies, complete with cell phones, who experience similarly pedestrian or unromantic worries (one of their former members has colon cancer). Even the supposedly untainted romantic rebels are fully imbricated in capitalism and its dangerously excessive consumption, figured by cancer of the colon. The turn-of-the-century romantic-modernist *salon* has now become a postmodern marketplace, where the inhabitants even buy stocks on the web.

Northern Exposure's complicity with postindustrial capitalism clearly differentiates it from another traditionally modernist form of utopia—the Marxist commune. Thus Marxist critics may object to my designation of this program, or perhaps *any* network television program, as utopic. Since class is a particularly blurred social category in Cicely, class struggle does not define these inhabitants' lives or politics. For example, Joel's social position is deliberately ambiguous since he is both a yuppie doctor and an indentured servant controlled by his overseers, Maurice and the state of Alaska. When he does try to go on strike, he fails to gain any sympathy for his plight, perhaps because he cannot rightfully claim the status of "oppressed" since he also claims the privileges of the ruling elite. Class conflict is also blunted by the fact that friendships often cross traditional class boundaries; the millionaire aesthete Maurice and the petit bourgeois bar-owner Holling are the best of friends, and Maurice's elegant dinner parties bring together friends from all classes. In fact, few of the inhabitants seem to embrace class as a meaningful identity. This post-Marxist worldview resonated with my audience group, one of whom was "annoyed with Chris when he went on and on about the woes of capitalism and individualism just because Maggie bought a washer and dryer set." The utopian ideals of this program and its fanclub are not located in a resistance to capitalism, but that should not lead to the conclusion that the program supports the status quo in all respects.

The most important way in which *Northern Exposure*'s ideal community differs from modernist and humanist utopias is through its poststructuralist critique of humanist universalism. By including feminist and non-white characters as community leaders, *Northern Exposure* explicitly rejects the whitewashed and masculinized view of humanity that usually structures mass-market television texts. Cicely's welcoming reception of a carnival of "freaks," including a flying man, was perhaps the most strident statement of the show's celebration of human difference. In *Heterotopia: Postmodern Utopia and the Body Politic,* Tobin Siebers argues that "the desire for heterogeneity . . . characterizes the aesthetic and political ambitions of postmodernism" (4), whereas modernism aimed for order and wholeness. The postmodern, he contends, remains attracted to the "romance of community" (Siebers 8), but envisions a sense of "wholeness in which various parts are allowed their autonomy" (Siebers 7). *Northern Exposure* gestures toward a pluralistic utopia that would allow differences of opinion rather than striving for a totalitarian sense of the "common good." The postmodern belief in the multiplicity of truth is explicitly voiced by Chris Stevens. When he is on trial for parole violation, Chris refuses to take the oath "to tell the truth, the whole truth, and nothing but the truth" because he believes that truth is relative and plural and thus cannot be reduced to a singular "whole." In another episode, the town echoes Chris's stance when they solve a dispute between two sparring Native American families with different interpretations of past events by allowing them to erect, side by side, two different totem poles to depict their opposed stories. This exercise in revisionist historiography underscores the validity of multiple, and even conflicting, truths.

The pluralistic society of Cicely bears some similarities to the "radical, plural democracy" envisioned by Mouffe. Mouffe aims to retain the democratic, pluralistic goals of "individual freedom and personal autonomy" (*Return of the Political* 7) that were the foundation of modernity's liberal tradition, while using postmodern theory to critique the universalism and unitary identities of Enlightenment ideologies (such as Marxist notions of class). Mouffe also rejects the essentialist idea of a social totality implied by the term "common good," a concept inherited from communitarianism and traditional utopian theory. Instead, she proposes coalition-building among people of diverse interests, united not by identity or a sense of the common good but by a chain of "democratic equivalence" (*Return* 19), by a politicized sense of themselves as equal citizens in a democracy. While she uses postmodern theory to discredit some of the projects of modernity, she argues quite convincingly that postmodernists need not reject the democratic, "progressive" legacy of modernity as Lyotard does. Of course, it is important to acknowledge that Mouffe is talking about a political project and not a text. However, there has always been a strong connection between utopian political theory and fictional texts (e.g., Thomas More's *Utopia*), since both involve the creation of alternative spaces and practices.

Marxists and Mouffe herself might object that *Northern Exposure* is not sufficiently "radical" (owing to its complicity with capitalism) to be an example of "radical, plural democracy." She argues that although we should retain liberal notions of democracy, "economic liberalism" (i.e., bourgeois capitalism) must be thoroughly critiqued from a more radical socialist viewpoint (*Return* 7). Clearly, the analogy I am making between her political concept and the ideologies of this television program can only be taken so far. But I do take issue with critics of mass culture who believe that only the supposedly "transcendent" space of the avant-garde can spawn radical critique. Similar to Stuart Hall, who theorizes that popular culture exhibits a "double movement between containment and resistance" ("Notes" 228), I argue that moments of critique are not rendered completely ineffective just because they come from within the culture industries. Hutcheon's term "complicitous critique," rather than "radical critique," seems a more appropriate term for the kind of resistance that can be found in television texts. While *Northern Exposure* is clearly not Marxist or even socialist, its textual representations of politics do bear some similarities to Mouffe's vision of a postmodern utopia. Instead of a falsely universalist common good, Mouffe posits that a radical plural democracy would enable and even encourage civil forms of antagonism. Despite the general tone of harmony on *Northern Exposure,* the program recognizes the "permanence of conflict and antagonism" (Mouffe, *Return* 8) in this outback community. By depicting a mayoral election in the "Democracy in America" episode, *Northern Exposure* rejects facile consensus and embraces Mouffe's principle of dissent, which is usually repressed in fictional utopias. Because of an argument over the need for a stop sign, former friends Holling and Edna compete for the job of mayor, engaging in fiery debates that draw the whole town. Speaking through Chris as a patriotic mouthpiece, the writers stress the importance of dissent to the democratic process. As usual, Maggie and Joel (as election commissioners) spar over what party is best and how an election should be run.

After Edna wins the election, the antagonism appears to die down and friendships are restored, and Chris quotes Abraham Lincoln's speech to a divided union: "we are not enemies but friends. . . . passions must not break the bonds of our affection." *Northern Exposure* envisions a multicultural society in which passionate differences can be expressed without leading to disorder and violence.

This moment of closure is not facile, however, because it does not seek to erase all dissent; we are left with Maurice's libertarian despair that his oasis of freedom is being bureaucratized out of existence. Regretting his own efforts to civilize the wilderness, Maurice poignantly laments that the liberty he craves will be curtailed by law and government, the inevitable baggage of civilization: "one day two trappers are arguing about beaver pelts . . . the next day there is busing in Boston. It all starts with one single stop sign." While the episode and the program as a whole praise democratic government as a utopian process, Maurice's skeptical voice remains, urging us to consider the negative consequences of governmental arbitration: the restriction of liberty. This program's attempts at peaceful resolution, in which some people agree to disagree, should not be equated with a forced consensus. Here the postmodern values of dissent and difference coexist, rather than clash, with an emotional commitment to the traditional value of civic involvement. Furthermore, the program's sentimental, harmonious endings should not be so quickly dismissed as conservative structures. The ideological goal of these sentimental endings—to provoke an emotional investment in a (relatively) harmonious democratic community—still carries subversive potential in an increasingly violent world in which a truly pluralist democratic ideology is by no means pervasive.

Critics might argue, however, that this liberal utopian community masks a colonizing appropriation of the other or a domestication of difference, and there is indeed some evidence of this problem in the show's narratives. In the fictional universe of Cicely, Alaska, violence and hatred are simply willed out of existence, and difference never leads to blows. There are few reminders of the hierarchical and oppressive world from which Cicely offers an escape, almost as if it can be simply willed out of existence. Gays are not bashed here (they only have to endure Maurice's repressed hostility); a black man who rides in on a motorcycle is treated with the utmost of courtesy; no one ever utters an anti-Semitic joke. By eliminating all the oppressive structures that make difference an often painful reality for marginalized people, the program occasionally lapses into a problematic "feel good" sameness. The plotline in which Chris and the African American Bernard discover that they are twins in spirit, and quite literally brothers (who share a white father), may be a refreshing example of "race-blindness," but it also elides important differences created by racism and underestimates the tenacity of prejudice in any human society. The writers also domesticate the gay male characters and the lesbian co-founders by placing them in monogamous relationships and avoiding mention of their different sexual desires. Although the "gay marriage" episode was banned in the deep South (see Harris and Pryor), the "family values" depiction of Ron and Erick's gay wedding contained nary a kiss. Because it avoids any direct representation of how and why certain people have been persecuted for being "other," *Northern Exposure* misses the chance to offer a more subversive social critique. By simply allowing mainstream viewers to identify with marginalized people without feeling their pain, this kind of identification risks becoming an appropriation or a substitution of self for other rather than a more radically empathetic experience. As Sommer argues, such facile connections may last "hardly longer than the reading of a novel" ("Resistant Texts" 529) or the viewing of a television episode.

On the other hand, Grossberg suggests that this refamiliarization of the strange aids the project of democracy by wiping away the concept of othering. He suggests that "television empowers its fans by celebrating the ordinariness of the exotic" ("Putting the Pop" 187), and that "celebration, however much it ignores relations of domination, can be enabling" (170). Despite the caveats I noted above, *Northern Exposure*'s attempt to eradicate the concept of "othering" was highly desirable to this liberal audience. Since these viewers were already all too aware, rather than ignorant, of the violence directed at marginalized others in our society, they were ready to move beyond realism to revel in a fantastic alternative. In my view, there are more likely to be disastrous consequences from overemphasizing difference than from pointing out similarities. The kind of cross-group identification promoted by *Northern Exposure*, in which differences are respected but do not negate the possibility of human fellowship, offers a pointed political statement amidst an increasingly balkanized global landscape, where xenophobia and violence against ethnic and sexual minorities is widespread. The 1992 Los Angeles riots and the Serbian "ethnic cleansing" wars of the 1990s, among other examples, attest to the fact that multicultural communities are fragile constructions indeed. Utopian cultural products that depict harmonious democratic communities can provide crucial emotional nourishment. As one post on the newsgroup put it, "I like the way conflicts are resolved. Disparate personalities usually wind up at least being tolerant in the end. That's the kind of society I'd like to live in, instead of the one I've got. It's a great escape."

Some who decry the escapist qualities of television might argue that such representations, however utopian, do nothing to foster the value of community in the "real world." One of the questionnaire respondents offered a similar self-reflexive comment on the demise of the show: "It was the loss of a community I loved, which may be even more sad . . . because a good argument could be made that television has destroyed real community, thus making vicarious experiences of community (like *Northern Exposure*) viable." His argument echoes Baudrillard's fatalistic vision of our culture as a state of the "hyperreal," in which reality and referents are no longer accessible because our media-saturated world is completely defined by simulations, images, and surfaces. Baudrillard believes that we can no longer distinguish between virtual and real community because the signs are the same, and therefore the real is collapsed onto the representation. Rather than accepting such a totalizing and pessimistic theory of the effect of the media upon audiences, I draw upon the work of cultural studies practitioners like Richard Dyer and Grossberg. Not only was my audience group keenly aware of the difference between the uplifting sign and an often-depressing reality, but this "escapist" representation could possibly move them to change the real world that they inhabit. As Richard Dyer argues, even popular musicals can provoke utopian desires for change, for "temporary answers to the inadequacies of the society which is being escaped" ("Entertainment" 277). Fantasies of community thus respond to and form an antidote to the social fragmentation of (post)modern life. Grossberg also points out the power of a "functional positivity" in popular culture that is ignored by postmodern theorists who emphasize the negative: "Opposition may be constituted by living, even momentarily, within alternative practices, structures, and spaces, even though they may take no notice of their relationship to existing systems of power" ("Putting the Pop" 170). Because this optimism can remain long after turning off the tube, television can inspire agency and action among viewers with previously undernourished utopian imaginations. As one fan wrote, watching *Northern Exposure* causes her to experience "a sort of high, like all things in life are possible."

Because some of my questionnaire respondents discussed the show as a kind of drug, a welcome escape from their own less-than-idyllic lives, I wondered whether this program's "quick fix" could be preventing them from getting off their couches to fulfill their desires in the real world. In her study of romance readers, Radway hypothesizes that because these books satisfy women's fantasies for utopian gender relations, they may promote inertia and stasis (*Reading* 50). However, I hesitate to accept such a conclusion about either the Smithton romance readers or these *Northern Exposure* fans, precisely because they have made one significant and lasting change in their lives—they have created and joined a fanclub in hopes of meeting others who share their value systems. This process of building solidarity through identification should not be undervalued, because it can shore up faith in the possibility of realizing a utopian alternative. As one *Exposure* fan wrote, "the program made me want to live there, and to make that kind of society and culture come about." "There" could be anywhere they choose to make it, and these fans in fact created a friendly cyber-community as just such a utopian space, where empathy and respect are primary values. For example, when one man posted an emotional note about the parallels between one episode and an event in his own life in which he had damaged a friendship, many readers offered sensitive advice and continued their encouragement for several months. When an occasional "flame" takes place, others gently remind the flamers to avoid such "un-Cicelian" behavior. Although I saw evidence of some vitriol on the newsgroup in 1995, in 1998 it seemed like a much kinder and gentler place, complete with a welcoming committee to greet first-time posters, and a yearly group pilgrimage to Roslyn, Washington where the program was filmed. This pilgrimage involves important group bonding to reinforce their shared political ideology.

Yet the charge still remains—do such virtual communities on television and the Internet end up eroding real communities? For instance, David Morris posits that information technology has "achieved instant communication along with a vanishing sense of community" (151), although he ignores the creation of thousands of online communities such as alt.tv.northern-exp. In *No Sense of Place*, Joshua Meyrowitz contends that television is destroying our sense of locality, and *Exposure*'s episode about Shelly's satellite dish endorses this attitude by reclaiming Shelly from the "global village" back to her local community. I turn to David Morley for an important corrective to arguments such as these. Morley suggests that electronic media have *transformed* rather than destroyed the idea of community, by expanding it beyond local boundaries and therefore helping to widen and relativize individuals' perspectives ("Geography" 337). Because the newsgroup fanclub draws participants from many countries around the globe, it has become an even more plural communal space than its inspirational model of Cicely, Alaska. I would argue that this Internet group satisfies some of the most basic elements of any real community—a sharing of support, feelings, values, and attitudes through language. We need to consider that utopian representations can have the power to improve the real by offering people hope and alternative possibilities. Increasing the number of alternative representations has long been the goal of feminists, racial minorities, and gay activists, who believe that media could have a positive rather than a negative effect on the way we perceive and construct our own realities. I propose that Maurice's gradual recognition of his similarity to gay men Ron and Erick could serve a radical political function, educating viewers to reconsider homophobia. As Elihu Katz reminds us, those who view television as an escape mistakenly suppose that the "vacationing" viewers "do not bring anything back" with them (15). In fact, they usually return with new and perhaps improved strategies for dealing with real-life situations. The viewers who responded to my questionnaire should not be categorized as escaping from reality, since many expressed explicit concerns about democracy and the political climate, and only four of them indicated that they have no party affiliation and do not vote. Rather than a flight from reality that reinforces stasis, a viewer's enjoyment of *Northern Exposure* should be viewed as an effective "way of countering despair" (Radway, *Reading* 222). One man in the fanclub said, "I get both envious and sad that I am not a part of such a community," and his comment takes on more significance when one learns that he is Croatian and lives in war-torn Zagreb. The postmodern utopian communities of *Northern Exposure* and its Internet fanclub offer a much-needed respite for viewers disgusted and disheartened by a violent world.

The value of community has often been sentimentalized in popular culture. However, I have been arguing that *Northern Exposure*'s postmodern version of a humanist utopia took on a new and perhaps more subversive significance in the 1990s. Rather than fostering a troubling and naive consensus, this program's utopian sensibility allows for differences of opinion and of identity formation, but does not allow these differences to lead to violence, anarchy, or stasis. Although Iain Crawford argues that *Northern Exposure* seeks order and answers rather than destabilizing questions, I have argued that the answers it provides through its sentimental narrative devices are implicitly critical of the social fragmentation of postmodern life. Psychoanalytic theorists and media critics often assume that mass-market forms merely support conservatively defined identities and social formations, but this popular text promotes the liberal multicultural hope for a communion between self and other and a dissolution of unitary identities. Similar to the work of George Lipsitz, my case study of *Northern Exposure* and its fans explores "the potential of popular culture as a . . . site for experimentation with cultural and social roles not yet possible in politics" (Lipsitz 17). This hybrid cultural product suggests that postmodern ideas can be used to help build democratic utopian communities, rather than to shatter them. My study of the cross-group identification patterns of these fans also indicates that *Northern Exposure*'s lessons about deconstructing identity and forming political coalitions of "democratic equivalence" were well-heard, or simply that the text drew viewers who already perceived of themselves as postmodern fluid subjects. While some of these fans identified with characters in the program who mirrored their own subject positions, the majority did not. This series both reflected and contributed to the cultural questioning of subjectivity taking place on many fronts in the 1990s. This fanclub's hybrid taste for both high and popular culture also indicates another important cultural shift—a breaking down of the "aristocratic" hierarchies of taste that Bourdieu observed to be strongly aligned with class distinctions. *Northern Exposure* helps to foster a breakdown of cultural hierarchies and barriers to identification between individuals with differing social identities. Further, the program implies that ideology—in this case a liberal belief in democracy and multiculturalism—can play a larger role in identification than psychoanalytic theorists admit. In sum, this study of *Northern Exposure* and its fans underscores the need to think about emotional identification as more than just an unconscious response linked to bodily coordinates, and more than just a means of reinforcing hegemonic ideologies.

Chapter Five

Kiss of the Spider Woman and the Politics of Camp

With its thematic focus on identification and leftist politics, Manuel Puig's *Kiss of the Spider Woman* is a paradigmatic text of sentimental postmodernism. Since the text is also centrally concerned with the politics of mass culture and of homosexuality, it bears some relationship to the critical practice called "camp." Many critics have analyzed *Kiss of the Spider Woman* as a work of "gay fiction," but none has attempted to situate Puig's text or its film and musical adaptations in relation to camp as a gay or queer critique of heterosexual mass culture and its value systems. Any academic discussion of camp bears the burden of definition, since the term has been variously defined as a "depoliticized" form of send-up that converts the "serious into the frivolous" (Sontag), an "aestheticized sensibility" (Babuscio; Sontag), an "operation of taste" (Ross), and a radical form of "queer parody" (Meyer). I will be relying on Richard Dyer's sense of camp as a gay sensibility that involves a dialectical movement between "theatricality and authenticity" (*Heavenly* 154), between an ironic critique of mass culture and a sentimental immersion in it. Defined in this way, camp is kin to my concept of sentimental postmodernism as a hybrid style invoking both irony and sentimentality, both critical distance and emotional engagement, and both essentialism and anti-essentialism. I argue that *Kiss of the Spider Woman* exudes a camp sensibility in its aesthetics and in its treatment of the politics of sexuality, gender, and mass culture. The concept of camp is particularly useful for my study because it offers a bridge between aesthetics and the politics of identity—between the textual and the sexual.

Crucial to the camp positioning of *Kiss of the Spider Woman* is its merging of the aesthetics and narrative strategies of high-cultural postmodernism and of popular culture. The popular sensibility of *Kiss* is evident in its treatment of melodramatic film as a positive vehicle for intimacy between two prison cellmates (Molina and Valentin) and as a means to revivify Valentin's battered spirit. The novel could be described as a tragic love story that tugs at the heart strings, not unlike the B-movies that Molina cherishes and retells to Valentin. Another sign of the text's affinity for the popular is that it was adapted into a successful film (1985) and Broadway musical (1993). Despite these attributes of a popular sensibility, *Kiss* has most often been received as a high-cultural postmodern text. In the tradition of literary postmodernism and high modernism, Puig's novel challenges the reader with its difficult mixture of narrative elements, including footnotes and stream of consciousness style. *Kiss* upsets narrative expectations, criticizes the banality of popular culture, and deconstructs such accepted cultural dichotomies as male/female, rational/emotional, and homosexual/heterosexual. Many critics regard *Kiss of the Spider Woman* as a high cultural, critical meditation on popular culture, rather than as a participant in popular culture. I contend that the text establishes a symbiotic relationship between the popular and the postmodern that is crucial to its political impact upon audiences. Pamela Bacarisse argues that Puig's novels have drawn two distinct reading publics—serious critical readers with cultural capital, and a mass audience desiring sentimentality, illusion, and comfort (*Necessary Dream* 4). Rather than assuming that the text speaks only to discrete audiences with tastes for high or low, I propose that many audience members are attracted by precisely this "campy" conjunction of opposing aesthetics and worldviews, as the sentimental and the postmodern, the emotional and the critical, speak to one another dialogically in the text. In order to explore how viewers and readers negotiate the dialogic stylistics of this text, I interviewed thirty fans of *Kiss of the Spider Woman* (all residing in the Washington, D.C. area) about their responses to the novel, musical, and film versions. While these fans do not consider *Kiss* to be an example of camp (since they generally associate camp with its low-cultural forms, such as John Waters's film *Hairspray)*, I see evidence of a camp sensibility—merging the sentimental and the critical—in their own readings of this novel, film, and musical.

Kiss's dialogic strategy moves audiences to weigh the merits and limitations of various dichotomous poles, such as emotion vs. reason, fantasy vs. realism, and escapist kitsch vs. Marxist critical thought. The majority of the audience group interpreted the text as enacting a fusion or compromise between such extremes, and herein lies the heart of sentimental postmodernism's politics. The plot of *Kiss* concerns the developing relationship of two prisoners in an Argentine jail cell, two men who appear to represent opposite principles—the rational, macho, Marxist, heterosexual political prisoner (Valentin), and the emotional, effeminate, apolitical, homosexual B-movie *aficionado* (Molina). Through Molina's eyes we are led to criticize the rigidity of Valentin's Marxist worldview and his attempt to banish emotion, beauty, fantasy, and personal relationships in his pursuit of revolutionary change in the public sphere. On the other hand, Valentin allows us to see that Molina does nothing to resist his own oppression (or that of gays as a group) and uses kitschy film as a crutch to escape societal problems. To underscore the theme of dialogism, Puig constructed much of the novel as a dialogue between the two central characters, as in a play. As their dialogue progresses, the two men begin to see through each other's perspective, and their eventual union, both sexual and emotional, represents this larger merging of viewpoints. Although some of my interview group read the text as un-ambivalently Marxist, most felt that the novel and its adaptations criticize the tendency of Marxist thinkers to deny the human need for fantasy, aesthetic beauty, and emotional connection. I read *Kiss of the Spider Woman,* and sentimental postmodernism in general, as a counterpoint to Frankfurt School theorists such as Theodor Adorno, who disdained sentimental popular culture as a tool of fascism. Instead, *Kiss* suggests that a desire for love and aesthetic beauty should not be immediately dismissed as retrograde, because affect is crucial to sustaining political conviction on the Left as well as the Right. With its focus on film melodrama, the text implies that the micropolitics of human relationships is just as important as the macropolitics of Marxist revolution, and suggests that personal desires and dissatisfactions fostered by popular culture could lead to positive change in both the private and public spheres. Reappraising the role of popular culture in the political sphere, *Kiss* suggests that mass culture, and not merely the avant-garde, can provoke critical thought. The fact that this novel, film, and musical stir up intense emotions among its audiences works against fascism rather than for it, by fostering respect and sympathy for both leftist revolutionaries and sexual minorities.

As part of its project to underscore the micropolitics of the personal sphere, *Kiss* provokes readers to re-evaluate various categories of identity that have served both to enable and limit freedom. I argue that *Kiss*, in all three of its media forms, offers its audiences a means of reflecting upon their own ambivalent or shifting feelings about gender and sexual identities. When the voices of anti-essentialist feminists and queer theorists spread from academia to the mass media in the 1990s, some people where moved to question their once secure belief in stable identities. By offering us two main characters who appear to be opposites, *Kiss* invokes a dichotomizing view of identity familiar to fans of melodramatic popular culture. However, while the text seems to condone polarized and essentialist constructions of sexuality and gender in its initial characterization of Molina and Valentin, these binary rubrics blur, shift, and are subverted as the relationship between the two men progresses and eventually becomes sexual. Molina himself is an odd mixture of essentialist conceptions of subjectivity (transsexual, gay, feminine) and anti-essentialist ones (transgender, drag, queer). *Kiss* thus offers its readers the comfort of traditional unitary identities but also urges us to reconsider them without totally undermining their usefulness and emotional pull. This tension between authenticity and anti-essentialist performativity also characterizes the practice of camp. Since both the popular melodramatic and the postmodern senses of subjectivity are given full play in *Kiss*, the reader is encouraged to consider their competing merits and to think about the political implications of his or her own self-construction. This sentimental postmodernist text thus finds a receptive audience among ambivalent people who appreciate queer theory's attempt to allow broader coalitions but who still feel innately "gay" or "straight," and among people who accept the anti-essentialist position on gender but still feel most comfortable practicing acceptable forms of gendered behavior. Despite the fact that most of the interviewees appreciated the text's attempt to represent sexuality and gender as fluid, many of the gay and bisexual people in particular also expressed intense feelings of biological and essential otherness and an affinity with identity politics. *Kiss* and the viewers' responses to it suggest both the political promise and the limitations of queer politics, with its emphasis on performativity and surfaces over depth and rootedness.

Because *Kiss* invokes both traditionalist identities and postmodern anti-identitarianism, the viewer or reader is left with a great deal of interpretive freedom. A few of the interpretive choices audiences face are: Is Molina gay, transgender, or transsexual? Is Valentin straight, bisexual, or gay? Do the two men become less polarized in their gender roles, or remain static? Is this a story about the fluidity of gender and sexuality, or about the essential fixity of those characteristics? In the interviews, I set out to examine how people's own identities and ideas about gender and sexuality might affect their interpretations of the text's characters and its narratives concerning identity. These 30 individuals—13 gay men, 2 lesbians, 4 bisexual women, 1 bisexual man, 6 heterosexual women, and 4 heterosexual men—did not usually respond in neat patterns according to their sexual and gender self-identifications; I often found that particular interpretations cut across many of the groups. This group thwarted the naive expectation, based on a vulgar understanding of identity politics, that all gay men or straight women would read the text in a similar way. I do not mean to imply that the self-professed identities of the interviewees had no influence upon their interpretations, but rather to show that such identities are fractured, multiply determined, and layered. Interpretations were clearly affected by how each person conceives of identity in the abstract, and those understandings turned out to be highly individual, politicized, and sometimes contradictory. What sexual identity means to these thirty individuals was hugely variable, influenced by their response to a plethora of concurrent debates. Sparked by the AIDS crisis, queer activism (Queer Nation, ACT-UP), and scientific attempts to discover a "gay gene," public debates in the mid-1990s addressed whether sexual identity is politically chosen or preordained; socially constructed or biologically influenced; fluid or static; essential or performative; based on a continuum or an either/or binary; and based on sexual desires, sexual behavior, or affiliation with a group culture or politics. For many interview subjects, their sexual identity was also complicated by their race, gender, class, and age. Despite these numerous complicating factors that serve to individuate identity, I did find that a few types of textual interpretations usually accompanied particular ways of thinking about identity. There was a strong correlation, for example, between a pre-existing belief in biological essentialism or polarized schemas and a reading of the text as a representation of the fixed and biologically determined nature of identity. Those who embraced fluidity and rejected either/or polarities of sexuality and gender tended to read the text as an exemplar of ambiguity and felt that Valentin and Molina transcended categories. Yet a significant number of people echoed the mixture of discourses already present in the text by using language that indicated both a popular, melodramatic view of identity as fixed and a postmodern sense of identity as fluid. These diverse audience responses to *Kiss of the Spider Woman* suggest that identity is no longer, or perhaps never was, a static given that overdetermines audience interpretations and response.

The interviews revealed an astonishing diversity of identity within supposedly homogeneous groups, and they also revealed a complex pattern of cross-group identification that has important political implications. In *Identification Papers*, Fuss acknowledges that if identification allows crossing of gender/race/sexual boundaries, it could potentially encourage coalitions and foster empathy for oppressed groups (8). The text of *Kiss of the Spider Woman* enacts such a crossing, as Valentin and Molina slowly retreat from their polar positions and mutual distrust to the point of identification and intimacy with the other. This textual model encouraged my audience group to loosen their own self-conceptions and to discover affinities for the other within the self. The individuals I interviewed revealed a strong capacity for identifying with characters who did not share their own identity affiliations; women and gay men identified with Valentin while heterosexuals and people with masculine personalities identified with Molina. This finding challenges identification theories which reduce identification to a simple process of self-recognition, of finding resemblance and solidifying one's identity. It was also striking that many people identified with both men at once, or they identified as well as disidentified with the same character. These ambivalent forms of identification, which have often been underemphasized in theoretical work on identification, further attest to the complexity of identity. In short, my ethnographic study of responses to *Kiss of the Spider Woman* underscores that identification is a politically charged, emotionally powerful process that can promote self-criticism, a loosening of identity, and counter-hegemonic coalitions.

Reception and Production Contexts

Since I analyze fiction, film, and musical theater in this chapter, it is necessary to differentiate these specific media contexts and the historical and cultural conditions influencing reception. A brief explanation of the construction of my audience sample is also in order. To solicit participants for my study, I placed notices in the volunteer sections of two free newspapers in Washington, DC—*The City Paper* (a liberal weekly covering politics, arts, and events) and *The Washington Blade* (a weekly concerning issues of interest to the gay community). I also placed flyers in coffee shops and video and book stores in Dupont Circle, a middle-class urban neighborhood with a large percentage of gay residents. These choices were based on some assumptions about the likely American audience for *Kiss*—that they would be culturally literate and possibly well-educated, generally liberal (given the political and sexual themes of the text), and either homosexual, bisexual, or "gay-friendly" heterosexuals. Although my choice of venues for solicitation may have limited the participants, I nonetheless found quite a diverse group in terms of age, race, ethnicity, religious background, and sexual identity. Out of 30 people, there were 8 white Protestants, 10 Catholics, 7 Jews, and 4 who practiced Asian religions (Buddhist, Taoist, Hindu). Nine were racial minorities and/or people of mixed race, with ethnic affiliations ranging from Malaysian to Jamaican. 60% of those who volunteered to be interviewed were under 35, 20% were 36–50, and 20% were over 51. Yet the group was homogeneous in terms of class (mostly middle class, with a few lower-middle and upper-middle), education (80% had at least a B.A.), and political affiliation (73%

were Democrats, socialists, or leftists); the solicitation venues or the appeal of the text itself might help to explain these similarities. The demographic categories of the greatest relevance to my study were those of gender and sexual identity; I interviewed eighteen men and twelve women, ten heterosexuals, fourteen gay or bisexual men, and six lesbian or bisexual women. The skew towards a larger number of gay men was not surprising, since *Kiss* is often marketed as a text addressing issues of male homosexuality; in Dupont Circle, one video store displayed the film in a section on gay themes, and Puig once spoke at the area's gay bookstore, Lambda Rising.

The group of thirty could also be subdivided according to which media version of *Kiss of the Spider Woman* that they read or saw. It could be argued that my audience group is not in fact responding to the same text, but to three different texts. I decided to examine audience responses to all three versions of *Kiss*, rather than merely the novel (as master text), because the popularity of the film and musical in the United States created a resurgence of interest in the novel. Many of my interviewees had in fact encountered one of the adaptations before the original. Twenty-five people had seen the film, sixteen had read the novel, eight had seen the musical, and eighteen had consumed more than one media version of *Kiss*. While some may question any generalizations one could make about response because of this multi-text factor, I consider it a rich opportunity to address the effect of media context upon reception. For example, each of the three versions is positioned differently on the high art/popular culture continuum, which may result in different kinds of identifications and audience response. Each version may even attract slightly different audience populations. These differences may be caused in part by the status of the medium in question and by how each text is positioned as a genre within its medium. For example, although all three versions blend elements of both high and popular culture, the novel is more highbrow than the film or musical. Not only do novels carry more cultural prestige, but Puig's postmodern text was reviewed and marketed as a serious and difficult piece of literature. While Hector Babenco's film contains arty aesthetics and an unconventional plot and thus was marketed to art-house theaters, many of the people I interviewed echoed the popular belief that the medium of film should be classified as entertainment rather than art. Just as the film of *Kiss* is an arty text within a popular medium, the Broadway musical version occupies a similar position as an award-winning, serious-themed show with a difficult score, within a medium that is often perceived as lowbrow and escapist. The slightly different cultural positioning of these media versions results in different emotional registers and audience expectations. With its use of music and dance, the musical aims to tug directly at the heart strings, and the fans I interviewed cited the emotional catharsis as their favorite aspect of the show. Although many people were emotionally moved by the novel as well, it often provoked a more intellectual response from those I interviewed, who praised the book's narrative technique and ideological messages.

It is not surprising that the people in my audience group who had read the novel and those who had seen the musical differed the most in terms of cultural tastes, and in fact only two people had consumed both novel and musical versions of *Kiss*. The novel-readers tended to be college-educated with somewhat highbrow tastes, favoring canonical and postmodern artists and expressing disdain for musical theater and television. On the other hand, the fans of the musical were more likely to have lowbrow tastes, and their responses were primarily emotional and visceral rather than analytical. As one musical devotee remarked, "I'm a literal person and I don't try to figure out what the hidden messages are. . . . To me, a show is more of a treat to the senses, a fantastic escape." Despite some evidence of a polarization between the musical and novel audiences, it is also significant that many individuals did not fit into such neatly separable taste cultures. Those who had seen the film version of *Kiss* enjoyed a wider variety of cultural products, from low-budget indies to Hollywood blockbusters, from James Joyce to television sitcoms. The two people who had both read the novel and seen the musical were college-educated gay men who felt equal affinity for both high and low. The fact that fourteen people had encountered both the novel and the film suggests a substantial overlap in the audience appeal of these two media versions. Although the individuals that I interviewed did not always exhibit such predictable tastes, the fact that the producers and writers of the film and musical significantly altered the "parent text" of the novel suggests that they aimed their texts at distinct taste communities. In this way, assumptions about reception—about which kinds of people are drawn to a particular medium and genre—can be said to have influenced textual production, resulting in versions with different politics and thematic emphases. Both the film and the musical are considerably less radical than the novel in their treatment of homosexuality and of Marxist and fascist politics, and I attribute this difference in part to the media context. The ending of Puig's novel, which depicts Valentin's morphine-induced dream after he has been tortured, implies that the "straight" Valentin has indeed fallen in love with Molina, because he fantasizes about a composite lover who is both Molina and his girlfriend Marta. Valentin is imagining a conversation with his beloved Marta, but Marta speaks lines of dialogue that Molina had once said to him, such as "That's the only thing I don't ever want to know, the names of your comrades" (281). The film's ending significantly alters the sexual politics of this dream by depicting Valentin rowing away in a boat with Marta only; Molina is nowhere to be seen. Perhaps an expectation that an international film audience would be somewhat uncomfortable with a homosexual "love story" influenced the screenwriter Leonard Schrader and director Hector Babenco to mute the romantic gesture of the novel's close.

The musical moves even further away from a homosexual romance narrative by implying that Valentin has sex with Molina mainly to induce him to carry messages to the Marxist revolutionaries; their relationship is reduced to friendship and Valentin's motives are primarily political. In the song "Anything for Him," Valentin rationally decides to trade on Molina's selfless affection for him. By appeasing viewers who cannot fathom the idea that Valentin might sexually desire and even love Molina, the musical offers the weakest challenge to heterosexist norms. Although musical theater is often considered a gay genre, the white, middle-class mainstream (in terms of sheer numbers) still make up the greater part of the audience for expensive Broadway musicals. While writer Terrence McNally had previously penned a few plays with gay themes, in adapting the widely known *Kiss of the Spider Woman* into a musical he was faced with the opportunity to reach a broader, more mainstream audience, given the film's recent success at the Oscars. McNally and lyricist Fred Ebb thus appealed to the assumptions of the heterosexual members of their target audience by not allowing Valentin to deviate too far from the heterosexual type, and their strategy paid off quite literally. The musical became a Broadway blockbuster that spawned a national tour, and McNally won a Tony. His new-found fame and financial clout gave him the freedom to address gay audiences in his later plays *Corpus Christi* and *Love! Valor! Compassion!*, which tackle such controversial themes as AIDS and a homosexual Jesus (see Zinman). The writers of the film and musical versions of *Kiss* were clearly hesitant to take the same political risks that Manuel Puig did in writing his novel, perhaps because their projects were more influenced by the commercial imperative.

The different imagined or intended audiences for each media version—Spanish-speaking leftist intellectual readers, English-speaking art-house film viewers, and American, Canadian, and British fans of musical theater—also may have affected the writers' differing treatments of Marxist and fascist politics. Puig imagined an audience of Latin American intellectuals and rebels critical of government oppression, so he assumed the reader's basic sympathy for Marxist causes and the knowledge that more moderate resistance often proves ineffectual against a totalitarian state. By assuming that his readers will sympathize with Valentin, Puig is able to criticize some of Valentin's methods without implying a rejection of his basic ideology. Because the film was made for an international audience with limited knowledge of the oppressive Argentinean political situation, the screenwriters watered down Valentin's politics and made his "crimes" less threatening—rather than a perpetrator of violent revolt, he is merely a journalist who gives his passport to an old man trying to escape the country. Critic Philip Swanson called the film's dilution of Valentin's radicalism a "sell-out to liberal elements in the American motion-picture industry" (339). Whether or not one deems this move a "sell-out" to American liberalism, it seems clear that the screenwriters aimed to retain sympathy for Valentin among an international viewing audience that might equate dissidents with terrorists. In fact, some of my audience group used the word "terrorist" to describe Valentin, which suggests that the film wasn't watered down enough for them.

Because the musical version of *Kiss of the Spider Woman* is aimed at U.S., Canadian, and British theater-goers who in general accept capitalism and are fearful of violent revolt, the text softens Valentin's Marxism even further in an attempt to build sympathy for him. Whereas in the novel and film Valentin's bourgeois background provokes intense guilt which complicates his political stance, the musical rewrites his origins, depicting him as a starving orphaned beggar who dreamed of a better future. By locating the roots of his Marxism in his poverty, the musical makes Valentin more benignly sympathetic to liberal democratic or even centrist theater-goers. Theater critic Toby Silverman Zinman astutely argues that McNally's early plays reveal that he "is not at heart a political playwright." While McNally and lyricist Ebb tried to distance the musical from radical Marxism for an American audience, they also edited out the complicated treatment of fascism in the novel and film. Although the two preceding versions confronted audiences with Molina's fondness for the aesthetics and romance of Nazi films, and thus blurred the line between good and evil, the musical avoids any mention of Nazi cinema and describes Molina's favorite film as a melodrama about a woman in love with a Bolshevik student revolutionary (rather than a Nazi officer), a plot which simply mirrors Molina's love for Valentin. This textual shift absolves the audience from trying to understand how Molina's love for beautiful aesthetics led him to be seduced by Nazi propaganda, and from thinking about the larger problem of divorcing aesthetics from politics and morality. In the musical, Marxist revolutionaries are also stripped of any menace or even of an articulate political agenda; they function only as romanticized signs. The show's writers may have assumed that moderate American audiences desire types of good and evil rather than ambiguity, and thus they simplified the musical's politics and stripped its characters of some of their complexity. While the musical offers a camp treatment of Molina's favorite movies, particularly the over-the-top Bolshevik tale, the version of camp employed here has less of a critical edge than it does in the other two media versions.

Many of those I interviewed were unable to distinguish between the three versions and believed they all expressed the same "basic message" (although this was interpreted variously). Of the eighteen people who had consumed more than one media version, their experience of one medium often bled over into their interpretation of another, to the point of creating a sort of conglomerate text. A few gay viewers even wishfully projected a romance narrative upon the musical because they had glimpsed some of it in the film and/or novel. Reading the novel was generally the most dominant experience among my audience group, coloring how they viewed the other two versions. Even if they read the novel *after* encountering the film or musical, they tended to attribute Puig's work the status of "master text." The in-depth character development of the novel, and its extended treatment of Marxism, fascism, and homosexuality, led some people to use that fuller understanding to interpret, reinterpret, or even to misread the other versions. Although I did find some differences in interpretation and response that could be attributed to the particular media text in question, these differences were often mitigated by the "conglomerate text" effect.

Given that the three media versions of *Kiss* target slightly different populations, I am particularly interested in how my U.S. audience sample imposed their own cultural values upon a novel that was not written primarily for them. The national context of this group clearly had an effect on their reception of *Kiss*. For example, the understanding of sexual identity among urban Washingtonians, particularly those who define themselves as gay, varies greatly from a Latin American cultural construction of homosexuality. Most of my audience sample either disregarded the text's original context or were ignorant of the differences. In an interview, Manuel Puig noted that his novel was directed at Spanish-speaking readers, most of whom have been denied information about the origins of homosexuality. In order to educate people, he included footnotes summarizing the history of theoretical discourse about homosexuality and intended them to be taken seriously (Christ 28). The fact that many of my interviewees read the footnotes as ironic send-ups of "out-dated" Freudian theories indicates their distance from the intended audience of Latin Americans in the 1970s. Most importantly, social constructions of homosexuality in the U.S. are quite different than in some parts of Latin America, where only the receptor, the one who is sexually penetrated, is considered to be *maricón* (fag, queer); such penetration implies a loss of masculinity which Latin Americans associate with homosexuality (Foster 2). The active penetrator who adopts the macho role is often considered to be straight and may even be married. As David Foster contends in *Sexual Textualities*, many Latin Americans do not equate gay sexual acts with a gay identity, and they frown upon homosexual identity politics as a foreign concept (4–5). Argentinean readers might view Valentin and Molina's relationship through this lens (although Puig attempts to challenge such gender-stereotyped notions), and they might be less likely than my U.S. audience group to consider Valentin to be gay or bisexual. To understand or criticize the novel's take on sexual identity, the American readers invoked contexts that would have been foreign to a Latin American audience—gay liberation and gay pride, a belief that gay sex acts imply a gay or bisexual identity, the disassociation of homosexuality and gender inversion, and the Kinsey scale.

Yet these fans are not simply reading against the grain of the text, because Puig himself was well aware of U.S. sexual theories and included only European and U.S. scholars in his footnotes. The novel was also written while Puig was living in Greenwich Village right after the Stonewall riots, and his text seems to offer an implicit commentary on gay liberationism and identity politics in the 1970s. In a 1979 interview, Puig applauded the self-respect fostered by gay liberation in the U.S., but he also saw "danger in the American attitude" of viewing homosexuals and heterosexuals as different and segregated species (qtd. in Christ 28). In *Kiss*, Puig clearly criticizes the gender stereotyping inherent in the Latin American construction of sexual roles, but he also appreciates the ability of that construction to break down the rigid barrier between heterosexuals and homosexuals, thereby enabling people like Valentin to explore their potential for bisexuality (Christ 30). *Kiss of the Spider Woman* mediates between Latin American and United States' constructions of sexuality in the 1970s, a dialogic which my U.S. audience group translated into their own cultural terms and debates of the 1990s—gay liberationism vs. queerness, essentialism vs. anti-essentialism, pre-Stonewall inversion vs. transgenderism, sexual acts vs. identities, and gender polarities vs. androgyny. The fact that the later film and musical were produced in English also gave audiences justification for reading the texts in a U.S. cultural context. Not only did this audience group read Puig's novel out of its original cultural context, but they also read it out of historical context. In a sense, they and I are interpreting the 1976 novel (translated into English in 1978) in an anachronistic fashion by connecting it to recent debates about identity politics vs. queer anti-essentialism. It is important to remember, however, that ideas we now identify as "queer" were in circulation in the U.S. and other cultures long before the late 1980s and 1990s, when they became codified as queer theory. Manuel Puig might be called proto-queer in his desire to move beyond the limits of either/or identity choices to embrace a "natural" bisexuality. In a 1987 interview concerning the writing of *Kiss*, Puig made the anti-identitarian comment that "a sense of identity should never be based on sexual orientation" (qtd. in Bacarisse, *Impossible Choices* 101). His sensibilities may have been influenced both by a Latin American suspicion of gay identity and by anti-essentialist ideals in circulation in 1970s U.S. culture. In an article on the history of gay identity, Steven Seidman argues that a strain of mid-1970s American gay culture was incipiently queer in its pursuit of the ideals of androgyny and bisexuality, despite the hegemony of essentialist discourses of gay liberationism at the time (108–10).

Not only do I read *Kiss* as queer before the term came into vogue, but I also argue that the text is infused with an uncanny prescience, as if it is criticizing queer politics from a belated point of view that audiences of the 1990s share. Despite Puig's anti-identitarianism, *Kiss* shows respect for Molina's deeply felt otherness and refuses to treat sexuality as merely a performative surface phenomenon, and this point of view resonated strongly with my audience group. I contend that *Kiss of the Spider Woman* can be read as pre-queer, proto-queer, and post-queer all at the same time. The temporal conflation is further fueled by the fact that the film and musical adaptations were created in the 1980s and 1990s, when discourses concerning sexuality were rapidly being transfigured; thus the storyline took on new valences and political meanings for audiences, some of whom read it as radically queer while others saw it as a throwback to a pre-Stonewall era. A fascinating article by David Román and Alberto Sandoval considers the symbolism of the musical version—blood imagery and kisses of death—as a treatment of the AIDS crisis. While they saw the musical version as *au courant*, Dennis Harvey gave a negative review to the film, arguing that it was as a tired representation of the pre-Stonewall gay as "tragic outcast" (Dennis Harvey, <http://www.planetout.com/popcornq/db/getfilm.html?1938>). At the root of this diversity of response is the text's hybridity. It elicits sympathy for both identity politics and queer politics, but ultimately endorses neither and rests in the space between. It looks forward but also backward, reappraising both old and new paradigms. This temporal and cultural liminality—this mediation between different national cultures and moments in the history of discourses of sexuality—makes *Kiss of the Spider Woman* an ideal text to shed light on the complex process of audience reception.

Pop Cultural Kitsch Meets Highbrow Postmodernism

Audiences use the extra-textual discourses of a particular historical moment to make sense of *Kiss*, but their readings are also shaped by the text's own strategic mediation between melodramatic popular culture and formally experimental high culture. Although each media version of *Kiss* is positioned differently on the continuum from low to high culture, they all participate in a fusion of the popular and the postmodern. However, it is easy to see why critics have tended to stress the elements of *Kiss of the Spider Woman* that might be considered high modernist or postmodern. From page one, the novel immediately announces itself as highbrow by challenging the reader to distinguish the characters from each other. Instead of a traditional introduction to the characters and situation, *Kiss* begins *in medias res* with a dialogue already in progress and omits the speakers' names, which are not revealed until the end of the chapter. The film begins with a similarly disorienting technique, eschewing the standard establishing shot and instead offering the viewer a disembodied voice and a slowly roving camera that reveals glimpses of a bare room and a man's body dressed in drag. Both novel and film deliberately frustrate the passive reader/spectator in order to encourage a more active and critical interpretation process.

In the novel, Puig employs many experimental narrative techniques that force the reader to work hard to make meaning, thus increasing the potential for alienation or confusion but also for intellectual pleasure. The variety of narrative techniques—such as dialogue, stream of consciousness monologues, academic footnotes, play scripts, and impersonal official reports—works to shatter a perspective of omniscience and to draw attention to form, two aesthetic projects that are often associated with high modernism and literary postmodernism. Puig's "remarkable interior monologues" even prompted a reviewer to compare him to James Joyce (Wood 19). By refusing closure, the novel invites comparison to postmodern fiction by Don DeLillo or Thomas Pynchon. Puig's text closes with Valentin's surreal dream narrative, which leaves many questions unanswered: Does Valentin love Molina? What motivated Molina to pass on the message to Valentin's comrades—love, a movie-inspired desire for a tragic fate, or an awakened political conscience? *Kiss*'s experiments in form and its attempt to engage audiences in active, critical interpretation might satisfy even Adorno's criteria for modernist art. The most characteristically postmodern feature of the text is its academic-style footnotes (mostly concerning theories about homosexuality), which interrupt immersion in the narrative and push the reader to make intellectual connections between the footnotes and the storyline above. The absurd and often random placement of the footnotes, however, frustrates a reader's desire for legibility even further. The connections that can be gleaned between the footnotes and the narrative are often ironic ones. For example, the scene in which Valentin succumbs to diarrhea is accompanied by a footnote concerning Freud's beliefs that the anal retentive drive is at the root of repression and that anal fixation leads to homosexuality (141). Hutcheon argues convincingly that Puig's footnotes exemplify postmodern parody and irony, because the authority of these "experts" on sexuality and politics is undermined by their failure to explain the behavior of the characters (*Politics* 85). While Puig thwarts a desire for simple keys to unlock the characters' psyches, he also rewards the careful reader by offering more subtle connections, such as clever intertextual and allegorical doubling between the inset narrated films and the lives of Molina and Valentin. For example, "The Enchanted Cottage," the film that Molina revisits in his mind but refuses to share with Valentin, rests on the theme of looking beyond surfaces to see "not the body but only the soul" (111). This metaphor applies to Molina's struggle with the disparity between his interior female self and his masculine exterior, while the love story between an unlikely couple mirrors Molina and Valentin's relationship.

Kiss of the Spider Woman marks its distance from typical melodramatic film and formula fiction not only by fostering active reading and viewing, but also by deconstructing the dichotomies commonly employed by popular texts. Melodramas often rely heavily on a victim vs. villain structure in which innocence triumphs over evil, and *Kiss* invokes such a structure by immediately drawing our sympathies toward men unjustly imprisoned and tortured by a fascist government. But midway through the text, we discover that Molina is no longer simply a victim, because he has consented to the warden's bargain to wheedle information out of Valentin in exchange for an early parole. Neither is Valentin an uncomplicated victim, for despite his own egalitarian principles, he oppresses Molina by harshly belittling his values and feelings. By urging Molina to pass a message to his revolutionary comrades and by minimizing the danger of that venture, Valentin is also inadvertently responsible for Molina's death. Both characters are multi-faceted, capable of both kindness and treachery, unlike the pure types of melodrama. Bacarisse sees in the novel a Foucaultian message that power and oppression are ubiquitous (*Necessary Dream* 100), an idea that challenges the melodramatic faith that evil can be eradicated. The grim ending of the text, in which evil remains unchecked, thus diverges from typical melodramatic closure; Molina is killed while trying to deliver the message, and Valentin is once again tortured in prison. In addition to questioning melodrama's polarization of good and evil, the novel and film versions of *Kiss* also deconstruct the cultural dichotomies of masculine/feminine and gay/straight, identity binaries that are often reinforced by popular texts. Believing that all humans exhibit both masculine and feminine traits, Puig argued that "the woman most desperately in need of liberation is the woman every man has locked up in the dungeons of his own psyche" (qtd. in Christ 26). Puig's deconstruction of gender binaries is evident in the characterizations and plot structure of *Kiss of the Spider Woman*. For example, although Valentin at first embodies the stereotype of the macho male, his emotional longing for his girlfriend Marta and his desire for fantastic escape through film are more powerful than his attempts to repress them. In the novel's final dream narrative and in the last shots of the film, Valentin embraces the "feminine" world of comfort, love, and peace, imagining himself in a romantic beach landscape resembling one of Molina's movies. On the other hand, while Molina seems stereotypically feminine and extremely emotional, he also displays purportedly "masculine" behavior by bravely double-crossing the warden. By the end of the text, this once effeminate man becomes masculinized as he agrees to act politically by contacting Valentin's comrades, stands up to his godfather for the first time, and rationally settles his bank accounts before carrying out his final life-threatening mission. Just as the two men move away from their initially gender-stereotyped behavior, even to the point of merging or switching places, the text also blurs their place in a binary rubric of sexual identity. The once securely macho heterosexual Valentin willingly engages in gay sex, and in the novel he appears to feel love and desire for Molina. While Molina seems uncomplicatedly homosexual at first, we learn that he feels like a heterosexual woman at heart. Their sexual union allows both men to redefine themselves in a more fluid and liberating way, as they are transformed into "someone else, who's neither a man nor a woman," neither gay nor straight, "but someone who feels . . . out of danger" (235). By disrupting binary understandings of gender and sexuality, *Kiss of the Spider Woman* denaturalizes these qualities and underscores their constructedness and fluidity. This poststructuralist, anti-essentialist sensibility once again situates *Kiss of the Spider Woman* as a postmodern text, pushing audiences to reject dualistic models that exaggerate and oversimplify human difference.

One could also discern in the text a high modernist critique of popular culture's potential to alienate people from reality and to limit their perspectives and desires. Valentin voices the perspective of Marxist critics of popular culture by lambasting Molina for loving the beauty of a Nazi propaganda film and for ignoring its distortion of history and truth: "it can become a vice, always trying to escape from reality like that, it's like taking drugs or something" (78). Valentin also rightly points out that Molina has internalized harmful gender stereotypes from melodramatic film, such as the idea that submission to violent men is pleasurable for women: "you've been fed an old wives' tale. . . . To be a woman you don't have to be . . . a martyr" (244). The end of the text also suggests that Molina's "political" heroism might have been merely an attempt to enact the romantic death of a film heroine, and thus Puig underscores the problematic glorification of feminine self-sacrifice in popular cinema. In addition to this feminist critique of kitsch's stereotypes, Puig's novel offers an allegory about the stupefying effects of mass culture via Molina's retelling of the film *I Walked with a Zombie.* The living dead of the film who "don't have any will at all beyond the witch doctor's" (167) could be read as figures for the passive mass audience, controlled by the witch doctors of Hollywood. Stephanie Merrim sees Puig's text as a tragic exposé of the way that "the characters have been rendered 'zombies' by the culture" of popular movies (157). The art-house film and the musical versions of *Kiss* also work hard to distance themselves from the kitschy inset films that Molina tells. In the musical, campy overacting in the number depicting the Russian melodrama provokes laughs from the audience, and Philip Swanson has noted that the film version of *Kiss* "asserts the superiority of Hector Babenco's film over popular B-movies" by highlighting the clichés and absurdity of the Nazi melodrama (337).

All of these characteristics have led to a frequent classification of *Kiss of the Spider Woman* as modernist, postmodern, or at least high cultural. I argue, however, that the text does not merely mock kitsch culture, but also exudes a pop sensibility itself. *Kiss* differs greatly from high modernist texts like *Ulysses* whose ironic inclusion of pop cultural references does nothing to alter their status as high cultural *objets d'art.* Despite its formal difficulty, *Kiss of the Spider Woman* also solicits emotional engagement and identification, much like Molina's favorite popular films. As one interviewee said of the text, "it's designed to pull at your heartstrings, and it works." Many were moved to tears because they saw it as a story about the basic human need for intimacy and love. Just as Molina pines for the romance of Leni Lamaison and her Nazi officer, they long for such a connection with another person in their own lives. Molina's belief that "there are reasons of the heart that reason doesn't encompass" (259) emerges as a truth for the whole text, one which even Valentin learns to accept. The reader is even encouraged to respect kitschy love ballads because they "contain real truths" about human emotional life (139). According to critic Gustavo Pellón, Puig demonstrates "that the human element of sincere emotion can redeem even the most banal mode of expression" (198). This questioning of reason's supremacy and insistence on the importance of emotionality and romance places the text in a melodramatic lineage. The high value that *Kiss* places on emotionality also links it to camp; for example, Dyer attributes gay men's campy identification with Judy Garland partly to the fact that her songs register "intense, authentic feeling . . . and suffering" (*Heavenly* 149). *Kiss*'s attempt to foster identification with its characters and immersion in its fictional world is clearly a popular strategy at odds with the alienation effect favored by the avant-garde. One gay man said he "cried like a river" at the age of fifteen upon encountering a positive, brave gay character that he could identify with. This solicitation of identification is accomplished through media-specific strategies: the novel reveals the characters' private thoughts through first-person narratives and stream of consciousness; the film offers point-of-view shots and subjective dreams and memories; and the musical's songs dramatize the character's feelings. As László and Larsen argue in their study, texts that offer "inside POV" increase the emotionality of a reader's involvement in the text. Puig's novel not only induces identification, but also makes the subject an explicit theme of the narrative. As Molina and Valentin discuss at length which film characters they identify with, the reader/viewer of *Kiss* is prompted to ask himself the same question of Puig's characters; this parallel implies that the inset popular films and the formally experimental outer text are not as different as they seem. Although leftists have often criticized popular culture for attempting to seduce audiences, *Kiss of the Spider Woman* endorses such a strategy. As one interviewee aptly put it, "there's this strong theme of seduction, as Molina and Valentin seduce each other through story-telling, and I was entranced and seduced by that plot myself." This reader, who normally considers himself a "lowbrow kind of guy," was also attracted to the story for its gradual building of suspense and tension, which he compared to detective fiction.

Although I have noted earlier that *Kiss of the Spider Woman* eschews the melodramatic prescription of happy and moralistic closure, it could also be argued that the ending borrows elements from tragic popular romances. Molina's "noble sacrifice" for Valentin's cause recalls Leni's romantic death defending the interests of her lover (in the Nazi film), and the ill-fated relationship of Molina and Valentin echoes the tragic love between the singer and the alcoholic journalist (in the Mexican film). By mirroring these popular plots in his own tale, Puig acknowledges their emotional power. At the close of Puig's text, even Valentin acquiesces to his desires for fantasy, escape, and love, finally accepting the value of Molina's melodramatic worldview.

The last shot of the film version, in which Valentin and Marta row off into the sunset in a boat, may be read as a parody because it is such an obvious melodramatic cliché; however, many viewers did not read this scene as ironic but rather experienced it as a respectful and poignant treatment of the human need for escapism. One reader in my study found this ending to be uplifting, much like popular texts, "since Valentin was finally free for the first time." As literary critic Jonathan Tittler notes of the novel, "escapism is not disparaged out of hand" (56). Even as it tries to critique such banal closure, *Kiss of the Spider Woman* clearly evokes the outlines of popular tragedies and melodramas and even endorses some of their romantic and escapist values.

Similarly, although the text deconstructs the dichotomies of melodrama, the remnants of such rubrics are still present, appealing to audiences with popular tastes. About one-third of my audience group read the text in terms of familiar types and polarities (masculine/feminine, gay/straight, victim/villain, fascist/Marxist) and did not notice any questioning of dichotomies. Their reading of the text, which differs from the predominant critical take on the novel, was influenced by their differing cultural sensibilities and tastes. While I and many other readers saw moments of deconstruction in the text, it is also clear that the author has respect for the emotional pull and clear world picture that binary cultural rubrics afford people, even as he resists the harmful effects of stereotypes. Like Molina, Puig was addicted to popular melodramas, watching as many as three or four daily (Manrique 24). *Kiss of the Spider Woman* mounts a defense of popular culture by suggesting that such films can work to open up the identities of viewers, rather than merely reifying traditional stereotypes. Although these movies solidify Molina's stereotypical feminine behavior, they help Valentin to face his emotions, uncover his *anima*, rethink his macho heterosexual identity, and connect with another person. The films' emphasis on empathy and identification humanizes Valentin and allows him to explore his complexity as an individual. Thus the text counters the critical view of melodramatic film as a duping mechanism which merely sutures viewers into limiting identities. Thus, by implying that popular texts, and not only the avant-garde, can foster progressive change, *Kiss of the Spider Woman* challenges artistic hierarchies and the critical assumptions that accompany them. Such assumptions include the beliefs that only formally experimental, non-realist aesthetics can have transgressive politics, that popular culture never fosters critical thought, and that the emotional strategies of melodrama are merely manipulative and escapist tactics that foster conservatism or even fascism. While Puig's novel notes the drawbacks of both sentimentality and the rationalist alienation promoted by avant-gardists and high modernists, the text also attempts to fuse their merits, by fostering critical questioning and active reading as well as emotional engagement, human sympathy, and the recognition that the personal is political.

In focusing on this fusion or mediation, I take issue with those critics who argue that Puig's ironic tone totally undermines any sentimental moments in the text. Stephanie Merrim, for example, reads *Kiss* as a parodic exposé of mass culture's stupefying properties (157). Merrim echoes the viewpoint of Jameson, who believes that the presence of irony and poststructuralist sensibilities in postmodern texts preclude any investment in deep feeling (*Postmodernism* 15–16). By presenting irony as omnipotent and sentimentality as anemic, these critics reveal a prejudice that blinds them to the complexity of hybrid texts. Literary critics Bacarisse and Naomi Lindstrom are among the few who recognize the hybridity of *Kiss of the Spider Woman* and its postmodern mediation between high and low culture. Bacarisse notes that Puig does not mock his characters but instead employs irony as a means of identifying with them as victims of life's ironic situations (*Necessary* 99–105). Here irony works to increase identification and sympathy rather than to undermine it. In *Impossible Choices*, Bacarisse further points out that Puig refuses to observe the "'Great Divide' between mass culture and the canon of high modernism" (2) because he sees "no vital difference between highbrow and lowbrow art, which are both valid indicators of personal and collective truths" (9). While several critics have noted the novel's dialogic vacillation between high and popular culture, many of them still display a preference for critical distance and a prejudice against kitsch reminiscent of the Frankfurt School. Like Bacarisse, Gustavo Pellón focuses on Puig's ambivalent "double vision" as a merging of criticism and empathetic participation in popular culture, and he rightly points out that many critics have missed Puig's appreciation of kitsch (193). However, Pellón nonetheless reveals an anti-popular bias by referring to kitsch as a "parasitic art form" that betrays viewers into self-deception, "intellectual passiveness," and "servility" (199). Since he deems Puig's attempt to merge high and low culture a "fascinating contradiction" (199) that ultimately is impossible to sustain, he underestimates the political power of such hybridity. Similarly, Philip Swanson views the dialectic at work in *Kiss* (novel and film) as a problematic contradiction rather than a productive tension, and he equates popular culture with conservatism (341). Arguing that Puig's texts "consistently deconstruct any ideology or sentiment they appear to be expounding or expressing" (332), Swanson wrongly concludes that the novel's dialectic leads to "self-cancellation" (332) and confusion rather than a plurality of ways of seeing or a productive double vision.

I am not the first critic to recognize the dialogism of *Kiss of the Spider Woman;* however, my paradigm of sentimental postmodernism treats such hybridity as politically potent rather than regrettable and avoids the anti-popular biases exhibited by so many of these critics. In addition, nearly all of the critical articles on the text's dialogism offer formalist readings, rather than situating the strategy in cultural or political context as I aim to do. Laura Rice-Sayre astutely points out that "most critics have taken refuge in a formalist discussion of the plurality of styles, the multiple play of discourses, and the polysemic qualities of the text and have tended to ignore or even deny the political content and form the novel's dialogue embodies" (248). Santiago Colás counters this tendency in his book *Postmodernity in Latin America*, offering useful readings of Puig's postmodern mixture of high and mass culture against the backdrop of Argentinean Peroniste politics. However, his argument focuses only on the macropolitical, rather than investigating the text's considerable investment in micropolitical change. Furthermore, the few critics who analyze the political content of *Kiss* and explore its surrounding contexts are mainly concerned with identifying the sources of Puig's ambivalence. None has considered what effect his ambivalent texts have upon audiences or has attempted to locate the politics of the text in its articulation by readers and viewers.

For a brief example of the effects of the hybridity of sentimental postmodernism, I turn to my students' responses to *Kiss of the Spider Woman.* We read the novel and watched the film for a unit on postmodern narrative technique, and the previous text on the syllabus was John Fowles's *The French Lieutenant's Woman*, which the class found to be a clever but dry exercise in parodying Victorian culture. Because Fowles's characters did not solicit identification or even sympathy, the students were minimally engaged although they found it to be an intellectually challenging read. Even though they were also challenged by Puig's narrative style, these formal innovations did not result in reader alienation or ironic detachment. In contrast, many of the students were moved to tears by *Kiss of the Spider Woman*'s affirmation of the power of human intimacy. Because they identified so strongly with Molina and Valentin, their debates about the political meanings of *Kiss* were also more heated than their discussions of Fowles's highbrow text. Their ability to think critically was not hampered by their emotional responses, as detractors of sentimentality often argue; in fact, it was enhanced. In contrast to disaffected highbrow postmodernism, the emotional engagement fostered by this hybrid text gave it more power to affect these students on a political and ideological level, to get them thinking about the meaning of gender and sexuality. But unlike typical Hollywood melodramas and sentimental fiction, *Kiss* upsets rigid notions of identity rather than confirming them. Because the text deconstructs rigid character types, heterosexual students were able to identify with the effeminate gay character Molina, which helped them to rethink homophobia and gender stereotypes. It even prompted them to communicate more respectfully with a gay student in our class. This fusion of emotional and critical strategies is central to the cultural and political power of *Kiss of the Spider Woman* and of sentimental postmodernism as a style.

Camp as Sentimentality-cum-Irony

Sentimental postmodernism, with its ambivalent attitude toward popular culture and its mixture of sentimentality and irony, shares some qualities with the strategy of "camp." The term is often used to describe a gay or queer sensibility or political strategy that critiques the absurdities and incongruities of mainstream heterosexual culture by exaggerating them. Camp has come to be associated with postmodernism and poststructuralism because of its emphasis on surfaces, play, irony, performativity, parody, and a denaturalization of gender and sexual roles. Owing to the influence of Judith Butler's analysis of drag in *Gender Trouble*, many theorists of camp read it as a poststructuralist, anti-essentialist strategy (see Bergman). For example, Moe Meyer argues that camp must be seen as a specifically queer form of postmodern parody that enacts an "oppositional critique of bourgeois essentialism" (18). In line with a reading of camp as a poststructuralist tactic, many critics see irony as its chief trait. For example, Scott Long defines camp as a critical stance toward kitsch that "enjoys its distance: by definition it refuses to identify with the films except in mocking fashion" (87). Rather than reading camp as poststructuralist, I align myself with those critics who treat camp as a mediation between ironic critique and an emotional engagement in mass culture and the depth models of identity employed therein. Andrew Ross notes that gay camp often involves an appreciation of mass culture's "feminine" emphasis on emotionality (70). Jack Babuscio and Susan Sontag see camp as a "tender feeling" of identification (Sontag 119) not equivalent to mockery because it "implies fervent involvement" and earnestness rather than mere disdain for the object being camped (Babuscio 23). The seriousness with which drag queens often take their performance of gender also suggests this duality—even as their performance questions the naturalness of sex roles, some queens with transsexual desires may nonetheless be sentimentally attached to femininity as an essential identity (see Newton). My analysis of the dialectic at work in sentimental postmodernism is echoed by Dyer's focus on camp as "passion-with-irony" (*Heavenly Bodies* 155). Dyer claims that a gay camp "sensibility holds together qualities that are thought elsewhere to be antithetical: theatricality and authenticity . . . intensity and irony, a fierce assertion of extreme feeling with a deprecating sense of its absurdity" (154). Feuer has extended Dyer's point to argue that camp "embraces both identification and parody—attitudes normally viewed as mutually exclusive—at the same time and as part of the same sensibility" (*Seeing* 135).

Despite its overwhelmingly serious rather than playful tone, I argue that *Kiss of the Spider Woman* exudes a camp sensibility and encourages such a political strategy among its audiences. Molina's excessive attention to the *mise en scene* of melodramatic film is a perfect example of camp's "emphasis on sensuous surfaces, textures, imagery, and the evocation of mood as stylistic devices . . . fascinating in themselves" (Babuscio 22). It could be argued that Molina's subtle transvestitism (in the film version, he wears earrings, makeup, a scarf, and a woman's robe) also participates in the theatrical, denaturalizing aspects of camp, although Molina is simultaneously invested in the authenticity of gender norms. By making such declarations as "my real name is Carmen [the tragic opera heroine]" (65), Molina suggests the performativity of gender and ironizes the essentialist discourse of "realness." Bacarisse also points to the identification of Molina and his friends with actresses: "this marginalized group's 'camp' view of their own situation . . . [is] accurately reflected in subservient, frustrated, suffering, feminine images" (*Impossible* 105). While Molina might appear to be a campy reader of melodramas in that he fetishizes their glitzy surface aesthetics and feminine emotionality, I would argue that his reading of these texts lacks an oppositional attitude toward their gender stereotypes, heterosexist values, and conservative (even fascist) politics. In my view, Molina lacks the critical distance and oppositional intent to qualify him as a true practitioner of camp. But the critical eye that Molina lacks is provided by the text of *Kiss of the Spider Woman* as a whole. Babenco's film version clearly parodies the Nazi film within it, and the musical version also mocks extravagant, upbeat numbers, particularly in the song "Morphine Tango," whose own incongruity in the midst of this darkly serious play underscores the general absurdity of musical plots. However, these mass cultural objects are not merely critiqued and mocked, but are also fondly enjoyed for their beauty and treated as valuable conduits for emotional release. By uniting the emotional investment of Molina and the critical detachment of Valentin, *Kiss of the Spider Woman* adopts the dualism of a gay camp attitude. In an interview, Puig once defined his own version of camp: "ridiculing and trying to destroy something one loves in order to prove that it is indestructible" (qtd. in Bacarisse, *Necessary Dream* 53).

Most of my audience group interpreted "camp" to mean a humorous or silly form of send-up, and thus they would not apply the term to such a serious and moving text. Nonetheless, some of their responses to *Kiss* could be described as campy in the more expansive sense that I have been theorizing. Many were emotionally engaged in the story and in the mass cultural films that Molina retells, while also maintaining some intellectual distance to question their ideology. One self-described "fag hag" who loves campy films noted that she could see the Nazi film through both Molina's and Valentin's eyes: "I'm Jewish and I loved how Valentin told Molina—'You moron, this is fascist propaganda!' But at the same time, Molina was right, it was a beautiful film." Another highly intellectual, leftist reader reported that she "connected in a visceral way" to Molina's rendition of *Cat People*, because she loves the popular genres of horror and the fantastic. She stated, however, that even when she's enjoying pop culture "for what it is," she never turns off her analytical mind or leftist viewpoint. For these viewers/readers, *Kiss of the Spider Woman* encouraged a camp reading process that satisfied their popular desires as well as their intellectual cravings and leftist ideologies.

Political Camp and the "Aestheticization of Politics"

I view camp not merely as a dualistic sensibility that holds sentimentality and irony in tension, but also as a political strategy. Critical discussions of camp have been inevitably circumscribed by assumptions about the politics of mass culture. Most theorists who praise camp as a subversive strategy view it as an ironic practice in opposition to sentimental kitsch, which they assume to be inherently conservative (see Meyer; Butler, *Gender Trouble*). On the other hand, those who criticize poststructuralism and postmodernism for being apolitical, passive, or lacking in seriousness tend to see camp's politics in a different vein. Andrew Ross views camp as an anemic form of political resistance, too fascinated by the capitalist culture industry which it purports to critique. I view camp's politics as offering a limited subversion and a partial critique from within, rather than an opposition from a pure space outside of the hegemonic culture and its value systems. This political standpoint is typical of sentimental postmodernism. The camp strategy at work in *Kiss of the Spider Woman* borrows from both poststructuralism and Marxist politics but fully endorses neither.

The political aims of *Kiss of the Spider Woman* are wide-ranging, involving a re-evaluation of critical assumptions about camp, kitsch, sentimentality, irony, Marxism, and the avant-garde. The plot line exploring Molina's investment in the beautiful surfaces of the Nazi film "Her Real Glory" raises questions about the politics of sentimental mass culture, questions that were addressed earlier in the century by Marxist-influenced Frankfurt School theorists Adorno and Benjamin. *Kiss of the Spider Woman*'s postmodern perspective implicitly questions Adorno's fear of mass culture and his belief that only the formalist experimentation of high modernism can foster radical critique. By acknowledging the radical as well as the conservative potential of sentimentality, Puig also invites us to reconsider some of Benjamin's ideas in "The Work of Art," particularly his critique of kitsch's "aestheticization of politics." While maintaining a leftist perspective, *Kiss of the Spider Woman* eschews the Frankfurt School's categories for judging the political value of cultural objects and suggests that affect can be a useful tool for the Left as well as the Right. Although Benjamin and Adorno wrote before the advent of postmodernism, their ideas about mass culture, aesthetics, and politics are relevant to this discussion because they have had a lasting impression on contemporary cultural criticism, from Marxist-influenced cultural studies to critics of postmodernism such as Baudrillard and Jameson (see Jay xvii). Both Benjamin and Adorno argued that the beautiful aesthetics of mass culture—and the sentimental, comforting emotions it engenders—result in audience passivity and regressive politics, a conclusion which Puig's novel challenges. Although it is crucial to note that much of Benjamin's work treats mass culture more positively, in his most influential essay "The Work of Art" he reveals concerns about fascist kitsch's beautification of war and reactionary politics: "the logical result of Fascism is the introduction of aesthetics into political life . . . [Mankind's] self-alienation has reached such a degree that it can experience its own destruction as an aesthetic pleasure of the first order. This is the situation of politics which Fascism is rendering aesthetic. Communism responds by politicizing art" (587–88). Objecting to a fascist "aestheticization of politics," Benjamin condemns the attempt to falsely recreate art with "aura" that invokes ritual values, beautiful aesthetics, sentimentality, and mystification. As Arato and Gebhart explain, "works with aura produce concentration, empathy, absorption, and identification on the part of the reader, or audience—modes of response that lead according to . . . Benjamin to political and esthetic passivity" (209). At this point in his career, Benjamin favored "political art" such as that produced by the Soviets and playwright Bertolt Brecht, art that alienates and shocks audiences to produce a critical estrangement rather than enraptured identification. Although Benjamin reacted against the identification and absorption that we associate today with popular narrative film, he saw potential for mass culture to provoke critical distance, albeit in the montage style of silent film that we might now consider avant-garde rather than popular.

Exhibiting a much stronger anti-popular bias than Benjamin, Adorno was harshly critical of the passivity of audience's response to the beautiful aesthetics of kitsch. Adorno condemned all products of the "culture industry" as conformist, repetitious, and complacent. Arguing that mass culture enslaved people into acceptance of the status quo, Adorno saw little difference between the Nazi propaganda machine and the American liberal culture industry (Jay 297). He saw radical potential only in the critical, noncommodified "autonomous art" of formally innovative high modernism (Arato and Gebhart 217). In my view, he wrongly assumes that a particular form implies a particular politics. Critical of social realism and directly political artists, Adorno argued in his essay "Commitment" that the shock, dissonance, and active response produced by modernist aesthetics are the best means of achieving the leftist goal of critiquing capitalist conformity (Arato and Gebhart 300). Adorno's insistence on the distinction between high and low art (Adorno and Horkheimer, "The Culture Industry" 135), and his total resistance to commodity culture, positions him as an opponent of popular forms of postmodernism. While he might have lauded *Kiss of the Spider Woman*'s experimental aesthetics, he surely would have objected to the text's sympathy for the values of mass culture.

Kiss of The Spider Woman offers a challenge to Adorno's generalizations about the politics of popular culture and to Benjamin's equation of beautiful aesthetics with fascism. While Benjamin is horrified by the Nazis' beautification of death and war, Puig asserts that aesthetic pleasure is crucial to human life, even if it serves to glorify death. Because Molina wanted to "die like some heroine in a movie" (279), he experiences his own death as an aesthetic pleasure, just as he had enjoyed the death of his Nazi film heroine. But the text urges us to empathize with his desire for beauty and sentimentality, which he believes give meaning to his life, rather than to judge him harshly as a masochistic dupe of the culture industry. Puig's camp strategy could be read as an "aestheticization of politics," in that camp's politics are primarily stylistic and aesthetic. *Kiss* asks us to rethink the assumption that the "beautiful" is automatically prone to fascist political manipulation, by reminding of its association with a different form of leftist critique—a queer politics of gesture and campy play with surfaces. As Angela McRobbie argues, "glamour, glitter and gloss should not so easily be relegated to the insistently apolitical" (*Postmodernism* 20). More importantly, *Kiss* reminds that empathy and identification, which Benjamin and Adorno disdain for discouraging critical thought and fostering political passivity, may in fact move people to take political action, perhaps even in a leftist direction. Molina decides to act politically and risk his life precisely because he loves and respects Valentin. And although Valentin believes that emotion will interfere with his political goals, it is presumably his own empathy for the poor and oppressed, despite growing up bourgeois, that moved him to commit his life to the Marxist cause in the first place. Valentin's Marxist anti-emotional dogma, which leads him to renounce his bourgeois lover Marta, is ironically shown to be more repressive and less humane than the message of "Her Real Glory," a fascist film which admits the complexity and power of love, even if it involves betrayal of one's beliefs or nation. Here Puig seems to be previewing the call of Grossberg and Mouffe, who have argued that the Left has much to learn from the Right's effective use of affect to mobilize people. In "Postmodernity and Affect," Grossberg argues that the disjunction between affect and ideology fostered by modernism and Marxism has unfortunately resulted in a postmodern political apathy.

Perfectly illustrating Grossberg's argument about the importance of affect to political consciousness, *Kiss of the Spider Woman* offers a warning to the Left as well as a strategy for its revival. Although Puig recognizes Adorno's complaint that film culture can dupe and limit people, the author sees leftist potential in mass culture's utopian spirit, which fosters a desire for change even as it shapes one's emotions in limiting ways. *Kiss* implies that because Valentin lacked the emotional aspects of a utopian spirit, his rationalist politics were ineffectual. As the text progresses, Valentin regains this utopian feeling though "escapist" popular culture, a possibility which Adorno ignores. Listening to the kitschy ending of the zombie film induces Valentin to imagine a happy ending to his own violent internal monologue: "the rich one sleeps peacefully after bestowing his wealth upon the poor one" (214). The novel's last sentence also attests to the human need for a utopian space where love triumphs: "this dream is short but this dream is happy" (281). It could also be argued that Molina's obsession with love stories gives him hope for a social acceptance of homosexual romance. Rather than merely being pacified by the culture industry and the capitalist ethos underlying it, Molina expresses some dissatisfaction with his shallow life of surfaces: "being a window dresser all day, enjoyable as it is, when the day's finished, sometimes you begin to ask yourself what's it all about, and you feel kind of empty inside" (70). He recognizes that his own life lacks a plot and therefore a purpose: "when does my life start?" (254). Popular film actually *fosters* his longing for a more meaningful and emotionally fulfilling life, a longing which leads him to take political action at the end of the text.

Puig defends pop culture's "aestheticization of politics" but he simultaneously aims to make art that is more directly political and leftist. His vision of "the political," however, differs from that of the Frankfurt School and more traditional Marxism. Puig revels in surfaces and explores the subversive qualities of camp, but he does not see aesthetics as the sole means of achieving an anti-fascist political point. Rather than pursuing leftist goals via an aesthetic of defamiliarization as Adorno recommends, the text urges a more direct form of political action in the diegesis or narrative content. Despite its ironies and playful aesthetics, *Kiss of the Spider Woman* could be called a social protest novel or film; several of my audience group even labeled it "leftist propaganda." Towards the end of the novel, Valentin seems to be speaking for Puig when he urges Molina to turn his campy, ironic form of resistance into something more likely to effect change, by joining some group (possibly of other gays), "even if it's a group that just does a lot of talking" (215). Valentin's attempt to raise Molina's consciousness about exploitation materially influences his post-prison behavior, leading Molina to recognize his own self-worth and to stand up to his overbearing godfather for the first time. And although Molina is killed once he attempts a bolder form of political praxis, the text still implies that such direct forms of protest or subversion are necessary and laudable, even if they are often doomed to fail. At some moments, the text uses the lens of Marxism to critique the passive politics of a poststructuralist camp agenda. Puig values Valentin's revolutionary struggle to spread class consciousness and to undermine the corrupt government, but *Kiss* does not conform to a Marxist worldview. Rather than focusing on the macro sphere of governmental structure, *Kiss* stresses the micropolitical sphere of sexual and gender relations. This shift towards the micropolitics of personal identities reflects Puig's skepticism about the possibility of grand epistemic change, a quality which gives the novel a post-Marxist perspective. As such, Puig's fiction differs from Sartre's socialist *littérature engagée* although they share a basic desire for social change. Many critics have read the ending of *Kiss of the Spider Woman* as fatalistic or dystopian, because neither Valentin nor Molina succeed in furthering the "revolution" (see Pellón; Bacarisse, *Impossible Choices* 149–50). Santiago Colás argues that the text reflects a postmodern recognition of "utopia's impossibility and of the tragedy of believing in its inviolable realization" (75). In contrast, I would not call this postmodern text anti-utopian, because it places considerable hope in the power of individuals to make change on an intersubjective scale. Molina and Valentin may not bring down the fascist state, but they do succeed in changing each other in an intensely emotional and powerful way.

The change in these two men should be seen as "political" because they come to a greater awareness of the broader social consequences of their own identities and relationships. Molina is awakened to the dignity and revolutionary implications of homosexuality, and of his identification with the feminine, amidst such a heteronormative and macho culture. Meanwhile, Valentin comes to recognize his own hypocrisy in desiring power over Molina and thus relaxes his own machismo. As he chastises himself for rejecting Molina's kindnesses, Valentin worries that the "enemy," the oppression ubiquitous in the outside world, has infiltrated their own cell (202). The novel here seems to be calling attention to the Foucaultian notion that the enemy is within, that there is no place of pure innocence or resistance outside of power structures. *Kiss* focuses attention on the micropolitical "level where power is wielded over one subject by another" (Tittler 53), but it does not condone a passive acceptance of the inevitability of oppression. Rather, it urges us to struggle against this Dionysian will-to-power as does Valentin. The text implies that possible antidotes to such hierarchy are love and compassion. Although the ending suggests that a socialist or communist revolution is nearly impossible in such a repressive state, it does offer some hope for change on the level of the individual. Despite the fact that many literary critics read *Kiss* as dystopic in macropolitical terms, most of my interview subjects were inspired rather than disheartened by the ending. In the text's positive treatment of love and intimacy between two seemingly incompatible men, these viewers and readers saw a rare utopian glimpse of liberatory sexual and emotional possibilities.

In their response to the text, most of my audience group focused on the sexual politics of the relationship between the two men rather than the macropolitical plot about Marxism and totalitarian governments. Many saw the text's message as similar to the ideas of Marcuse included in the novel's footnotes; as one bisexual woman put it, "the sexual is political and being queer can be a revolutionary transgression." Several people argued that Molina is a more revolutionary figure than Valentin, because of the courage required to live daily life as a cultural "deviant." One gay social worker with radical politics argued that Molina and Valentin both undergo huge political transformations because they question gender and sexual norms that they had previously taken for granted. He stated that such personal growth "is the real battlefield for any revolution. Because none of us goes through those individual changes without thinking that things in general have to change." Most of my audience group saw *Kiss of the Spider Woman* as a transgressive political text, one that urges audiences to question stereotypes and to understand the systemic nature of gender and sexual oppression. They also recognized in the text a distance from Marxist versions of radicalism. Eight people, who were mainly drawn to the text because of their own sympathies with Marxism, overlooked its criticism of Valentin's ideology. But the predominant reading among these thirty people was to describe *Kiss* as leftist or liberal because it critiques both fascism and Marxism at once. As one student of Latin American political history said, "it really is targeted at the middle ground, at people who are horrified by the oppressive government but are also dissatisfied by unbelievable extremes." A bisexual woman, whose ex-girlfriend is involved in the international socialist movement, liked the film because it pointed out Marxism's incompatibility with human nature and questioned the feasibility of violent revolution. A woman who is now anti-Marxist after eight years of living on a kibbutz, where "if you don't nail it down it's stolen," similarly appreciated the text's revelation of Valentin's hypocrisy. While *Kiss*'s anti-fascist message appealed to many people's progressive, reformist politics, the text also echoed their bourgeois discomfort with the notion of radical communist revolt, a sentiment particularly common among the gay people I interviewed. Rosemary Hennessy and Dennis Allen note that "lesbigay" is often experienced as a bourgeois identity, because homosexual self-definition has been strengthened by the capitalist consumption of cultural objects and signifiers. The practice of gay camp clearly involves an immersion in the capitalist culture industry; one cannot mock without first consuming. Indeed, Puig's footnotes point out that this consumerist tendency has placed gays "on the periphery of movements for class liberation" (213). *Kiss of the Spider Woman*'s camp sensibility marks it as a post-Marxist and postmodern text, focusing on the micropolitics of gender and sexuality rather than class struggle.

Interpreting the Politics of Sexual and Gender Identity

Participants in my audience survey saw the text as centrally concerned with sexuality and gender, but their readings were by no means univocal. Their various interpretations of *Kiss* were influenced by many factors, including their self-identifications and their ideas about gender and sexuality as abstract concepts. The fact that the text represents the identities of Valentin and Molina in ambiguous and multiple ways also complicated the interpretation and identification process. My interview subjects produced such complex and even contradictory response narratives that they put into question sociological reception studies and identification theories which box people into simple identity categories. Although some patterns of interpretation correlated to a self-professed identity, more important to their reception of *Kiss* was each person's particular understanding of sexuality and gender, such as beliefs in the fluidity of gender, in a biological basis to sexuality, or in the notion that homosexuality involves gender inversion. Understandings of gender and sexuality have experienced so much contestation and change in recent years that they clearly do not operate as static, unconscious givens in the lives of these audience members. This text enacts that contestation and encourages people to reflect upon the politics of their own subjectivities.

Kiss of the Spider Woman highlights political tension between an essentialist conception of gender and sexual identity and a postmodern anti-identitarian queer ideology. Twelve people in my group read the text as a typical melodrama in which Molina and Valentin function as opposite types (gay vs. straight and feminine vs. masculine), a reading which confirmed their belief in polarized identities. In contrast to this group, eighteen people professed at least some belief in the fluidity of gender and sexual categories, and most of them interpreted the text as an anti-essentialist attempt to blur the outlines of those identities. But even these people influenced by postmodern reconceptions of subjectivity were unwilling to abandon or denounce traditional rubrics for understanding difference, both in this text and in their own lives. Although *Kiss of the Spider Woman* allows diametrically opposed readings because it both installs and deconstructs identities, it also appeals to people with split loyalties to both queer and gay-liberationist camps, and to both difference-based and anti-essentialist constructions of gender. *Kiss*'s adjudication between surface and depth models of gender and sexual identity offers viewers and readers a means of exploring their own ambivalence about such identities.

Audience members find their own ambivalence or inner conflict mirrored in the characters of Molina and Valentin, whose identities are multiply coded. While Molina uses the term "gay" to refer to himself, it is clear that this umbrella identity strains to fit his complex individuality. In one sense, he represents the apolitical pre-Stonewall homosexual who bases his identity on an earlier psychoanalytic "invert" model that elided the difference between sexuality and gender. Today, however, Molina might identify himself as transgender or a preoperative transsexual rather than gay, because he sees himself as a heterosexual woman imprisoned in a man's body: "my friends and myself, we're a hundred percent female. We don't go in for those little games [i.e., falling in love with each other]—that's strictly for homos. We're normal women; we sleep with [straight] men" (203). His essentialist beliefs in the homosexual invert or transsexual model often lead him to adopt stereotypical behavior, such as limiting himself to the receptive role in anal sex with Valentin because "that's the natural thing" for women to do (244). Judith Butler has argued that the transsexual identification with a "real," inner gender is a "literalizing fantasy" that tries to naturalize a process that is socially constructed (*Gender Trouble* 89). When Valentin dreams of Molina becoming the seductive spider woman, Molina is wearing a mask, which recalls Butler's theory of gender as performative. Yet Molina believes her gender identity to be innate, a female soul underneath the mask of a biologically male body.

Although Molina appears to embrace depth models for both sexuality and gender common in the 1970s and earlier, he also exhibits sensibilities akin to postmodern reconceptions of identity as a shifting surface. This connection is not merely an anachronistic reading, since queer theorists of the 1990s resurrected and politicized earlier homosexual interests in camp, drag, and the performative qualities of gender. Marking Molina as proto-queer are his campy declaration that "my real name is Carmen" (65), his investment in the surface aesthetics of kitschy films, and his job as a window dresser, an artist of the surface. Further, his identifications with women could be likened to an anti-essentialist *transgender* identity, rather than to a *transsexual* understanding of gender as natural (see Butler's distinction between these terms in *Bodies That Matter*). Despite Molina's own beliefs in innate femininity, his performance of femininity—his queeny behaviors and donning of women's fashion accessories—nonetheless highlights a disparity between the outside and the inside, between the surface of gender and the depth of biological sex. Nowhere in the novel, film, or musical does Molina indicate a desire to literally change his body to match the inner woman, a somatic alienation which Jay Prosser argues is endemic to transsexuality. Instead, his emotional identification with discursive femininity in film narratives could be read as more of an anti-essentialist or deliteralizing move in line with Butler's sense of transgenderism as a subversive disruption of gender boundaries. The character of Molina, therefore, offers audiences a myriad of interpretive possibilities because he combines both literalizing (essentialist) and deliteralizing (anti-essentialist) conceptions of gender and sexuality.

Interpreting Valentin's identity also poses challenges for readers and viewers since he is multiply coded as both macho and feminist, and as a heterosexual, bisexual, and latent homosexual. While some saw him simply as a heterosexual macho type, he eventually relaxes his anxieties about expressing emotion and vulnerability and even voices some feminist sentiments. Despite his desire for power over women and his belief that sensitivity "can get in a man's way" (29), he also questions gender stereotypes by asserting that "art's not just something for women" (76) and "the man of the house and the woman of the house have to be equal with one another. If not, their relation becomes a form of exploitation" (244). His machismo is mitigated by his political awareness of the oppression women face. Valentin's sexuality is even more ambiguous than his gender ideology. Many critics read him as unequivocally straight despite his sexual liaison with Molina, but such a reading depends on a static, unitary notion of sexual identity. This reading implies that having sex with Molina is merely a gesture of friendship or a simple substitution (given the absence of female partners in prison) that never puts Valentin's heterosexuality into question. Several people in my group, however, saw this sexual act as a surfacing of latent homosexual desires that were repressed in the world outside prison. Puig's choice of the name Valentin also alludes to film star Rudolph Valentino, who was accused of being gay because of his androgynous appeal. It's also possible to read Valentin as bisexual, if one believes that he desires and/or loves both Marta and Molina. Puig has admitted that one of the "experts" of the footnotes, Dr. Anneli Taube, is actually a fictional stand-in for his own pro-bisexuality stance (Bacarisse, *Impossible* 107). Taube/Puig expresses hope that individuals would not be forced into identifying with either heterosexuality or homosexuality, or with either masculinity or femininity (207–13). All of this variation and ambiguity forces audiences to ponder Valentin's place amidst their own rubrics for understanding identity, and perhaps even to reconsider those categories themselves.

How these audience members read and responded to Molina and Valentin was clearly affected by their own definitions of sexual and gender identity. Invoking a wide variety of discourses, they disagreed about whether these identities are: biologically determined or socially constructed; fluid or rigid; political choices or preordained givens; based on a continuum or an either/or binary; determined by internal feelings, social behaviors, or cultural identification; and whether they are influenced by other social identities such as race. Several people, both gays and straights, connected gender and sexuality, arguing that being gay is like "getting in touch with one's feminine side" (or masculine side, if lesbian). Even though many feminists (e.g., Gayle Rubin) and queer theorists (e.g., Sedgwick) debunk inversion theories and aim to separate sexuality from gender in their analyses, many people continue to feel that they are inextricably linked categories, an experience which should be respected rather than dismissed as outmoded. Everyone named sexual and gender identities for themselves when asked, many who "belong to" the same category had differing ideas about what it means to them. Within the homosexual group, those who used the word queer experienced their identity differently than those gays and lesbians with more assimilationist politics, and "butch" homosexuals were often strikingly different from so-called "femmes." A few individuals in my group had changed their sexual identities and gendered behavior over time (e.g., one feminine-identified bisexual man was formerly macho and married), a phenomenon which is rarely discussed in theoretical writing on identity. My ethnographic study adds to an understanding of "sexual difference *within* homosexuality" which Butler argues "has yet to be theorized in its complexity" (*Bodies* 140). In addition, these interviews also shed light on differences within the "norm" of heterosexuality, which gay critics tend to treat as a monolithic and uncomplicated identity. Among this audience group, social-constructionist heterosexuals and biological-essentialist heterosexuals spoke such a different language that they rarely interpreted the text in the same way. The rich landscape of difference revealed in my interviews challenges the assumption that identity determines how people read.

The ambiguous identity of Valentin, in particular, provoked wide-ranging ideological interpretations. Interview subjects from all the sexual identity groupings (gay, lesbian, heterosexual, bisexual) read Valentin as straight, but for divergent reasons. It is not surprising that nearly all of the biological essentialists read Valentin as unequivocally heterosexual; they argued that he did not love Molina romantically and had only engaged in sex as an act of friendship or human need. The heterosexuals were also more likely than the bisexuals or homosexuals to read Valentin as heterosexual, possibly because more of the straight people were biological essentialists resistant to fluidity and bisexuality. On the other hand, seven gays and lesbians also argued that Valentin must be seen as straight, even if he is repressing homosexual desire, because that is how he chooses to present himself socially; they defined identity as a conscious and political identification unaffected by isolated sexual encounters. For example, one gay man argued that Valentin did not become gay even though he had romantic as well as sexual feelings for Molina. He reasoned that the extreme prison circumstance allowed Valentin to "transcend" his heterosexuality briefly, but it was merely an isolated "exception that proves his chosen rule." It was important to pay attention, therefore, not just to what types of people interpreted Valentin as straight, but why they did so, and their reasons were connected to larger philosophical debates about the meaning of identity. Thus, the question of whether Valentin feels romantic love or at least sexual desire for Molina turned out to be central to the fifteen people who believe that Valentin became bisexual or gay, or had been repressing such "innate" tendencies all along. Many argued that the romance glimpsed between the characters, more so than their sexual intercourse, showed a true shift in Valentin's identity. The large majority of those who read Valentin as bisexual and in love with Molina were themselves gay or bisexual; two straight women agreed with them. In this case, the identity of the viewer/reader did have a strong influence upon interpretation. Because it can be difficult to divine a character's emotions in a text, particularly a visual one, some of these gay and bisexual viewers projected their own emotions onto Valentin to justify their reading of the text as a love story. This helps to explain why some people found the kissing scene in the film to be forced and awkward while others broke down and cried at the sight of such a "tender moment." One recently divorced man who now identifies himself as gay interpreted the musical as a passionate love story (a reading which goes against the grain of the characterizations put forth in the lyrics), arguing that Valentin experiences the same "change of heart" that he did himself. Reading *Kiss of the Spider Woman* as a love story is not simply a matter of projection or wish-fulfillment, for there are many hints in the novel that Valentin's feelings for Molina go beyond friendship. The readers of the novel were much more likely to characterize it as a romance than were viewers of the film or musical, in which the characters remain more polarized. Even if one aims to explore the role of the reader in creating meaning, the text's role in suggesting certain interpretations to audiences should not be overlooked.

I found much less diversity in the survey group's categorization of Molina. The vast majority interpreted him to be an effeminate gay man and were hesitant to label him transsexual or even transgender. Nine out of the ten heterosexual research subjects saw Molina as simply gay, because many of them accept the stereotypical equation of gender inversion with homosexuality and have little knowledge of transsexuality. For example, one heterosexual woman made the questionable claim that "95% of gay men are feminine like Molina." On the other hand, both straight and gay people resisted the inversion stereotype but still concluded that Molina was gay rather than transsexual. They did not take his belief that he was really "a woman inside" seriously, arguing that his effeminacy was either an attempt to "follow what society tells him a gay man is supposed to be" or internalized homophobia, "the desire to be considered a normal female rather than an 'abnormal' gay man." The biological essentialists and those with difference-based ideas about gender also dismissed the concept of transgenderism and asserted that Molina was a man at the core. Transgender and transsexual were more acceptable and viable identities in the minds of the sexual minorities in the group. A few gay men were willing to consider Molina genuinely transsexual because they seemed personally anxious to disassociate homosexuality from gender inversion. But many other gay men were quick to argue that an identification with the feminine has been an important part of gay culture and doesn't necessarily imply transsexuality. As one man put it, "Molina may not have peed standing up, but he was definitely a gay male and wanted to be male. He wanted a woman's life, not to *be* her." The analysis of this audience group's interpretations of Valentin and Molina's identities underscores my larger point—that although a person's own sexual label sometimes predicted how he or she would read the characters, these interpretations were more strongly correlated to ideological notions about the roots of sexuality and the nature of identity. While heterosexuals were likely to read Valentin as heterosexual, and bisexuals to read him as bisexual, the gay men exhibited the widest range of interpretations of Valentin, because their ideological understandings of sexual identity were the most varied as well. While most people identified Molina as gay rather than transsexual, their reasoning revealed diverse ideologies that put into question the concept of a homogeneous identity cohort.

Each individual's belief in either essentialist or anti-essentialist models proved to be the strongest influence on interpretation. Molina's story attests to the value of essential, deeply felt identity (in this case, a feminine essence), whereas Valentin's character development (towards a more androgynous, bisexual self) works to question the limitations of a unitary and static sense of identity. It is also possible to read Molina as undergoing a subtle identity shift away from the pole of stereotypical and abject femininity. Whether people in my audience group read the characters as static and typed, as in a melodrama, or whether they saw a transcendence of identity rubrics usually corresponded to whether they espoused essentialist or postmodern ideas about identity. Everyone recognized the polarities set out, but not everyone recognized the attempt to break down those dichotomies. Almost all of the sixteen people who interpreted the text's message to be about the fluidity of sexual or gender identity were either anti-essentialist themselves or at least accepting of the continuum principle. Nearly all the bisexuals and self-defined "queers" read Valentin and Molina as blurring identity boundaries. Many were tired of identity politics ("sexuality is pretty negligible in the end and I wish it weren't such an issue") and were glad the characters were able to "transcend" their identities, even if only temporarily. Most of those who lauded the characters for transcending identities were either women or feminist men whose frustration with gender prescriptions leads them to view identity politics as limiting rather than enabling.

Despite *Kiss of the Spider Woman*'s efforts to question binary notions of identity, twelve people nonetheless read the text's characters as polarized and static. Although essentialism has come under fire in academic discourse, people outside (and inside) the academy continue to rely on traditional identity constructs in order to make sense of life as well as texts. Three of the four straight men in my group saw no identity shifting in the text, and this reading confirmed their biological essentialism and difference-based ideologies. One straight man had been troubled when a formerly straight college classmate came out as gay and began wearing lipstick. His comments revealed a desire for an orderly division of sexuality: "it was kind of strange that he thought he was one way but then it turns out he was not." It is not surprising that this interviewee chose to ignore any ambiguity in Valentin's sexuality, since this possibility disturbed him. However, these essentialists should not be dismissed simply as "bad readers," because the text itself takes great pains to garner sympathy for Molina, who himself views life through the lens of binary oppositions and experiences femininity as a deeply important identity. Inspired by the film's attempt to foster respect for difference, one essentialist gay man argued: "it made me convinced that you should always be true to the way you are. That's what I really admired about Molina—he's accepted his difference from the norm and he's not letting it bother him." These twelve people felt that *Kiss of the Spider Woman* offered a testament to the importance of accepting innate difference— "the way you are."

In the preceding analysis, I have been arguing that *Kiss of the Spider Woman* appealed to and was interpreted differently by two distinct groups—those who accept melodrama's polarized notions of identity and those who embrace postmodern fluidity—but I would also like to complicate the picture a bit. In fact, it was common for individuals to express seemingly contradictory ideologies about identity at once. For example, one gay man argued that bisexuality does not work because "you're either gay or you're not," yet he later stated that he believed in a sexual continuum like the Kinsey scale in which people can fall somewhere in between. Many who outwardly rejected either/or logic and accepted bisexuality nonetheless used polarizing language (e.g., "gay side," "different teams" or "the opposite sex"). By frequently invoking the Kinsey scale, many people echoed the contradiction inherent in its very construction. This scale supports the "queer" belief in fluidity or bisexuality by suggesting that individuals can have both homosexual and heterosexual desires, but it nonetheless reinscribes polarized thinking by designating heterosexual as 0 and homosexual as 6. While my research reveals the folly of dividing audiences into simple sociological identity groupings, it also suggests caution in boxing people into single ideological categories, because in-depth interviews often reveal instability in their beliefs. Audience researchers studying identity must acknowledge the contradictions, multiplicity, and incoherence that muddy the waters and make reception patterns more difficult to identify or interpret. Also, some people contradicted their professed ideologies inadvertently, while others were conscious of ambivalence or were willing to cede some ground to an opposing ideology. For example, one essentialist gay man who distrusts bisexuality saw Valentin as inhabiting a different "planet" from him, yet later in the interview he stated that he "appreciated and was pleasantly surprised by Valentin's ambiguity." A bisexual queer woman also showed respect for those she disagrees with: "I try to blur identity distinctions without dishonoring the people for whom that is really a necessary means of living. Believing that sexuality is biological may be a very real feeling for some people, even though it's not for me." A gay man who is a social constructionist nonetheless accepted Molina's belief that his "natural self" is female. *Kiss of the Spider Woman* encouraged some readers and viewers to respect the power of feelings of difference at the same time as they seek more fluid and less restricting conceptions of selfhood.

The majority of the participants in this group expressed some anti-essentialist ideas. Yet many were unwilling to toss out the notion of essence even if they rejected the biologism or binary logic that plagues essentialist thinking. One bisexual, anti-essentialist woman has a disorder in which she rips out her hair, partly because of anxiety caused by her mother's rigid prescriptions for appropriate feminine behavior. Despite her rebellion against gender-socialization and heteronormativity, she wears dresses and makeup and paints her nails: "Because I'm bald, when I'm without all that externally feminine stuff, people look at me as if I'm a man, and I don't like that." Even one social-constructionist straight man who once had a "gay phase" and did female impersonation said, "there are limits on how feminine I'd want to seem to others. I like my masculine traits—I'm brave and unafraid of risk-taking." This fallback on comfort zones of stereotyped gender behavior may seem to be merely a conservative deployment of essentialism, but I argue that feelings of embodied identity should not be so quickly dismissed, particularly when they are felt by "subaltern" rather than hegemonic groups (see Spivak 205). For instance, almost all of the gay, lesbian, and bisexual people in the survey asserted their sexual difference as a deeply felt identity, even if they did not use biological rhetoric. Very few embraced the anti-identitarian spirit of queer theory, and only five claimed an identity as queer or "post-gay" (most of the queer contingency were bisexual). One assimilationist gay man who takes pride in his "normalcy" nonetheless stated that his homosexuality "is a big sense of who I am; it's like being African American." Even though he chooses to blend in to the heterosexual mainstream, this man still experiences his sexual difference as an embodiment similar to race. As Jay Prosser urges in his study of transsexual narratives, critics need to relax their zeal to deconstruct "feelings of embodiment," because it often results in a dismissal of the fact that "body, sex, feeling, [and] belief in an imminent self" are of crucial importance in people's lives (16–17). My interviews with this audience group illustrate Prosser's point; faith in identity politics and embodied difference is still alive and well in this urban middle-class gay community. Straddling the line between gay identity politics and queer ideologies is perhaps what makes these people such devoted fans of *Kiss of the Spider Woman*.

This text suggests not only the political promise of queerness—its inclusivity and potential for coalition-building, and its deconstruction of limiting stereotypes and false binaries—but also its limitations, which include a lack of seriousness and an underestimation of the emotional power of identity moorings. On the pro-queer side, the majority of the viewers and readers applauded the text for fostering fluidity and questioning rigid binary oppositions; one bisexual man valued *Kiss* for its message to "tear down the walls and stop limiting yourself, stop pretending you're one or the other." Many audience members were moved by the text's hope that "people who appear to be very opposite to each other can learn to respect, admire, and even love one another," a message which could be read as a criticism of a politics of solidarity based only on shared, fixed identities. When Valentin respectfully tells Molina that "if you enjoy being a woman, you shouldn't feel any the less for it" (243), his statement could be read as a queer criticism of the gay liberation movement's exclusion of transgenderists and its narrow conception of difference. Instead of a politics based on sameness, *Kiss* calls for a recognition of multiple differences that would allow the building of a queer coalition of gays, transgenders, straights, and bisexuals, of people like Molina and Valentin. Most of the audience group applauded *Kiss*'s queer ideology concerning fluidity and inclusivity, yet these viewers also recognized the drawbacks of surface models of identity, particularly their political anemia. Puig's novel was written before poststructuralism became a widespread theoretical paradigm, but it nonetheless gestures towards an anti-essentialist future while also offering a warning to those bent on dismissing depth models and identity politics. Despite its efforts to question rigid identities, *Kiss of the Spider Woman* redeems the gay liberation movement's attention to the serious depths of sexual identity, instead of merely celebrating the playful surfaces that queer theory privileges. Molina himself seems to tire of a campy life of surfaces and drag play when he remarks: "being a window dresser all day, enjoyable as it is, when the day's finished, sometimes you begin to ask yourself what's it all about, and you feel kind of empty inside" (70). Expressing an incipient but undirected desire to do more than just find pleasure in his own difference, Molina hopes to actually *make a difference* by participating in the revolution. This moment in the text resonated deeply with one audience member, a man who claimed a strong identity as a "black gay man" but also expressed an affinity with the moniker queer because he tries to "interrogate and play with gender" (see Appendix A for the complete interview). Despite this man's willingness to consider identity as a performative surface construction (he once participated in a gay performance art troupe that wore skirts), he also worries about the political usefulness of drag culture and about its anti-feminist tendencies. Because he is a politically active social worker, this black gay/queer man was glad to see Molina adopting a more serious tone after his release from prison: "when he goes back to his drag friends, they don't have meaning to him anymore. This whole game he played with gender is no longer important; it tells him nothing about himself. He grows up and decides to act politically, to put himself on the frontlines instead of merely playing." These statements echo the concerns of Steven Seidman, who worries in *Fear of a Queer Planet* that the queer poststructuralist model could devolve into "an empty politics of gesture or disruptive performance that forfeits an integrative, transformative politics" (135). *Kiss of the Spider Woman* presents a warning to queers who have wholeheartedly embraced pre-Stonewall drag and camp as subversive strategies without paying attention to their drawbacks; in a violently homophobic world, a campy politics can be like a feather "trying to stop an elephant" (Bergman 12). My study of the interpretation patterns of this audience group serves as a reminder to the academic community that although queerness and anti-essentialism are gaining discursive prominence, they are by no means unilaterally or uncritically endorsed even among educated liberal or leftist communities.

I contend that *Kiss of the Spider Woman* resonates so strongly with audiences, and was so successful in its screen and stage adaptations in the 1980s and 1990s, because it spoke to people trying to negotiate shifting and conflicting cultural ideas about sexual and gender identity. While *Kiss* allowed some audience members to confirm a pre-existing ideological preference for surface or depth models, the textual hybridity encouraged others to envision a strategic compromise between them. Whatever these audience members decided about the characters' identities or about the text's message concerning sexuality or gender, they all recognized that something politically important was at stake.

Identification and Disidentification Patterns

The complex relationship between identity and identification, and the political promise of cross-group identification, are central themes of *Kiss of the Spider Woman*, in which two characters with seemingly opposed identities come to identify with each other. A crossover identification with the feminine is also the central motivation for Molina's obsession with melodramatic film. In the early moments of the novel when they are discussing the film *Cat People*, Molina asks Valentin "who do you identify with?" (25), and Valentin's predictable answer is based on his macho identity. As the novel progresses, however, the once simple question takes on more political resonance, and the answers to it become more unpredictable. While at first Valentin disidentifies with the emotional landscape of Molina's films, he is gradually seduced into identifying with both Molina and his popular film narratives, which causes him to rethink his previously rigid sexual and gender identity. Meanwhile, Molina's previous identification with abject, passive femininity wanes as he begins to recognize the worth of Valentin's political stand against oppression. The boundaries between the two men slowly dissolve as they retreat from their polar positions to the point of identifying with the other.

This cross-group identification has subversive power because it urges audiences to free up the rigid distinction between self and other. After the two men in *Kiss* have sex, Molina's desire for Valentin turns into an identification, so strong that he searches his own face for a mole that he knows is Valentin's. He reflects: "it seemed as if I wasn't here . . . like it was you all alone. Or like I wasn't me anymore. As if now, somehow . . . I . . . were you" (219). As Leo Bersani argues in *Homos*, "the desire to have is never entirely distinct from the desire to be" and "the boundaries between having and being are bound to be more blurred in same-gender desire than in heterosexual desire" (63). Bersani believes that the sameness of homosexuality is subversive because it involves giving up "knowing where he ends and the other begins" (129). While Bersani is only interested in identifications among people who share a sexual identity, I argue that cross-group identification can also yield a subversive dissolving of boundaries. Although *Kiss of the Spider Woman* is more invested in difference than is Bersani, it does attest to the political value of a search for sameness, of finding some aspect of yourself in another person. Molina and Valentin feel very differently gendered, but they both move closer to androgyny and to a recognition of sameness. Even their language becomes less gendered and less polarized as the text progresses, and it becomes increasingly difficult to tell who is speaking in the late portions of the novel. Seeing ourselves as primarily similar to others, rather than different, could be a positive change for heterosexuals as well as homosexuals, since it could lessen misogyny (Bersani 147) as well as homophobia.

The boundary-shattering identifications present in the plot were mirrored by the identification patterns that I found among these audience members. Some heterosexuals and macho individuals identified with Molina, and many women and gay men in the group identified with Valentin, a finding that challenges theories based on a one-to-one correspondence between a viewer's social identity and his or her identifications. Furthermore, identification theories that employ an essentialist model of either/or identity poles would be at a loss to explain the fact that many of the people I interviewed identified with both men at once. Others both identified and disidentified with the same character, and this simultaneous recognition of difference and sameness has not been given adequate attention by theorists. I contend that the text itself fosters such ambivalent and multivalent forms of identification as part of its larger project of re-envisioning the relationship between identity and solidarity. Yet, as essentialist theorists might predict, some people did identify with characters who appeared to belong to their social group. Twelve out of the twenty gays, lesbians, and bisexuals identified with Molina on the basis of shared "sexual otherness." Likewise, all of the straight men identified with Valentin. Since Valentin's sexual identity was interpreted variously, people of all groups (straight, gay, and bisexual) identified with him based on the perception that he shared their orientation. While sexual identity was sometimes cited as a reason for identification, so were politics, cultural interests, and personality traits. Some connected with Molina because of his apolitical stance or his love of popular culture, while others identified with Valentin's intellectualism or his angst over his class background. Ten people identified with Valentin's Marxist ideology, which underscores that identification can reflect a conscious political affiliation. Not surprisingly, my audience group most often identified with the two men for the reasons that they were in prison—Valentin's Marxist identity and Molina's sexual difference.

Many people also cited "same gender" as a reason for connecting with a character, and this was sometimes a simple case of essentialist identification (i.e., men identifying with male characters on the basis of their masculine traits). However, the majority of the group defined gender in an anti-essentialist way, as a set of cultural behaviors, predilections, and feelings not necessarily determined by the sexed body. For example, some women (four heterosexuals and one lesbian) crossed groups to identify with Valentin for being realistic, goal-oriented, tough, strong, and active, all qualities associated with masculinity. While one literalist woman could not identify with anyone because "there were no women in the film," many other women crossed the sex divide to identify with Molina for his emotional, romantic, and nurturing traits. Since Molina straddles genders himself, claiming to be "a woman inside," what does it mean to identify with him on the basis of "shared gender"? These instances of identification on the basis of shared masculinity or femininity flout essentialism by highlighting the distinction between gender characteristics and the sexed body, with the result of relaxing the boundary between men and women. Cognitive researchers Crawford and Chaffin conducted a study that also questions essentialist ideas about gender and reading. They argue that how one positions oneself on a scale of masculinity and femininity leads to differences in interpretation. Along the same lines, 7 out of the 12 women in my survey identified primarily with Valentin, rather than with the feminine Molina, with whom they might have been expected to identify. Freudian and Lacanian theory implies that a heterosexual woman would desire rather than identify with Valentin, but only two women (one straight, one bisexual) expressed sexual attraction for him. Furthermore, these two women felt both desire *and* identification for Valentin, which puts into question the Freudian opposition between these psychic processes. Some women identified with Valentin because they shared his masculine personality, but many feminine-identified women crossed over both the sex and gender divide to see something of themselves in him. What they empathized with, primarily, were his political and intellectual struggles. A woman whose bourgeois desires conflict with her leftist ideology had experienced similar inner turmoil: "he wants to go out and help people, but he wants to hang out in a beautiful penthouse and sip a martini. I identify with that—I'm not sure if I'd rather have the money or the satisfaction that what I'm doing has a higher purpose." A bisexual woman who has been "ridiculed for having different views" said that she identified with being "persecuted for something you believe in" as Valentin was, while a lesbian activist shared Valentin's resolve to fight against such persecution. Obviously, these instances of cross-gender identification should not be dismissed as a sad act of transvestitism, of women wishing they were men. These feminist women identified with Valentin because they are already like him—intelligent, political, and committed to egalitarian principles.

For similar reasons, several gay men crossed the sexuality divide to identify with Valentin, whom they read as straight. Psychoanalysts might read these identifications as a sign that these gay men unconsciously valorize normativity, but that would be an error. One "black gay political activist" in my group said: "I see myself like Valentin, trapped, not allowed to be the full round circle that I could be, in a hostile situation. Since my identity and my sexuality have a political base, I identify with Valentin rather than Molina." A political identity can often be more important to one's self-concept and identifications than the mere fact of sexual orientation, or sex, or gender. Such cross-group identifications between gays and straights, and women and men, highlight the fact that a singular identity category cannot wholly define people or their ability to relate to others. The man in the previous example is not only homosexual and male, but is also queer, black, feminist, leftist, masculine-identified, a social worker, and a college graduate. The unpredictable identifications stemmed from the fact that each individual embraces multiple identities sometimes at odds with one another. For example, many of the gay men in the group—eight out of thirteen—were surprised that they disidentified with Molina. Although these men were at first attracted to the text because it featured a gay character, they did not see themselves reflected in this effeminate man. Their gender identification as butch prompted some of them to connect more strongly with a masculine straight man than with a "queen." While these examples disrupt the equation of homosexuality with gender inversion, another example upsets a stereotypical view of heterosexuals as rigidly gender-normative. One heterosexual male senior citizen crossed the sexuality divide to identify with Molina because he is also feminized—he loves musicals and old melodramas and is the submissive partner in his marriage. These examples of men identifying with people of other sexualities but similar gender affiliations serve as a reminder that the vectors of sexuality and gender are intertwined in unpredictable ways and must be analyzed in conjunction, as Judith Butler also suggests (*Bodies* 239). Since homosexuality and heterosexuality are not homogeneous identities, they do not always lead to simple group solidarity.

My study also revealed that disidentifications—such as those expressed by masculine gay men for Molina—were often felt more strongly than identifications. Psychoanalysis maintains that a disavowal of the other is crucial to the formation of a self, and this proved to be true for some people I interviewed. Nine gay men disidentified with Valentin for exhibiting traits stereotypical of heterosexual men—homophobia, machismo, and violence—or because they felt he was "denying his gay side," while three women were alienated by Valentin's "masculine" inflexibility. Two straight men disidentified with Molina's gay-ness, as did a gay man and a bisexual woman who were not yet "out" when they encountered the text. What made this process of disavowal more interesting to me, however, was that many people disidentified with the character with which they might have been predicted to identify. Ten gay men and five women were turned off by Molina's femininity, and four men (three gay, one straight) disidentified with Valentin for being too macho. It's interesting that more gay men disidentified with Molina (ten) than with Valentin (nine), a finding which flouts essentialist expectations. Butler contends that disidentification is not merely a refused identification, but an "identification one fears to make only because one has already made it" (*Bodies* 112). I did see a few examples of this process of projection, of denying something within the self by rejecting another. Some gay men seemed to be trying too stridently to distinguish themselves from the effeminacy that Molina represents. When I asked one gay man whom he identified with, he said, "Well, not Molina. I'm not a transgender, I'm not a drag. . . . I did identify with him in the aspect that he was gay. But not to the standpoint that I would want to emulate that sort of thing. I have no desire to be a woman. I've always been proud of the fact that I am not the least bit interested in going with someone who is in a dress. I'm embarrassed for those people." Despite the fact that this man was wearing a baseball cap and a Redskins t-shirt, he struck me as quite feminine in mannerisms. Other people were more conscious of the fact that a particular character made them uncomfortable because he hit too close to home. One woman psychoanalyzed her own ambivalent feelings about femininity: "the things I didn't like about Molina—his self-destructive romanticism—are probably things I do myself, which is why I got annoyed with him." Disidentification may sometimes reflect a fear of something hidden within the self; on the other hand, such disavowals can also be consciously politicized. Several men, both straight and gay, rejected an identification with Valentin because they stand against homophobia and machismo, while many people disidentified with Valentin's extremist Marxist politics. Two gay men disidentified with Molina not because they feared femininity but because they read him as a self-loathing homosexual who "internalized homophobia" by wishing he was really a woman rather than a gay man. A few anti-essentialist feminist women were similarly critical of Molina for buying into stereotypical notions of femininity. Reflecting on her disidentification with Molina, a bisexual feminist said, "Why is he so hung up on being a woman? The idea of what it means to be feminine freaks me out sometimes. There's nothing like a drag queen to heighten this femininity that I'm not sure I always want to be a part of." More than just an unconscious fear of the other, the process of disidentification clearly plays a role in helping people to articulate their own ideologies and to establish their own political identities.

The disidentification patterns that I found illuminate broader social trends and attitudes as well as the construction of individual subjectivities. I believe there to be some cultural significance in the fact that both the men and the women in this group showed a much stronger disidentification with femininity than with masculinity, even though the text itself seems to criticize masculinity more harshly. Nine of the twelve women saw themselves as primarily feminine rather than masculine, yet the majority of them nonetheless disidentified with Molina's performance of abject femininity on the grounds that it was anti-feminist. This disidentification pattern could be seen as evidence of the positive cultural power of anti-essentialist feminist critiques of gender stereotypes. On the other hand, anti-essentialist feminism may have further exacerbated our culture's general disdain for traditionally feminine traits. The general devaluation of femininity common in Western cultures was clearly a root of the gay males' disidentification with Molina's femme persona. Very few of these gay men offered feminist critiques of Molina's behavior; instead many of them expressed a thinly veiled fear of being tainted by femininity and a strong reaction against gender inversion theories of homosexuality. While feminism has allowed women in our society to break free of some of the constraints of the feminine gender role, men—even gay men—still appear to be enthralled with masculinity and the power it confers. When I asked the men what masculinity meant to them, many cited a long list of positive traits (strength, bravery, protectiveness, honor, access to "perks") and only occasionally offered negative ones (rigidity, competitiveness), while the women usually led with what they disliked about femininity. This audience group's stronger disidentification with Molina than with Valentin highlights the fact that femininity is less valued than masculinity even among liberal Americans, despite the gains of feminism. In fact, anti-essentialist feminism may be inadvertently deepening the devaluation of femininity.

Several participants in the survey disidentified with characters of the basis of gendered traits, but very few rejected an identification because of the sexual identity of a character. Only four gay people disidentified with Valentin for being straight. Likewise, Molina's homosexuality led four people to disavow any connection to him—two straight men and two people who were not yet "out of the closet" when they encountered the text. The relatively small amount of homophobia among this group is probably due to the fact that *Kiss of the Spider Woman* draws readers and viewers who are already tolerant, if not gay-friendly. Nonetheless, I was surprised and heartened to see so few people rejecting an identification with their sexual others, because it suggests that the social divide between homosexuals and heterosexuals is becoming less stark, or at least that people are not reducing the sum total of a person's being to his or her sexuality. In fact, most of these viewers and readers understood subjectivity to be multi-faceted and perceived individuals to be an amalgam of multiple identities. This understanding led to a more complex and ambivalent identification process, since twelve people were able to disidentify as well as identify with the same character in the text. Identification thus did not mandate an acceptance of the whole. For example, many gay men made comments like this one: "well, I identify with Molina for being gay, but he's so different from me—I'm not queeny." One woman likened herself to Valentin for his realism but criticized his rigidity. These examples underscore that identification and solidarity do not necessarily result in an erasure of difference. Instead of a facile unity based on the principle of homogeneity, these audience members experienced a looser connection that did not totally collapse the boundary between self and other. Some of the subjects in the survey voiced disidentifications in order to maintain some sort of boundary between themselves and others; in contrast, several were able to see the other *within* themselves. Upsetting facile polarizations, fourteen people in the study group identified with *both* Molina and Valentin. Since each person's subjectivity is made up of disparate loyalties, ideologies, and identities that can rarely be mirrored in another single individual, readers and viewers may feel affinity for more than one character in a text, even when the characters seem polarized. Lacan prefigured this idea when he theorized that we are all "split subjects" in a state of contradiction or vacillation between self and other. Rather than relying on an either/or logic of exclusion based on unitary notions of the self, the best current studies of identification focus attention on the vacillating or ambivalent self, particularly with reference to gender ambivalence (see de Lauretis; Clover; Rodowick).

Moving beyond Lacan's binary logic, this case study reveals the multiplicitous rather than merely ambivalent nature of identification. Four of the five bisexuals in my study identified with both Molina and Valentin equally, because they felt both gay and straight sexual desires or they defined themselves as androgynous and thus were able to identify with both genders. Six women (bisexual, straight, and lesbian) also connected to both characters, and it might be tempting to explain this by turning to de Lauretis's theory that female spectators are particularly capable of a "double identification" with both the masculine subject position, defined by the active desiring gaze and force of narrative movement, and with the feminine object position of the passive image or "space of narrative movement" (143). But how would de Lauretis explain the fact that eight men (straight, gay, and bisexual) also experienced this double identification? Furthermore, gender was not necessarily the crucial or only factor in the double identifications these people experienced; in other words, not all who identified with both men did so on the basis of gender androgyny or bisexual fluidity. Psychoanalytic film theorists who have discussed the possibility of vacillating or multiple identifications tend to see this vacillation only in terms of sexual difference (Mayne 90). While identification theorists have tended to privilege either gender or sexuality (or occasionally both) as the most meaningful identity axes, I found the identification patterns of these people to be much more complex, involving various and intersecting identities. Sallie Munt's concept of the "multivalent self" as a set of "intersecting plates" (2) aptly describes the multiple identities embraced by many in this audience group. For example, the gay men who identified with both men did not exhibit androgynous feelings as did the bisexuals; four of them identified with Molina's homosexuality but also connected to Valentin as either a political activist or a repressed, closeted gay man. The multivalent identification of one "straight" man (Joe) poses a serious challenge to polarized and unitary theories of identity. Joe identified with Valentin's leftist politics but also with Molina's rejection of politics, since he has become jaded about the efficacy of his past activism. While Joe stated that he identified with Valentin for being masculine, he also connected with Molina's gender flux since he used to impersonate female singers when he was an adolescent. Now he defines himself as straight like Valentin (and like him, he desired Sonia Braga, who played Marta in the film), but his experimentation with homosexuality in college gave him a kinship with Molina. Lastly, since this man is socially ostracized because of a mental disability, he identified with Molina's dignity in being different: "Molina was not willing to put up with anyone who didn't appreciate him, and I'm like that too." Joe's multiple and contradicting identities enabled him to experience a network of identifications with various groups. This layering of present identities over past ones was experienced by several other people in addition to Joe. This palimpsest effect, which records the impact of time upon identity, has not been emphasized in apparatus film theory, which treats identity as static rather than dynamic. Even when identities shift over time, such a change in identification often does not completely erase all connection to a person's past selves. A twice-married, bisexual, transvestite male in my group identified with Valentin as his past self (straight, political, masculine), and with Molina as his present self (gay, apolitical, feminine). Another formerly heterosexual and currently homosexual man identified with both characters since he had experienced their different sexual desires. One gay man had gone through a "silly campy stage" when he was younger, so he could see that part of himself in Molina, while his current persona as masculine and serious made him identify with Valentin as well. More attention needs to be paid to this diachronic factor and the layering of multiple identities that results with the passage of time.

Time proved to be an important factor in many people's responses to the text, for they had encountered *Kiss of the Spider Woman* during a particularly sensitive period of their lives when their own identities were in flux. For example, this cultural text played a crucial role in aiding a few young adults in my study to identify themselves as gay or bisexual. One man recalled sneaking out to see the film when he was fifteen because he was dying to witness a screen kiss between two men: "There were no positive gay role models in film or on television at the time, and I was so hungry for it. This film probably set my tastes and my interests." A bisexual woman saw with hindsight why the novel had so perplexed her: "I hadn't articulated my own bisexuality at that point. Maybe that's why I was responding so strongly, asking what was going on here with the sex between these two men. Maybe that's why it was important to me to try to figure that out." Another young man who now identifies as gay came across the film when he was in high school, when "the theme of repressing sexuality was a very cogent issue" for him. Although he was too afraid to identify with Molina's "out homosexuality" at the time, he was able to see himself in Valentin as a person with latent gay desires. By allowing a "safer" identification with the sexually ambiguous Valentin, the text offers an important point of entry and connection to viewers and readers who are tentatively questioning their sexuality. Identifying with Molina and Valentin allowed many people to acknowledge their own non-normative sexual desires and to enjoy a feeling of solidarity rare in their everyday lives.

Kiss of the Spider Woman also helped heterosexual viewers to reflect on their own identities. By identifying with homosexual and bisexual characters, many straights in my audience group were able to solidify their identities as non-homophobic liberals. In his article "Self-Relevant Reading in Literary Understanding," László Halász contends that readers usually seek confirmation of their preconceived worldviews, yet he admits that a reader can sometimes "restructure[e] his/her schemata in accordance with new information" (241). Cognitive psychologist Keith Oatley is more optimistic about the power of cultural texts to provoke "cognitive transformation" (54). I have observed such cognitive transformation among heterosexuals in my audience group who were moved to question their beliefs in the polarity of heterosexuality and homosexuality. Since the beginning of the text presents Valentin as a clearly heterosexual character, many straights slipped into an easy identification with him only to have the rug pulled out from under them. Because Valentin himself begins to question his sexual identity, the text moved some readers to consider the idea that "sexual identity as well as gender identity is fuzzier than most of us would like to think," as one woman put it. In addition, several heterosexual viewers and readers were surprised by their identification with Molina, which also worked to destabilize their beliefs in a clear opposition between self and other. Even though most of the heterosexuals in my audience group were attracted to *Kiss* because they were already tolerant or gay-friendly, the text still played a role in furthering their questioning of heteronormativity, and in confirming their political commitment to fight oppressive institutions. As one heterosexual woman noted, reading this text inspired her both to join Amnesty International and to begin reading *The Washington Blade*, a gay publication with a strong left-wing agenda.

Kiss of the Spider Woman had an even more powerful political impact upon a more conservative audience group that I observed informally—my students at the University of Virginia, where the student culture is not known for being gay-friendly. This group provides a useful counterpoint to the self-selecting liberal Washingtonians that I interviewed. When I taught *Kiss* (novel and film), my students experienced the transformative and subversive power of identification. While some homophobia marked their discussions of the first few chapters, their sympathy for Molina grew exponentially to the point of intense grief at his death. A closeted gay student in our class was so encouraged by this outpouring of empathy that he came out to his classmates during our discussion and was treated with remarkable sensitivity. Not only did the text encourage heterosexuals to overcome prejudice by identifying with their social others, but the text also offered a rare identificatory moment for this minority student. Molina's relationship with Valentin inspired this gay young man to turn an unrequited passion in his own life into his first reciprocal relationship. Of all the novels and films that I have taught, *Kiss of the Spider Woman* stands out as the one that "moved" students most intensely; the feelings it provoked led them to new ground, to reconsider their attitudes, politics, and identities. The experience of teaching this text is in fact what first led me to investigate the political effects of sentimental postmodernism upon audiences. My ethnographic study confirmed what I had glimpsed in these students' reactions—that sentimental postmodernism is indeed a "dynamic" cultural hybrid, dynamic in its ability to move audiences emotionally and politically, through the powerful tool of identification.

Conclusion

Cross-Group Empathy before and after 9/11

Without these detailed case studies of the impact of sentimental postmodernism upon readers and viewers, an analysis of the politics of this hybrid style would be incomplete and highly speculative. My contextual and empirical work with audiences is crucial to the conclusion that much of the political power of sentimental postmodernism can be found in the intense identifications that it fosters both within and across sexual identities, genders, and ethnicities. Much of the current critical work about identification has been produced by textual scholars writing from psychoanalytic perspectives. While these textual theorists have given us valuable insights concerning the ambivalent and fragmented nature of sexuality and gender identification, they have hastily dismissed empirical work as overly simplistic. Ethnography need not be viewed as inimical to theory or speculative textual analysis, for it can be a valuable means not only of corroborating and nuancing existing theory, but also of opening up new avenues of inquiry. Just as the founders of psychoanalysis revised their ideas through encounters with patients, cultural theory about subjectivity and identification can be greatly enriched by an interface with the object of critical speculation—spectators and readers. We need to be reminded that these objects of speculation are in fact subjects whose own narratives have much to tell us about the meaning and political significance of cultural texts.

These case studies suggest that we must look beyond both textual analysis and the unconscious in order to fully understand identification as a process of social and political articulation. While my study of *The Piano* underscored that identification is affected by the conscious feminist politics of viewers, the chapters on *Kiss of the Spider Woman* and *Northern Exposure* highlighted the radical potential of "excorporative" cross-group identification. All three case studies illuminated the political nature of identification, but, contrary to most theories, they also suggested its potential to move audiences to resist rather than support the status quo. As I have argued, sentimental postmodernism aids audiences in confirming and strengthening their own liberal and leftist political identities as feminists, multiculturalists, antiracists, and members of the queer coalition.

My findings about the progressive potential of cross-group identification also have larger relevance outside of this particular conjunction of audiences and texts. Contemporary scholars who address cross-group sympathy tend to view such cross-over affiliations with skepticism, as a form of false consciousness, passive empathy, or an imperialistic drive to incorporate the other into the self. As of late, there has been a boomlet of books on the complex issue of cross-race affiliation, but many of them take a decidedly pessimistic tone (see Berlant; Sanchez-Eppler; Gubar; Rogin; Sommer; Roediger; Wald). It is worth pausing to consider whether this current critical strain ultimately grants too much power to the ability of race to ground and divide us. I am also dismayed by what I see as a critical move away from the commitment to anti-essentialist coalition-building—best expressed in Bernice Johnson Reagon's 1983 essay "Coalition Politics: Turning the Century"—and towards a reinvestment in situatedness and identitarian thinking. This critical shift could be glimpsed at a conference at Cornell University in the fall of 2001, a few months after 9/11. Entitled "The Future of Minority Studies: Redefining Identity Politics," the conference featured scholars lamenting the loss of identity-rootedness amidst the knee-jerk reactions against essentialism. My own ethnographies have shown the ways in which identities continue to moor people, even as they struggle against their circumscribing effects. But as Reagon reminds, coalitions must be seen as a crucial strategy of survival given the realities of globalization. Twenty-plus years after Reagon's essay, the violence of domestic hate groups, world-wide terrorist organizations, and the resurgence of a right-wing U.S. national government make leftist coalition-building ever more politically urgent.

The hope in cross-group empathy evident in sentimental postmodernism need not be seen as a "dated" pre-9/11 sensibility. In the years after September 11, 2001, we have witnessed a hyper-vigilance concerning the policing of borders and an entrenchment of ethnic, religious, and national differences. In the face of a post-9/11 "us vs. them" mentality, I offer my book's arguments concerning the subversive potential of empathy and identification across group boundaries, with the aim of provoking a re-evaluation of critical investments in identitarian thinking. Given the increasing animosity between Islamic nations and the West, as well as sharp divisions between "blue" and "red" states within the United States, the liberal utopian ideology of these pre-9/11 sentimental postmodern texts may seem like a relic of a different era. Yet these textual inducements of cross-group empathy may nonetheless offer important strategies for left-leaning cultural producers in the twenty-first century. Much empirical research has concluded that empathy inhibits aggression, and thus social scientists have pointed to the absence of empathy as a telling feature of inter-group violence, such as the Israeli/Palestinian conflict (see Deigh 218–20). Do empathy-inducing narratives have any power to combat xenophobia and clannish mentalities, at least among the reading or film-going public? Skeptics might argue that such cross-group identifications in cultural space do little to effect change in the public sphere. As discussed in chapter two, a similar argument has been waged against sentimentality and the sympathy it aims to engender for marginalized groups. Yet empirical research suggests that reading literature does have observable effects upon ethical attitudes. In his book *The Moral Laboratory,* Jèmeljan Hakemulder surveys psychological studies of reading to conclude that fiction-reading—and empathetic role-taking in particular—promotes ethical reflection, moral self-knowledge, and a reconsideration of our beliefs about others. This book has argued that sentimental postmodernist texts turn the ethical field of intersubjective relations into a more explicitly political stance, as a liberal critique of the limitations of identity politics that nonetheless respects deeply felt experiences of difference.

In response to those who doubt the impact of cultural texts upon political attitudes or praxis, I would counter that "politics and culture do not exist in separate, watertight compartments" (Rogin 23). George Lipsitz convincingly links culture and politics in his book *Dangerous Crossroads*, an analysis of the cross-cultural affiliations enabled by the globalization of popular music. Lipsitz writes: "cultural production plays a vital role in nurturing and sustaining [political] self-activity. . . . Culture enables people to rehearse identities, stances, and social relations not yet permissible in politics. . . . Popular culture does not just reflect reality, it helps constitute it" (137). Similarly, I argue that the cross-group affiliations enabled by sentimental postmodernism may serve as sustenance or even a catalyst for an investment in counter-hegemonic politics. My attention to the connection between popular culture and political coalition-building is echoed by Donna Haraway in "A Cyborg Manifesto." Haraway describes the imagery of the cyborg in science fiction as "a myth system waiting to become a political language" that offers a "way out of the maze of dualisms in which we have explained our bodies and our tools to ourselves" (181). As Lipsitz and Haraway suggest, popular film, fiction, and music offer important sites for imagining alternative spaces and social relations, and these imaginings may shape the realities of a future political world. It is worth remembering that Michael Moore's emotionally wrenching left-wing documentary film *Fahrenheit 9/11* nearly turned the tide of the 2004 U.S. presidential election.

As I have argued throughout this book, sentimental postmodernism provoked strong emotional responses among viewers and readers in the 1990s, fueling their desires for political and social change. Adopting the strategies of critical high culture and emotional popular culture, these hybrid dialectical texts challenge both postmodern cynicism and sentimental complacency. Sentimental postmodernism aims to discourage a facile identification with the Other that merely fortifies the self and leaves hegemonic ideologies unchallenged. By provoking both empathetic connections and critical reflection about identity, these postmodern melodramas foster a deeper respect for cultural difference and a utopian hope in the viability of a pluralist and feminist democracy. The ethnographies of audience response presented here attest to the potential of visual and literary texts, and of the emotional identifications they enable, to shape people's idealizations and to sustain their political commitment to making the ideal real.

Appendix A

Annotated Transcript of an Interview for the *Kiss of the Spider Woman* Case Study

Annotated Interview with "C.G." *(African American gay male, college-educated, social worker)*

Note: I chose this interview to offer in full text not only because it was representative of the responses offered by this audience group, but because it also shed light on how social differences between interviewer and subject can sometimes affect the dynamics of an interview. The interview starts out with a strong rapport between the two of us, perhaps because I generally agreed with his interpretation of the book and with his politics. Once we got to the section of the interview concerning his own cultural tastes, then a miscommunication tied to racial difference occurred. See my annotations (italicized, and in brackets) concerning how this tension affected the latter part of the interview.

KCD: Where did you come across my advertisement?

CG: *The Washington Blade* (gay newspaper).

KCD: Have you read the novel, or seen the film or musical? When and how many times?

CG: I've read the book first, then saw the film. I don't know where I heard of his name, Manuel Puig, but I had kind of understood that he was a gay writer and that he was doing fiction from South America. And early on I had read a book of collected short stories from gay or homosexual South American writers, and it led me to read the novel. A few years after I read the book and a few years after the movie was out, I saw the movie at a friend's house when I was living in Detroit. A Latino friend of mine, and we talked about the movie. As well, I've seen *Cat People*.

KCD: Would you describe yourself as a fan of the novel or film, or did you have any negative reactions to it? What do you like or dislike about it?

CG: I think there is a big difference between the movie and the book. The book interrogates sexuality and it does it from many different perspectives. You have the whole notion of [inaudible word], the guy in the prison cell tells movies. You also have a running commentary of footnotes about current constructs of sexuality. There's a bit of like a folk sense of sexuality running through the movies that he tells. In the movie version, the situation has been flattened out. It may seem that it's a story of a straight man and a gay man in a prison situation, but it's actually a more generalized story about human compassion. Someone who wanted to see the movie as they saw the book would be frustrated. I've seen the movie several times since. I'm no longer frustrated at what the movie was trying to do; I understand the limitations of the movies. But the book is so much different, where I wouldn't connect the two. I wasn't interested in seeing the stage play. I love musicals, it's just—I can't imagine how they could take that one step beyond. The movie had nothing to do with the book, and I assume the stage play with Vanessa Williams as the Spider Woman would have nothing to do with the movie and totally nothing to do with the book. And I wasn't interested anymore.

KCD: You say the book is primarily about sexuality. What kinds of statements about sexuality do you see going on there?

CG: First the book is really a South American product. It's so much a South American product that it doesn't make as much sense. Especially through gay sexuality and even straight sexuality. The book also dealt with the whole political . . . the masculinization of power and the feminization of oppression. It went beyond roles, beyond what's a man and what's a woman, what's a homosexual and what's a straight person.

KCD: And you see the South American context as crucial to that.

CG: I think it's very crucial, without a history of machismo, without an understanding of how South Americans deal with the whole notion of sexual identity, it would be kind of a corrupt reading. I don't think they would think, as in this country, that if a man has sex with another man then it is probably a gay encounter. From my understanding and reading of homosexuals in Latin America, I don't think they would see it that way. So our notion of gay is radically different than how they construe homosexuality. I read one book which suggests they think of it as homosexualities—plural.

KCD: That question is interesting to me, because Puig wrote the novel when he was living in New York City, so he's dealing both with a South American context for homosexuality, but then all the footnotes are very Euro-Anglo constructions of it.

CG: Yes.

KCD: So I'm interested in, how do we read this? Do we read this as we would understand American characters interacting?

CG: I think there is enough of a cultural context for us to approach it, otherwise it makes no sense to us. I think the large part of the reading comes from the recitation of some of the movies. Because he is able to crystallize the psychology of sexuality through these movie images which are really connected to American notions of man and woman. I was more excited about the *Cat People* movie, more than the movie about the Nazis which takes a central point in the film. The movie about the cat woman and the movie at the end were more interesting. The cat woman, I remember this line from the book—"in the park all the trees were bare." For some reason I'll never forget that line, and when I read that I was blown away, and there were more lines like that. I guess there was this whole thing that if a person was fully sexually liberated, they would become a beast. That was part of how he told the story. The actual movie is a little bit different.

CG: But you were asking, do the footnotes help it make sense to Americans, if the Latin American concepts of sexuality are different? To me the footnotes are so out of place, became so repetitious, and at that time during the seventies, were called into so much question, that when I was reading it in the early '80s, they seemed a tad bit ludicrous.

KCD: Do you think that that was an intentional effect?

CG: Well, I think that was intentional. In the '70s, particularly with the feminists, by the time I got to the book around the mid-'80s, there was a lot of talk about Freud being an asshole. I remember this woman I worked with who used to come in to the office and she used to say that men had breast envy. She used to juggle her breasts in front of us—"Do you want one of these?" And I also read some stuff that said maybe Freud was just talking about white Jews at the end of the nineteenth century, and maybe he was not talking about the British upper class, or blacks. There was a whole question about the universality of psychology. There was a whole new look at Skinner as well.

KCD: Do you think Puig was participating in that questioning?

CG: Yes, that was the light in which I read the footnotes. I think I read them as senseless. Even though at the time I'm sure I consciously took them in. I think they were extremely important to the book. They were there to prove a point. But after reading them, you really want to get back to the story, but you really had to read the footnotes. But I think it's important that they become senseless, that you are forced to read them and want to get back to the action of the story because they appear out of context, and they don't point directly to what you are reading. They are another text that's running almost counter to the main text.

KCD: Do you think the representation of sexual identity is very different in the main text than in the footnotes?

CG: Oh yeah.

KCD: One of my questions is, how would you describe Molina's and Valentin's sexuality—are they gay, straight, bisexual, transgender, transvestite, transsexual? Do you put them into American categories such as those I listed?

CG: In the movie you do. Well, Molina is gay and Valentin is straight. In the novel, when I read that part when they really had sex I almost started crying, because I was thinking, my God will it ever come about? It's not all about what you are or who you are or what you might mean to somebody, it's actually two human beings coming together. In the book they were kind of driven to express physical warmth. No so much as a titillating move, are they going to make out, or they had nothing else to do. It was an actual practical and physical move that said a lot. That leaped above all the script, all the psychobabble that's underneath the main text. Beyond just basic human need. There was something going on beyond just staying alive in the cell. To me Valentin was much more nuanced in the book than he was in the movie—he was just a gruff straight man with a beard in the movie. In the book, ideas were more central to his being and to his sexuality, and the same with Molina. In the book, Molina was trying to go beyond that notion of homosexuals as absorbed by sex. You get that a little bit in the movie when he's actually putting himself on the frontlines, but I think in the book you see how he goes about. . . . It's been a long time so I'm not sure if I'm remembering this well.

KCD: You're doing incredibly well!

KCD: Do you think that Valentin changes or that his sexuality changes?

CG: I don't think it changes in the film, and I don't think it changes in the book. But in the book something else happens. Valentin starts to question himself because of his interactions with Molina. He questions his sexuality.

KCD: Do you see Molina undergoing any transformation?

CG: Yeah. It's really hard but, in the movie it's almost like the typical homosexual scheming, doing little plots, it's how people perceive homosexuals. In the book he's more like a masculine homosexual, it's interesting to see how men have kind of written his personality against him. I think he is a very courageous person. He's not playing any games when he goes up against the warden and the guards and you really see that. You really see how they're changing in the book.

KCD: You seem to have seen Molina as sort of a stereotype of gay men, the effeminate stereotype. Did that bother you?

CG: In the movie I did, and in the book I didn't. From the beginning when he was telling those stories, he was after something. Not so much to entertain Valentin but also he was trying to make some sense of it for himself.

KCD: So it was not a stereotypical thing for you?

CG: No, not at all, not as the stories developed. There's something about Molina that's like the woman in the Arabian Nights who tells stories so that her life was spared. The telling of the stories is I guess what enables one to transform the world within themselves; I think that was a basic part of Molina's character. His telling the stories and Valentin's response allows us to see the changes in both of them. I didn't see Molina as a static character, even from the beginning of the novel.

KCD: Which characters did you identify with, or not, and why? Did the fact that Molina is more feminine and Valentin more masculine have anything to do with whom you identified with?

CG: As a black gay man with some political activism in my background, I see myself like Valentin, trapped, really not allowed to be the full round circle that I could be, in a hostile situation. I never thought about it that way. But at the time that I picked it out to read, I was interested in it because it had a gay character. So I expected to identify with Molina, but didn't.

KCD: Why not?

CG: It's kind of different things, but Molina was more free than Valentin in many ways. Then Molina began to see how trapped he was, maybe that had something to do with his transformation. Because I don't consider myself a feminized gay man, maybe I'm going back and not looking at how I would see the novel today. I don't see myself as a feminized gay man, although I have a greater appreciation for them now, realized what a difficult thing it is to be—a friend of mine said, "I'm not man enough to wear a dress." And I realized some of . . . how tough and courageous that is. It's not a game to them. I guess I see myself as more of a political person, and my identity and my sexuality has a political base, and that's why I would identify with Valentin rather than Molina. I guess it was more the external things about Valentin's character.

KCD: What do you think *Kiss* suggests about masculinity and femininity? Does the novel assert strong differences between men and women, or does it question those supposed natural differences?

CG: It's saying that they absolutely actually exist. What they are at the service of is another question. There are some real powerful women in the book, the spider woman. In the book, you get the sense that the activists in the movement, Valentin's girlfriend, there are heroic women in the book and in the movies. The movie that's told at the end of the book about the spider woman. There's also the maid, Mimi, in the Nazi film? There's also the woman in the *Cat People*, the woman that he really loves. So I don't think the movie is saying that there's no difference between man and woman, but it may be asking what are these different factors in the service of? What do they support, what do they mean? Is that clear?

KCD: Yeah, I think so. It's not answering any questions, merely asking them.

CG: Exactly. It's not saying that there's no such thing as a woman or a man. It says that there is actually a difference between the sexes, but what are these differences for, what regimes do they support?

KCD: What do you think of Molina's statements that he wants to be a woman? What do you think of that?

CG: I believe that there are men who, if allowed to fully express themselves, they should be women. I think Molina starts out with that in the book, but by the end of the book and even to a certain extent in the movie, I don't think he so much wants to be a woman as he wants to be more of himself, and if that's a feminized man, then that's alright.

KCD: He's not a transsexual in the making. You don't see him that way.

CG: Certainly in the movie and in the book one gets that suggestion, but it's stronger in the book that maybe that's something that by the end of his transformation in the book, maybe that's not something he truly wants. I get a little sense of that in the movie also, especially when he's released from jail and he goes back to his friends and they are utterly, they don't have a meaning to him anymore. So this whole game he played with gender is no longer important, it tells him nothing about himself. In that sense, no, I don't think he actually sees himself becoming the true woman he wanted to be. He changes his mind. He comes to terms with himself in different ways. Now he's in prison for being a pederast, not so much for having sex with men or seeing himself as a woman in a relationship.

KCD: I'm also interested in why Molina decided to contact Valentin's political comrades. Did he do it to be a heroine in one of his movies? You seem to read his actions at the end of the film as more of a kind of heroic, politicized action.

CG: Yes.

KCD: But Valentin leaves open the suggestion that he was just doing it to be like Leni in the film, to die a romantic death, this whole love fantasy that he has with Valentin.

CG: I think life in prison and what happened between him and Valentin was so powerful that he was transformed. I don't think his life meant anything to him anymore. I think he stopped living his movies. I think that Valentin at that point was not a good judge of what's happened to Molina. Just as Molina doesn't fully see what's happening to Valentin. Valentin suffers a lot of his pain alone, and if I recall the book isn't told from either point of view. The narrator is omniscient.

KCD: Well, there are many different kinds of narrative strategies. Sometimes it's like a play, or you get to read what characters are thinking to themselves.

CG: Exactly.

KCD: You don't get an overall perspective from an omniscient viewpoint.

CG: Exactly, that's one of the interesting things about this, all the different styles. I tried to read his book *Betrayed by Rita Hayworth*, but it just wasn't as good, and I really tried. Reading *Kiss of the Spider Woman* was initially tough, well it wasn't, well, I thought it would be, because it isn't written like most novels.

KCD: What do you think are the novel/film's messages about revolutionary leftist politics or Marxism? Does it support or criticize Valentin's ideals, or both?

CG: Oh, wow. Yeah, I think the movie goes beyond Marxism. I think it questions, he's from Argentina right? He [Manuel Puig] questions both angles very severely. He questions politics being so masculine and so high and human emotions and values being low and easily turned against us. He does question all of that. He isn't really so much supportive of Valentin or Molina's corners; he's actually talking about a transformation, and what happens to these characters after they go through the situation, because that makes them of value to us.

KCD: So you don't see Puig making a strong political stand on one side or the other?

CG: Exactly, but I think he is making a political point. I don't know if you'd call it an "ism" or not, but perhaps he's talking about the way people are actually constructed. Maybe he's talking about human needs. But I still don't want to go as far as to say what the movies suggests . . . if we just get along everything will be alright. I don't think he is saying that.

KCD: Some people who wanted to read it as this revolutionary book, well, the ending is so fatalistic. None of their efforts amount to anything. They get killed, nothing is changed in the outer world. But what you're saying is that the change is in them.

CG: Yes, Valentin and Molina are different, and maybe Puig is suggesting that that is the real battlefield for any revolution. Because none of us goes through those individual changes without thinking that things in general have to change.

KCD: Did any moments or scenes move you emotionally? Why? Would you say you were intensely involved in *Kiss* or just casually involved or distanced?

CG: The sex scene, but also I was really moved by the discussion of the movies, I loved the movies. Although I can only remember 3 of them, but I think there were 4 of them. I guess the movies were one. The *Cat People* movie really overwhelmed me, because the landscape, I don't mean the actual physical landscape, but place does become a main character in that movie, but just the idea of how hard life is and how difficult it is to fully express yourself, and the dangers and the responsibility of doing so. To me it's a little bit bigger than just sexual, it's something that the movie was about, and it's certainly something that Molina was talking about. I don't know if I was moved by the Nazi movie, but certainly the uniforms, the power and being subdued, it's kind of a rape fantasy. That was intriguing. And I remember really clearly about the revolutionary movie, and the woman and the guns. That sounds like a story that Valentin would like. Then there was the scene where they had sex. And as a sex scene, if one was looking to be titillated, that is not the book's point—there's no dialogue, there's few real descriptions. It was happening in the dark. But what's so overwhelming is that two people are hitting, and it could be a mother and child, it could be a brother and sister finally having a conversation where they understand each other. Just people actually, the impact of two people that were absolutely different connecting. Maybe it was something I was going through at the time or something. I remember actually crying.

KCD: Would you characterize it as a love story?

CG: No. I don't even think the movie is a love story. A lot of fantasy goes on in the movie, and Molina and Valentin read each other as not fully being there. But the circumstances that bring them together are so overwhelming that most of their humanity is like flattened out. They have to really rely on some essentials to get through. Even though Molina tries to create romance, the romance turns into something else. For some reason, I wouldn't describe it as romantic. It at least moves them toward transformation, I keep saying that.

KCD: But it's not a transformation to being in love with Molina?

CG: No. Yeah, I don't think they are in love, I don't think that is possible for them.

KCD Do you think Valentin maintains a straight identity?

CG: No, I think he questions his identity, especially in the book towards the end. He questions everything about himself, what he's doing, what's the point of it. Is he not as bad as the bad guys? Are Molina and the woman he loves, are they the victims, are they part of his obsession with power from another angle? What does it mean to be a man? Has he ever really been in love? Is he capable of feeling anything other than ideas? I think Valentin has asked himself all those things, and has no pat and sure answer. He just drops them all in the reader's lap.

KCD: Would you say you were a consumer or fan of popular culture, such as the kinds of films and songs that Molina loves? Or are you more critical or dismissive of such films as Valentin is at first?

CG: I refuse to take any movie seriously. I no longer believe that some movies. . .what's considered art is very questionable. The most trivial thing can be the most interesting thing to me. For instance, I like Steven Spielberg—I don't think he has anything worth saying, I don't think he's an incredible storywriter. I think he knows a lot about projecting visions and capturing pictures of people saying and doing outrageous things. I think that's all movies are, they are pictures from our minds. They are not the real world. They're not novels, they're not narratives in that sense. And to try to make them make sense like that is just silly. Often movies are workshop efforts; there are so many people coming from so many different perspectives with so many minute influences on it, that it's hard to take it seriously, from the viewpoint that they make one sense or one man is in control and that they will always hold their meaning. Things change over time.

KCD: You don't like assigning the label of art to films, but you would assign that label to novels?

CG: Yes. I have to say that. Because they are the work of one person at one particular time. Now what's great and what's not, a lot has changed since I went to college in the '70s with the *Norton Anthology* where all the men were white, and they were all European and supposedly they described American culture. What's great is open to question.

KCD: What are some of your favorite novels, films, or cultural objects?

CG: When I was a kid, I was really moved by James Baldwin. I felt I had found a kindred spirit. I remember being a teenager, like 16, reading *Notes of a Native Son*, and I remember Baldwin talking about being in Switzerland and what meant a lot to him as an American, what helped him with his identity, were listening to Bessie Smith's records and reading Henry James. So in my early 20s, that's what I did. I've read almost all of James's novels except for the *Ambassadors* and the *Golden Bowl*. I've listened to all of Bessie Smith. Those are parameters that shaped my notion of what's valuable in American culture.

KCD: Very different poles.

CG: But if you are American . . . I have this thing, and I'll be honest, it's kind of interesting. A lot of black people will not have a problem with me saying Henry James, I can read him, and I don't feel a divide, but what burns a lot of black people up is white people for instance don't think that Frederick Douglass speaks to their soul or define their political agendas. That's fucked up. They think that they are not white people if they are not with, if they are two white people together, they think that they are only white if they are dealing with somebody black or somebody outside their circumstances. Black people do not see white people that way. Most white people are fucked up by their educations, because they are not allowed to see really what . . . [*Note: Here his tone really changes from camaraderie to an attack. He is getting angry because I insinuated that Henry James was at the opposite pole from*

Bessie Smith, and he attributes this comment to my "white education." His comments about "white people" here are clearly directed at me.] Henry James to me in my mind and Bessie Smith don't separate; they are on one continuous plane. I feel sorry for a lot of white people because they can't see that. [*Note: Now I am getting upset that he feels sorry for me because he thinks I do not "see" or understand the value of Bessie Smith, that I reify racial difference, and that I do not understand the pathologies of whiteness. I feel misrecognized.]*

KCD: I think you misunderstood me. I just meant that, why did Baldwin pick those two? I think it has that resonance of high culture versus popular culture to many people, but that doesn't mean one has more value than the other, that Henry James is somehow more important than Bessie Smith because he's a white "artist" and she's a black musical performer. Baldwin is clearly trying to say they are both important parts of American-ness.

CG: And I got that point. [*Note: Here he seems somewhat relieved that he misunderstood my point, and also that I know Baldwin's essay. Yet there is still an edge to his voice, as if he means, "I don't need you to tell me how to interpret James Baldwin."*] So if I had to pick great novels and music, it would be influenced by seeing things on a continuum, and not seeing them different.

KCD: What kinds of things would you choose?

CG: James, Bessie Smith, Richard Wright, Anne Sexton, Alice Walker, Sylvia Plath. I think I had a limited education, I think I had the education of someone my age, I was heavily influenced by the time that I came to reason, by the '60s and the '70s, so I think that it's limited. I think there is a lot of literature in the world that I would think great if I had the opportunity to be exposed to it. I think my education is limited like most Americans, and polarized by race and class like most Americans. [Note: *I resisted commenting on this last point about racial polarization. I almost felt compelled to tell him that I have read and appreciate the black writers that he mentions, so that he does not continue to think I am simply the product of a narrow-minded "white education." I am still feeling judged by him at this point. It is interesting to note that the African American interview subject has more power at this moment than the white interviewer, because I am concerned that he is lumping me together with all other white people, and I would like to have the chance to convince him otherwise. I suppress these thoughts and move on.*]

KCD: Other than novels, is that primarily the kind of culture that you enjoy most? Do you go to films?

CG: I go to films and movies, I like poetry, I watch TV, I take in everything. How it moves me is how I assign value to it. I like Hawthorne. I'll give you an example. The first time I came to DC was 1993 and I came for the Gay and Lesbian march. I came with a group of men of color from Detroit. That's the first time I ever saw this city. The next real time I came was the Million Man march. I saw a lot in that march. First of all, and I think this was the experience of a lot of people, I had never been with that many black men before, and I had never seen myself from that perspective before. I had never felt so much peace before. At the march I saw all these weird things. I saw this white man with his two sons who were black, and I was reading in the paper later how his sons were embarrassed of him. I saw the socialists there in support of the march. I saw a stream of Japanese school girls in plaid dresses weaving through. Our identities. . . and this refers back to the film and the two characters . . . our identities are much more complex than we see, we would just flatten them out to be. That [his answer to the question] is kind of stream of consciousness.

KCD: Is this novel and film a good example of your tastes?

CG: Yes.

KCD: Not Arnold Schwartzenegger movies? [laugh] *[Note: I am joking now to try to get back to the easy rapport of the first half of the interview.]*

CG: I actually like him a lot. I don't know why I like him, I think he's funny. I wasn't expecting to like him. My friends would kill me if they knew, but I do.

KCD: How do you define and describe your sexuality—are you gay, straight, queer, lesbian, bi, transgender, transsexual, etc.? How and when did you come to identify yourself in this way? How important is your sexuality to your sense of yourself?

CG: I'm a black gay man. Probably I was close to the age of 30 when I identified myself as such. I think it's very important only in the sense that I want people to know that one can be human and be those things. I think all three of those things are despised a lot in this country now. To call me a black man would not be to define me clearly, to call me a gay man is not to define me very clearly, to call me a man says very little about the other two. Those three categories are not seen as being of any value in this culture. I don't think that most people value gay men, and they certainly don't value gay black men. It's very important to me that those things are lovable, that one should take a gay black man out to lunch, for people to find out about them and their humanity. [Note: *I smile here, to communicate that I value black gay men. It is interesting that he may be alluding to our own meeting (in a coffee shop) as just such a conversation, an experience of both difference and sameness (as he references shared "humanity").*]

KCD: Do you usually behave in a predominantly feminine or masculine way, or do you see yourself as having both stereotypically masculine and feminine qualities? Please define what you mean by "masculine" and "feminine" qualities.

CG: I think I can't help but to see things as a man in this culture. I don't think I have much of a choice with that. I think I like to play with gender. I have a friend in Detroit who calls me and says "Hey girl, what's going on?" And with some of my friends we call guys she. To me that's liberating. I used to have a performance troupe in Detroit and we used to perform in skirts. And I've never really cross-dressed but I'm trying to be free, I'm trying to be freer. I think I don't have a lot of choices, though, I think the die was cast before I even knew what was happening. They looked at what I had and they said, this is a boy. They had decided at birth what I was going to be and what was right for someone like me.

KCD: Do you think gender is more of a question of socialization and not biology?

CG: Expression of gender, yes, it's socialization.

KCD: Do you feel that sexuality is more influenced by biology or socialization?

CG: Sexual identity to me is as personal as a signature. I think there's a regime of doctors at work since the late 19th century who decided that we must be all of one thing for the good of the country. I don't think I have much choice in being gay, and I don't think that Molina has much choice until he realizes that he has a lot of choices. I like the word queer although I've been almost chased out of party for referring to myself as queer. I think a lot of queer men are questioning and interrogating gender and themselves and their decisions and how they view women. The interesting thing about Molina is that he sees himself as the type of woman that a lot of drag queens identify and hallucinate about. Those are not really women; those are men's constructs of women. They are really a male notion of what a whore would be like—her hair, the clothes. But that's not a real woman. A transgendered woman does not represent herself that way, like a drag queen. They are both trying for different things. Drag queens are extremely masculine; their notion of the woman, the kept woman, the whore, is a male fantasy. It has nothing to do with woman. I remember talking to some young drag queens in Detroit and they had these old-fashioned 19th-century notions of women being fountains of purity. And all their ideas of women were actually kept whores and harlots, even their beauty was brought by men's power and wealth, and not intrinsic of the women themselves. When we look at Marilyn Monroe do we really see her, or do we see the studios behind her that dyed her hair, that put all the women to work for hours to sew the gowns, or the makeup man or all the lights. If we look at her, like in the foreground we see all these men, men, men, men, making decisions on what a woman should look like.

CG: Aren't those the women that Molina wants to be like?

KCD: From the beginning, but not towards the end. He realizes in the process of the transformation that that notion of woman is a problem, and he doesn't internalize it. His choices just become different. He realizes that that is a problem, only so much that it stops him from being fully himself or understanding himself. It has to go. It starts out that he wants to be these women, but he actually unmakes that as he tells the movies.

KCD: What are your attitudes towards feminism? What do you think feminism is?

CG: I have a lot of admiration for feminism. There are so many different expressions of feminism, and it has gotten a bad sort of spin on it. It's more from people who look at the women who agitate as the women usurping power, but I think it's much more powerful than that. I think that the power of women has for many years been usurped by men, and their sexuality has been used for the purpose of glorifying men.

KCD: Even drag queens.

CG: I think that even drag queens know that they are men. That's part of their lure and glamour, which is different from a transgendered woman. What do I think of feminism? I think it's really good. I think it means many different things. How a Latina in South America may express her feminism or her sense of being empowered is quite different from a woman in Nigeria or who grew up on the upper west side of NY. But I think that I'm a man too, and I'm not someone who can sit here and comfortably talk about what I think feminism is, because I don't want to betray it. I want to respect it.

KCD: How would you describe your politics in general? What kinds of political issues are most important to you?

CG: OK, I've been in DC less than two years and I haven't been very active here at all. I'm from Detroit. I belong to this group of black gay men, we meet every year from all over the country. Most of us are social workers like I am. I work for Whitman/Walker clinic. Most of my gay black friends are social workers. I worked for the Crockett for Congress campaign, who was the first black man who was elected from the 13th district. A white woman actually gave me 10,000 dollars to finish school and to travel around the country; I love her dearly. It's kind of hard to define me. I don't know why I'm in Washington, I came here without a job and ended up with Whitman/Walker. My politics have to do with the different communities I belong to, the gay community, the black community, probably more black working class community. But also, since I'm college-educated, I'm from the black working class but I can't claim that perspective anymore. Also I see myself as just a basic American. I wouldn't really say that I'm a conventional Democrat or Republican. I'm not really a Marxist. I wouldn't really consider myself a political activist. I think I'm interested in those things, and I get ideas about them especially from my work. Also I'm a published poet, in national magazines, I've read before.

KCD: What are the subjects of your poems?

CG: It's just poetry. My book was about living and writing in Detroit.

KCD: I was just wondering how you got there from this question about politics.

CG: My poetry is part of the same thing. I think it's important that people express themselves.

KCD: So you see writing poetry as a political act?

CG: Exactly. I don't know how to separate a political act from writing poetry.

Appendix B

Transcript of an Interview for *The Piano* Case Study

Interview with "D.M." *(white female graduate student in literature)*

KCD: How many times have you seen *The Piano?*

DM: Twice.

KCD: Did you see it when it first came out in the theatre?

DM: No, I think I saw it on video for the first time. And then I rented it last night before meeting with you.

KCD: Have you ever discussed the film with friends, and was there disagreement or consensus about the film's merit or politics?

DM: I've actually never discussed it with any other women that I can think of. I've discussed it with my husband and he liked it as well. So actually we tended to agree more than disagree which is unusual because a lot of films that have a lot of gender issues we do tend to disagree. But it's actually kind of interesting that we agreed on this film.

KCD: Do you remember any emotions that you felt while watching the film? What evoked those responses?

DM: Probably fear and desire were the two primary ones. I found the scenes between Ada and Baines to be pretty erotic, especially where he is cleaning the piano with his shirt. I don't know why, call me weird, I do not have a thing for Harvey Keitel at all, but there was something very erotic about that scene for me. [KCD: That scene was actually Keitel's idea]. Was it really? I always thought of him as a cheesy actor, but he seemed to enter a totally different dimension in that film, which is really interesting. Fear, well, I guess the fear starts to mount as you realize that the husband is going to figure out what's going on, and when the daughter brings the piano key to the husband and there's that whole scene where he's coming back, the way he's walking and everything, and he's throwing her around, very much a kind of domestic violence scenario, and then when he chops her finger off, definitely pretty fearful. The other scene that stands out for me is the end when she is in the water going down. I wouldn't say that fear was the emotion, it was more like anxiety, I guess. I guess there's a real suspense about what's going to happen, the first time that you see it, because it's a movie that could quite plausibly end either with her dying or with her living, which almost any other film you can think of, you pretty much know whether the person is going to live or die. But with this one, you really don't know.

KCD: Did you have a different response from the first to the second viewing?

DM: I didn't have a radically different response. I think the second time I was paying more attention to the daughter, and being really amazed for being such a good actress. And just that whole dynamic of her and all the conflicts that she's acting out. The first time I was focused on the Ada/Baines relationship and the second time on the daughter.

KCD: What is the film saying about sexuality, in your view? Are the film's "sexual politics" radical or conservative, or somewhere in between? Could you talk more about your reaction to Ada and Baines's relationship, and also to the sexually charged scenes with Ada and Stewart?

DM: I guess I have some ambivalent feelings about it, because he does set her up to be a whore and he says that, and so, I don't like films with whores. Like for instance, *Pretty Woman*, I just had the hugest problems with it, because of the whole scenario, the whole prostitute with a heart of gold thing. I don't know, I just have a lot of problems with that, and with what that means for the position of women in our culture—that the romantic heroine is a prostitute.

KCD: Do you think of Ada as being in the position of a prostitute?

DM: But see I don't; it's different. And maybe this is just some weird S&M thing or something, but somehow it seemed like it's ironic, because he puts her in that position, yet he is actually the way that she gets out of the position that she was in to begin with, of being basically sold by her father to this man, and to me that's the gender paradigm that she actually escapes through the relationship with Baines. So I don't see the relationship with Baines as replicating her father or her husband in any way. But it is ironic, because he does set her up totally as sexual object, and it's a very voyeurism, exhibitionism thing where he's watching her, and he says "hike your skirt up" and all that stuff. But it's just so fascinating to me at the same time because it's totally different from pornographic stuff that I've seen. You could definitely call it erotica, but it does not follow the formulas of any pornography that I've ever seen. Firstly, because it's so slow, it's not like "Ok, let's fuck now," it's this thing that evolves over time. Secondly, I guess, because it is so tied into her artistic life as well, that what he's in love with or desires isn't even really so much her body as the soul that comes out through the music that she's playing. And then because at a certain point, and I don't know if I can even say what point it is, it starts to become as erotic for her as it is for him, kind of against her own will maybe, yet it does. To get into the language of the gaze, even though originally she was the object of his gaze, within the context of the film, he becomes at least as much of an object of the viewer's gaze, particularly the scene in which he's naked, which is totally focusing the gaze on the male body, and interestingly a male body that isn't really all that attractive in a conventional sense and yet it comes across that way very much so in that scene. And even in the scenes where they are actually naked together, it doesn't focus on her body anymore. It's both of their bodies that are being focused on. And another thing about the sex, too, is the scene where she comes back and then she hits him and is taking all her clothes off, and then the husband comes and the dog licks the hand and that whole thing, which is really funny. It's interesting that the first thing he does sexually is he gets up under her dress. To me that was very different from a kind of conventional scripted sex scene, because he is giving her pleasure. The first thing that happens is that he tries to give her pleasure, it's not like, "I'm going to stick my penis in you now." He's kneeling down and she's standing, and she's the one who's enjoying it.

KCD: What do you think about Stewart and Ada?

DM: I find that very interesting too, because she's basically torturing him. That is an S&M thing undoubtedly; she's being sadistic to this man. I wouldn't say I find that erotic in the same way as the scenes with Baines, but it is a kind of . . . she has the power in those scenes and that is an important reversal from most sex scenes that get portrayed in film or in literature. She's the one who's in control. She says STOP or he backs off, and it's kind of interesting that he does. You would think that he would go right on ahead. And then the scene too where after he cuts her finger off and he decides he's going to rape her while she's asleep, and then she opens her eyes and looks at him, and he just backs right off. [KCD: the evil eye?] Exactly, it's funny that you say that because my husband, part of what I'm writing about in my dissertation is the image of medusa and the kind of gaze, and my husband has read some of the stuff, and we were watching it last night and he said, "she's medusa!" at that moment, which is kind of the whole evil eye thing.

KCD: Do you think this is a feminist film, and how might you define feminist in the context of film?

DM: See I do, absolutely, and I'm really surprised that anyone could construe it as misogynist. To me it's one of the few, maybe the only film I've ever seen that explores women's erotic desires from their own point of view rather than from a male point of view. To me it's definitely clear in the beginning of the film that she is so caught in this patriarchy that is totally alien to her, and that she can barely function in, and the fact that she chooses not to talk, to me it just symbolizes the fact that she is so alienated that she can hardly participate in this society. And obviously the piano is the one way for her to communicate. It seems to me that her relationship with Baines becomes her way out of that, and her way of exploring her own sexuality, or I guess recovering, because you get hints that she did have a pleasurable sexual relationship with her daughter's father, but you don't really know what the deal was with that. But it definitely seems like Baines becomes her release from the father and the husband. It's ironic that it is brought about by this prostitution scenario, yet it is her pleasure. And I think you have to allow her that. In my dissertation I talked a lot about this concept of rapture in Petrarch, this pleasing rape, the male poet puts himself in a position where he's being ravished or raped by the beloved and yet he enjoys that. You know, I obviously say there are a lot of problems with this, because rape is not enjoyable; it's an awful thing. But at the same time one of my advisors kept trying to say to me that you have to consider the fact, and I go into all this S&M stuff too, that there are women who find a fantasy of such a scenario erotic. The point I think she's making is that you can't judge other people's sexual desire and if it's politically correct then it's OK, but if it doesn't match your idea of what's politically correct, then it's not OK. I think that happens a lot. It's really unfair to judge what should turn anybody on, I think. For women, particularly, because their sexuality has been so controlled and so prohibited, then what the heck, if it turns her on, it turns her on. Why shut that down because it should be some better scenario?

KCD: You mentioned a little bit about Ada's silence, and that you think it symbolizes some kind of resistance to patriarchy. What do you think about her attempts to speak at the end of the film?

DM: I wish that that wasn't there. I didn't like that whole last scene. I think the film should've ended with her coming back up out of the water, because it's kind of a recuperation into legitimate society. It's cheesy. The one thing I do like about the last scene is the metal finger and the way it makes a little tapping noise on the piano. I like that because it seems that she had to lose something to get free, and what she lost was the finger, and that loss is not something that can really be replaced. The fact that it is very artificial, it does replace it, and that you can hear that, I think really does symbolize that this loss is going to stay with her, and that she had to lose—it's like an animal in a trap, and the animal has to chew off their leg or whatever. That loss stays with you. I thought that that was good. But the fact that she starts to speak, I just don't think so. It just seems likes Baines took her for what she was without the speech. That's who she was; that's who she was for her daughter; that's who she was for herself; that's who she was for Baines. Nobody needed her to start to speak. It kind of turns her into this regular old boring person. She was much more interesting when she didn't speak. I don't like that black veil that she wears at the end. There's all this black and white symbolism through the whole film. She wore the white veil when she came originally, and the black veil is funereal. It really does kind of qualify what I saw as the liberation that she did achieve. It's almost like she's been shrouded again. I think it's interesting too that as she regains her speech she covers her face, like to gain one she has to lose the other. Because her face is so important through the whole film, as an expressive force. So I didn't like that at the end.

KCD: What do you think about the final scene that comes right after that, the shot of her "lullaby" where she imagines herself down with her piano?

DM: I don't know, I almost think that Jane Campion seriously considered ending the film that way.

KCD: You're right—she did initially.

DM: Oh, really, that's interesting. Because it really does seem like that was a very plausible ending, and it is kind of postmodern that she does give both of the two endings. But I wouldn't have wanted it to end that way actually. I liked the fact that . . . [KCD: that she rose to the top?] Yes, and that obviously was kind of a rebirth scene, very much. That's interesting too, because the men in that scene become very maternal; they are almost like the midwives pulling her out of the water, as she is being given birth to. I really liked that scene. I think the thing about the lullaby, I think it's almost like that is her . . . like her finger, it's a part of herself that she had to lose. The thing that's under the sea is a part of her that she had to lose. And I think the fact that she was really so ambivalent and could go either way about whether to live or die kind of qualifies the liberation which she does achieve, because if she really could go either way, then is this all as great as it's supposed to be?

KCD: But yet you still feel that it's liberating?

DM: Yes, I do, but a liberation that entails having to lose certain things.

KCD: What do you think about the film's racial politics, particularly the treatment of the Maoris, and of Baines's ambiguous racial identification?

DM: Yeah, I don't like it; I think it's definitely a *Heart of Darkness* kind of thing. I was thinking about that last night actually, that having to align him with the natives in order to make him sexual is just kind of a pretty low device. For me, that's not what was erotic about him anyway. She could have not done that, and it still would have functioned the same. So I think the husband being a representative of civilization and Baines being a representative of the primitive was really heavy-handed and not necessary.

KCD: Do you think that Ada is an artist? And what about at the end of the film? Critic bell hooks has bemoaned that Ada loses her artistry in the ending scenes.

DM: I do think she's an artist, and I think she's still an artist at the end, too. I guess the fact that she's a piano teacher undercuts that in some way, but the fact that she decided to get rid of the piano I don't think meant that she decided to get rid of her art. [KCD: That's what bell hooks argues.] I can see that argument, but I don't think that's that what it means in the context of the film. I think it has more to do with letting go of the past, and trying to find a new beginning. The piano is tainted and it's baggage that she's been carrying around for a long time. That's what she has to let go. I think too that it was almost like a mask that she wore, and it's much harder to go through life without that kind of a mask. So it's almost like she's saying, "OK, I can just have me, I'm still me without the piano," whereas before without the piano she was not even a self; she couldn't even exist without it. On the other hand, another thing I'm writing about in my dissertation is the way that the myth of Sappho contrasts with the Petrarch thing, because Sappho and Petrarch are both masochistic enraptured love poets, but the difference is that Petrarch gets to live and be famous, and in the myth of Sappho as people told it, she jumps off a cliff after she loses her lover, and she basically has to sacrifice her art for her love. So there definitely is this pattern of the woman artist who can't love and be an artist at the same time.

KCD: You see a little bit of that in this film, but you wouldn't ultimately place it in that lineage?

DM: Right, yeah, I wouldn't. I would say again about the metal finger, it's like she still has her art, but it's an art that isn't the same as it was before. I think too that people, not artists, critics maybe, have a way of thinking that the artist's art should be the most important thing for the artist, but if you're the artist yourself, then you want a life too. It's not really fair for everybody else to say that. I think she's trying to have both at the end. Maybe it's not perfect, but to think that she should have just stayed miserable and lonely with her piano for the rest of her life isn't really a fair explanation to her.

KCD: A couple of questions about you and your own feminist politics. Do you think that your gender of sexual orientation affected your response to the film?

DM: Definitely, because I think it set up a total identification between myself and Ada, and I certainly sympathized myself with her particularly, having been sold by her father and then a husband who was so totally stupid and unresponsive, nothing that she could identify or connect with in any way. I definitely identified with that.

KCD: And you mentioned that you found it erotic, in a specifically heterosexual way.

DM: Well, yes, definitely.

KCD: Could you briefly define your own feminist views? What ideas or people best represent feminism for you? Do you see yourself as politically radical or more mainstream?

DM: I would say I'm pretty radical. I got dumped by one dissertation advisor because I was too radical. I'm trying to think in terms of French vs. American feminism, where I would put myself. I think I'm a pragmatic feminist in the sense of what is going to be of benefit to actual women rather than theoretically what should happen, but I think that I'm also extremely aware particularly of issues of sexual violence, which is what I focus on in my dissertation. The fact that women have been so controlled sexually to the point that they don't even know what their sexuality is, and it has been defined by men so much. That's the thing I like about the film, that at least this is one woman trying to redefine what sexuality could be for her. I went to a talk a couple of years ago with the title, "Is there such a thing as feminist pornography?" It was interesting because almost everybody there was like, Hell no, there couldn't be, because pornography is just inherently evil and sexist in and of itself. And then one woman was trying to say, but well wait a minute, maybe representations of sexuality and sexual desire aren't bad in and of themselves. Maybe it's the ones that have been available to us. And I guess I kind of agreed with her, that that was possible.

KCD: What do you think about the anti-pornography movement as represented by people like Catherine McKinnon and Andrea Dworkin? You've already said that you don't think that this film is pornographic, but could you talk about your feelings about the larger movement to censor or control pornography?

DM: I guess I have a lot of mixed feelings about it, but ultimately I don't think it's a good idea. I don't think that trying to eradicate pornography is a good idea. I think that what needs to happen is that society needs to change to the point that images of women being hurt or dominated would no longer be erotic, but I think that trying to get rid of representations of sexuality is a bad idea, even if you don't like what's being represented. Because it has got to be the most personal and the most individual thing, and it just seems like one person's idea of it, whatever that idea is, shouldn't be everybody's idea. Except I mean obviously children, I would draw the line there. But if you want to start drawing lines, then there would be people saying that there should be no depictions of homosexual sexuality. I guess I'm just for sexuality not being governed by anybody from the left or the right, because I think that it's a dangerous trend. But on the other hand, I do see and agree with points that people have made about the ways that pornography, as most of it is these days, objectifies women. For young teenage boys, this is their first exposure. It does set up a pattern that I'm not too happy with, but that pattern isn't going to change if you get rid of pornography, I don't think. I think that pornography reinforces something that's already there, rather than vice versa. I think there's got to be other ways.

KCD: I'm wondering what you think of recent writers like Camille Paglia and Katie Roiphe, who react against a feminism that treats women as victims. They are reacting against the anti-pornography movement in a sense. What do you think of their ideas?

DM: I don't like them, but I think it's good that they exist. I don't agree with them, and I think I'd get really mad if I actually talked to them. I think they are both useful and dangerous at the same time. I think that it really is important for women to stop thinking of themselves as victims, and if we think of ourselves that way then we are going to keep in that position. But on the other hand, it really kind of feeds the fire of the right wing, as you get into this rhetoric of "Oh, women are somehow complicit in their own rapes." That's just not true. I mean rape is rape; there is no complicity definitionally in that. Paglia is kind of a gadfly that stirs things up a little bit, and forces people who I probably would agree with more to consider what they are saying and to make sure that they're not going overboard, so that they can perfect their positions better through her criticisms.

KCD: Could you talk a little bit about how you became feminist, and when? Was it through reading academic or popular texts, or through activism or personal experience?

DM: That's a very interesting question to me personally. I came to feminism very late. When I was in high school I was not a feminist; when I was in college, I was not a feminist. I think I started to turn towards feminism in the last year of my undergraduate years at college. And I'm trying to think why that was. I think maybe it was just the process of getting older and seeing how things really were in the world. I went into therapy because I had a really rough time with my relationship with my boyfriend. Even though my therapist was not much of a feminist, I think that once I started to talk about those issues actually, which I had never really talked about with anybody, I think that started to get me on that path. I really think actually that that's what it was, going into therapy and looking at my own life and what had happened.

KCD: Did you start defining yourself as feminist from that moment? Do you remember when you decided to openly call yourself that?

DM: Probably not for another year or so after that, and I think that I adopted the term after I did start to do some reading. I read de Beauvoir's *The Second Sex*. That was one of the first things that I read in my first year in my M.A. I think at that point I did start getting into academic feminism, and that became important to me. Also, my senior year I had a female professor who was teaching a class in nineteenth-century women writers and she was not a real gung-ho feminist. Starting to think in terms of women's writing was important for me.

KCD: Do you see *The Piano* in relation to those nineteenth-century texts?

DM: I see it as being very contemporary and not very nineteenth century at all. Nothing I read in the nineteenth century could have come up with a lot of the stuff that's in that film, particularly the focus on Harvey Keitel's body, which wouldn't have happened. The male body was not represented in that way. That's one of the things that I'm writing about right now. The male poets described women's bodies, but the women poets who adopt a lot of the same rhetoric are describing their own bodies, not the bodies of the male beloved. How many descriptions of bodies of men do you see?

KCD: Is there anything more that you'd like to add, about the film or your own feminism?

DM: The anti-pornography movement is kind of an antithesis to the oppressive order. To me, a better way to go is to find a third way that doesn't just construct itself through opposition to what was before. But then again the danger of postmodern deconstruction is that we get into a kind of "everything goes" scenario, which undercuts any kind of change or opposition. But I don't see the *Piano* as being a deconstructive mishmash.

Appendix C

Questionnaire for the *Northern Exposure* Fan-club

Part One: Information about Your Viewing Practices and Participation in the Newsgroup

1. How regularly do you watch *Northern Exposure*? a. Every episode, b. Every other episode, c. Once a month, d. Occasionally (a few per season), e. Rarely
2. Which seasons have you watched regularly, at least half of the episodes? Choose as many as are appropriate. a. First season (Summer of 1990), b. Second season (Spring of 1991), c. Third season (Fall 1991–Spring 1992), d. Fourth season (Fall 1992–Spring 1993), e. Fifth season (Fall 1993–Spring 1994), f. Sixth and final season (Fall 1994–Summer 1995)
3. Are you watching reruns in syndication? a. yes, b. no
4. Do you videotape episodes and save them? a. yes, b. no
5. Do you watch every moment of each episode you have tuned in to, or do you miss some of it due to distractions or other activities you are doing at the same time? a. Watch every moment attentively, b. Miss 1 or 2 minutes, c. Miss 5 minutes, d. Miss 10–15 minutes, e. Miss more than half of the show. If you answered d or e, what other things are you doing while watching?
6. What other television programs (both prime-time and daytime) do you watch regularly? (List up to 10.)
7. What are your favorite television programs that are no longer on the air, or are no longer producing original episodes? (List up to 5.)
8. Do you post to the newsgroup? If yes, how frequently?
9. As a reader of the newsgroup, do you find yourself usually disagreeing or agreeing with the views expressed in the posts? a. Agree wholeheartedly, b. Generally agree, disagree with only a few posts, c. Agree with half, disagree with half, d. Generally disagree, agree with only a few posts, e. Strongly disagree
10. What is your general impression of the newsgroup? What is their attitude toward the show?

Part Two: Attitudes and Opinions about *Northern Exposure*

Numbers 11, 12, and 19 are crucial to my research. Please answer these questions with as much detail as possible.

*11. What are your three favorite episodes? (If you don't know the titles, just give a brief summary.) Please explain your preferences in detail.

*12. Does the show ever move you emotionally? What emotions did you feel while watching? Can you remember which episodes or scenes sparked these emotions?

13. Who are your two favorite characters (regular or occasional)? Why do they appeal to you?

14. From the following list, which qualities of *Northern Exposure* contribute most to your enjoyment of the show? Please rank your top 10, with 1 being the most important. a. Native American cultural themes, b. Quirky cast of characters, c. Poignant happy endings, d. Literary and philosophical references, e. Joel and Maggie's relationship, f. Religious themes (Judaism, Catholicism, New-Age spirituality), g. Magical realism/fantasy ("sleep flying," Arthur the bear/man), h. Humor and wit, i. Intellectual themes, j. Sense of community, k. Frontier theme, Alaskan setting, l. Dream sequences, m. Parodies of films, literature, and other TV shows, n. Randomly weird events (like "The Fling"), o. Ironic juxtaposition of events, p. Frank discussion of sexuality, q. Interwoven sub-plots, r. Non-stereotypical roles, s. Character growth, psychological development, t. Mixing of cultures, u. Other (explain):

15. Is *Northern Exposure* similar to or different from other television programs (particularly hour-long series)? For example, how would you compare it to *thirtysomething*, *Twin Peaks* or *Picket Fences* (or any other show of your own choosing)?

16. Which type of interaction between Joel and Maggie do you prefer? Please rank them 1–5, with 1 being the most preferred. a. J and M fight verbally, romance and friendship thwarted, b. J and M are friends, little sexual or romantic tension, c. J and M express physical attraction, not romantic (Episodes: "It Happened in Juneau," "Our Wedding," "Ill Wind," "Love's Labour Mislaid"), d. J and M express romantic attraction (most of season 5 and early 6th), e. J and M maintain friendship after he moves to the outback.

17. Do you prefer romantic episodes, or anti-romantic episodes in which romance is thwarted, ill-fated, or a relationship seems purely sexual? (Anti-romantic episodes would include those in which Marilyn rejects the flying man, Ruth-Anne rejects the traveling salesman Gil, Heather rejects Ed, Michelle rejects Phil, Maggie rejects Joel, Barbara rejects Maurice.) Explain.

18. Which relationship do you prefer? Why? a. Joel and Maggie, b. Chris and Maggie

*19. Pick an episode that you have seen recently (or remember well) and explain what you think it was about. What were its main themes and messages? Which moments or plots stood out to you as significant? Please explain.

20. What do you think of Chris's philosophical monologues on KBHR? a. They

are the highlight of the show; I love them, b. I enjoy them most of the time, c. I dislike them; they are annoying, d. I ignore them; they are unimportant to the show, e. I don't understand them.

21. Are you familiar with the term "postmodern"? If so, do you think *Northern Exposure* is postmodern? Why or why not?
22. Do you think *Northern Exposure* is progressive or conservative on the following topics? 1 very progressive, 2 progressive, 3 moderate, 4 conservative, 5 very conservative; a. homosexuality, b. gender, c. race, d. religion, e. sexual themes in general
23. In particular, do you consider the show to be feminist, or not? Please explain what feminism means to you.
24. Why do you think the show slipped in the ratings and was cancelled? For each possible explanation (a–i), choose one of the following responses: 1 strongly disagree, 2 agree, 3 unsure, 4 disagree, 5 strongly disagree. a. Bad time slot and day, b. Rob Morrow's departure, c. Show became too sentimental, d. Phil and Michelle plots uninteresting, e. Acting went downhill, f. Writing and plots went downhill, g. Chris and Maggie's romance, h. Show became less intellectual, i. CBS mismanagement, j. Other (explain)
25. How did you feel when you heard the show was cancelled?

Part Three: Information about You

Note: This information will be treated as strictly confidential and names will not be used in the research report.

26. What is your gender? M or F
27. What is your race or ethnic group? a. African American, b. Asian American, c. Latino, d. Native American, e. White, f. Other (explain):
28. If you are not a United States citizen, please list your nationality.
29. What is your age?
30. What is your religion?
31. What is your marital status? a. Single, b. Married, c. Living with partner
32. Occupational category: a. Full-time paid employment, b. Part-time paid employment, c. Student, d. Working in the home or childrearing, e. Unemployed, f. A combination of these (please specify)

    If you work full or part time, please list your job position. If you live with a spouse or partner, please list his or her job position.
33. At what age did you leave school? Please list any educational degrees earned or in progress.
34. What is your political party affiliation? a. Democrat, b. Republican, c. Independent, d. Other (please specify)
35. What kind of housing do you live in? a. Rented apartment, b. Owned condo or apartment, c. Single family home, rented, d. Single family home, owned, e. Other (explain):

Works Cited

Acker, Kathy. *In Memoriam to Identity*. New York: Grove P, 1990.

Adorno, Theodor, and Max Horkeimer. "The Culture Industry: Enlightenment as Mass Deception." *The Dialectic of Enlightenment*. London: Verso, 1979. 120–67.

Allen, Dennis. "Lesbian and Gay Studies: A Consumer's Guide." *The Gay '90s: Disciplinary and Interdisciplinary Formations in Queer Studies*. Ed. Thomas C. Foster, Carol Siegel, and Ellen E. Berry. New York: New York UP, 1997. 23–50.

Andringa, Els, Ed Tan, Petra van Horssen, and Astrid Jacobs. "Effects of Focalization in Film Narrative." *The Systemic and Empirical Approach to Literature as Theory and Application*. Ed. Steven Tötösy de Zepetnek and Irene Sywenky. Edmonton: U of Alberta; Siegen: Siegen U, 1997. 203–09.

Ang, Ien. *Desperately Seeking the Audience.* London: Routledge, 1991.

Ang, Ien. *Living Room Wars: Rethinking Media Audiences for a Postmodern World.* New York: Routledge, 1996.

Ang, Ien. "Wanted: Audiences. On the Politics of Empirical Audience Studies." *Remote Control: Television, Audiences, and Cultural Power.* Ed. Ellen Seiter, Hans Borchers, Gabriele Greutzner, and Eva-Marie Warth. London: Routledge, 1989. 96–115.

Ang, Ien. *Watching Dallas.* New York: Methuen, 1985.

Arato, Andrew, and Eike Gebhart, eds. *The Essential Frankfurt School Reader*. New York: Urizen Books, 1978.

Babuscio, Jack. "Camp and the Gay Sensibility." *Camp Grounds: Style and Homosexuality.* Ed. David Bergman. Amherst: U of Massachusetts P, 1993. 19–38.

Bacarisse, Pamela. *Impossible Choices: The Implications of the Cultural References in the Novels of Manuel Puig*. Calgary: U of Calgary P, 1993.

Bacarisse, Pamela. *The Necessary Dream: A Study of the Novels of Manuel Puig.* Cardiff: U of Wales P, 1988.

Baldwin, James. "Everybody's Protest Novel." *The Norton Anthology of African American Literature.* Ed. Henry Louis Gates, Jr., and Nellie McKay. New York: W.W. Norton, 1997. 1654–59.

Barthes, Roland. *The Pleasure of the Text*. Trans. Richard Miller. New York: Hill and Wang, 1975.

Barthes, Roland. *S/Z*. Trans. Richard Miller. New York: Hill and Wang, 1974.

Baudrillard, Jean. "After Utopia: The Primitive Society of the Future." *At Century's End: Great Minds Reflect on Our Times.* Ed. Nathan P. Gardels. La Jolla: ALTI Publishing, 1995. 214–20.

Baudrillard, Jean. "The Masses: The Implosion of the Social in the Media." *Jean Baudrillard: Selected Writings*. Ed. Mark Poster. Stanford: Stanford UP, 1988. 207–19.

Baudrillard, Jean. *Seduction*. Trans. Brian Singer. New York: St. Martin's P, 1990.

Baudrillard, Jean. *Simulacra and Simulations.* Trans. Paul Foss, Paul Patton, and Philip Beitchman. New York: Sémiotext(e), 1983.

Baudrillard, Jean. *The Transparency of Evil: Essays on Extreme Phenomena.* Trans. James Benedict. New York: Verso, 1993.

Bell, Daniel. *The Coming of the Post-Industrial Society.* New York: Basic Books, 1973.

Bell, Daniel. "The Cultural Contradictions of Capitalism." *The Public Interest* 21 (1970): 16–43.

Benjamin, Jessica. *The Bonds of Love: Psychoanalysis, Feminism, and the Problem of Domination.* New York: Pantheon Books, 1988.

Benjamin, Jessica. *Shadow of the Other: Intersubjectivity and Gender in Psychoanalysis*. New York: Routledge, 1998.

Benjamin, Walter. "The Work of Art in the Age of Mechanical Reproduction." *The Critical Tradition: Classic Texts and Contemporary Trends*. Ed. David Richter. New York: St. Martin's P, 1989. 571–88.

Bergman, David. "Introduction." *Camp Grounds: Style and Homosexuality.* Ed. David Bergman. Amherst: U of Massachusetts P, 1993. 5–18.

Berlant, Lauren. "Poor Eliza." *American Literature* 70.3 (1998): 635–68.

Berlant, Lauren. *The Queen of America Goes to Washington City: Essays on Sex and Citizenship.* Durham: Duke UP, 1997.

Berlant, Lauren. "The Subject of True Feeling: Pain, Privacy, and Politics." *Cultural Pluralism, Identity Politics, and the Law.* Ed. Austin Stuart and Thomas Kearns. Ann Arbor: U of Michigan P, 1999. 49–84.

Bersani, Leo. *Homos.* Cambridge: Cambridge UP, 1995.

Best, Steven, and Douglas Kellner. *Postmodern Theory: Critical Interrogations*. New York: The Guilford P, 1991.

Bobo, Jacqueline. *Black Women as Cultural Readers.* New York: Columbia UP, 1995.

Bordo, Susan. "Feminism, Postmodernism, and Gender-Scepticism." *Feminism / Postmodernism.* Ed. Linda J. Nicholson. New York: Routledge, 1990. 133–56.

Bordwell, David, Janet Staiger, and Kristin Thompson. *The Classical Hollywood Cinema: Film Style and Mode of Production to 1960.* London: Routledge and Kegan Paul; New York: Columbia UP, 1985.

Bourdieu, Pierre. "The Aristocracy of Culture." *Media, Culture, and Society* 2.3 (1980): 225–54.

Bourdieu, Pierre. *Distinction: A Social Critique of the Judgement of Taste.* Trans. R. Nice. Cambridge: Harvard UP, 1984.

Bourdieu, Pierre. *On Television.* Trans. Priscilla Parkhurst Ferguson. New York: The New P, 1998.

Bourdieu, Pierre, and Alain Darbel. *The Love of Art: European Art Museums and Their Public.* Trans. Caroline Beattie and Nick Merriman. Stanford: Stanford UP, 1990.

Brooks, Peter. *The Melodramatic Imagination: Balzac, Henry James, Melodrama and the Mode of Excess.* New Haven: Yale UP, 1976.

Bruzzi, Stella. "Tempestuous Petticoats: Costume and Desire in *The Piano.*" *Screen* 36.3 (1995): 257–66.

Butler, Judith. *Bodies That Matter: On the Discursive Limits of "Sex."* New York: Routledge, 1993.

Butler, Judith. *Gender Trouble: Feminism and the Subversion of Identity.* New York: Routledge, 1990.

Byars, Jackie. *All That Hollywood Allows: Rereading Gender in 1950s Melodrama.* Chapel Hill: U of North Carolina P, 1991.

Byars, Jackie. "Feminism, Psychoanalysis, and Female-Oriented Melodramas of the 1950s." *Multiple Voices in Feminist Film Criticism.* Ed. Diane Carson, Linda Dittmar, and Janice R. Welsch. Minneapolis: U of Minnesota P, 1994. 93–108.

Christ, Ronald. "Interview with Manuel Puig." *Christopher Street* 3.9 (April 1979): 25–31.

Christian, Barbara. "The Race for Theory." *Feminist Studies* 14.1 (1988): 67–79.

Christie, Chris. "Theories of Textual Determination and Audience Agency: An Empirical Contribution to the Debate." *Gendering the Reader.* Ed. Sara Mills. London: Harvester Wheatsheaf, 1994. 47–66.

Chow, Rey. *Writing Diaspora: Tactics of Intervention in Contemporary Cultural Studies.* Bloomington and Indianapolis: Indiana UP, 1993.

Cixous, Hélène. "Sorties: Out and Out: Attacks/Ways Out/Forays." *The Newly Born Woman.* By Hélène Cixous and Catherine Clément. Trans. Betsy Wing. Intro. Sandra M. Gilbert. Minneapolis: U of Minnesota P, 1986. 63–132.

Clark, Kenneth R. "CBS Schedule Gives Alaska Some 'Exposure.'" *The Chicago Tribune* (8 July 1990): TV Week 3.

Clark, Suzanne. *Sentimental Modernism: Women Writers and the Revolution of the Word.* Bloomington: Indiana UP, 1991.

Clover, Carol J. *Men, Women, and Chain Saws: Gender in the Modern Horror Film.* Princeton: Princeton UP, 1992.

Colás, Santiago. *Postmodernity in Latin America: The Argentine Paradigm.* Durham: Duke UP, 1994.

Collins, Jim. "Television and Postmodernism." *Channels of Discourse, Reassembled: Television and Contemporary Criticism.* Ed. Robert C. Allen. Chapel Hill: U of North Carolina P, 1992. 327–51.

Collins, Jim. *Uncommon Cultures: Popular Culture and Post-Modernism.* New York: Routledge, 1989.

Collins, Jim, ed. *High-Pop: Making Culture into Popular Entertainment*. Oxford: Blackwell, 2002.

Corrigan, Timothy. *A Cinema without Walls: Movies and Culture after Vietnam*. New Brunswick: Rutgers UP, 1991.

Crane, Diana, Nobuko Kawashima, and Ken'ichi Kawasaki, eds. *Global Culture: Media, Arts, Policy, and Globalization*. New York: Routledge, 2002.

Crawford, Iain. "Reading TV: Intertextuality in *Northern Exposure*." *Mid-Atlantic Almanack* 3 (1994): 14–22.

Crawford, Mary, and Roger Chaffin. "The Reader's Construction of Meaning: Cognitive Research on Gender and Comprehension." *Gender and Reading: Essays on Readers, Texts, and Contexts*. Ed. Elizabeth Flynn and Patrocinio Schweickart. Baltimore: Johns Hopkins UP, 1986. 3–30.

Creed, Barbara. Untitled Entry. "Special Issue: The Spectatrix." *Camera Obscura* 20/21 (1990): 132–37.

Cvetkovich, Ann. *Mixed Feelings: Feminism, Mass Culture, and Victorian Sensationalism*. New Brunswick: Rutgers UP, 1992.

de Beaugrande, Robert. "Readers Responding to Literature: Coming to Grips with Realities." *Reader Response to Literature: The Empirical Dimension*. Ed. Elaine Nardocchio. Berlin: Mouton de Gruyter, 1992. 193–209.

Degli-Esposti, Cristina. "Postmodernism(s)." *Postmodernism in the Cinema*. Ed. Cristina Degli-Esposti. New York: Berghahn Books, 1998. 3–18.

Degli-Esposti, Cristina, ed. *Postmodernism in the Cinema*. New York: Berghahn Books, 1998.

Deigh, John. *The Sources of Moral Agency: Essays in Moral Psychology and Freudian Theory.* Cambridge: Cambridge UP, 1996.

De Lauretis, Teresa. *Alice Doesn't: Feminism, Semiotics, Cinema*. London: Macmillan, 1984.

Denzin, Norman K. *Images of Postmodern Society: Social Theory and Contemporary Cinema.* London: Sage, 1991.

Diawara, Manthia. "Black Spectatorship: Problems of Identification and Resistance." *Black American Cinema: Aesthetics and Spectatorship*. Ed. Manthia Diawara. New York: Routledge, 1993. 211–20.

Doane, Mary Ann. *The Desire to Desire: The Woman's Film of the 1940s*. Bloomington: Indiana UP, 1987.

Doane, Mary Ann. *Femmes Fatales: Feminism, Film Theory, Psychoanalysis.* New York: Routledge, 1991.

Doane, Mary Ann. Untitled article. *Camera Obscura* 20/21 (1990): 142–47.

Douglas, Ann. *The Feminization of American Culture.* New York: Knopf, 1978.

Dyer, Richard. "Entertainment and Utopia." *The Cultural Studies Reader*. Ed. Simon During. London: Routledge, 1993. 271–83.

Dyer, Richard. *Heavenly Bodies: Film Stars and Society*. New York: St. Martin's P, 1986.

Eco, Umberto. *The Role of the Reader: Explorations in the Semiotics of Texts.* Bloomington: Indiana UP, 1979.

Elsaesser, Thomas. "Tales of Sound and Fury: Observations on the Family Melodrama." *Home Is Where the Heart Is: Studies in Melodrama and the Woman's Film.* Ed. Christine Gledhill. London: BFI Publishing, 1987. 43–69.

Felski, Rita. *The Gender of Modernity.* Cambridge: Harvard UP, 1995.

Fetterley, Judith. *The Resisting Reader: A Feminist Approach to American Fiction.* Bloomington: Indiana UP, 1978.

Feuer, Jane. "Narrative Form in American Network Television." *High Theory/Low Culture: Analyzing Popular Television and Film.* Ed. Colin MacCabe. Manchester: Manchester UP, 1986. 101–14.

Feuer, Jane. *Seeing through the Eighties: Television and Reaganism.* Durham: Duke UP, 1995.

Feuer, Jane, Paul Kerr, and Tise Vahimagi, eds. *MTM: Quality Television.* London: BFI Publishing, 1984.

Fish, Stanley. *Is There a Text in This Class? The Authority of Interpretive Communities.* Cambridge: Harvard UP, 1980.

Fiske, John. *Understanding Popular Culture.* Boston: Unwin Hyman, 1989.

Foster, David William. *Sexual Textualities: Essays on Queer/ing Latin American Writing.* Austin: U of Texas P, 1997.

Foster, Hal. "Postmodernism: A Preface." *The Anti-Aesthetic: Essays on Postmodern Culture.* Ed. Hal Foster. New York: The New P, 1998. ix-xvi.

Foucault, Michel. "Preface." *Anti-Oedipus: Capitalism and Schizophrenia.* By Giles Deleuze and Félix Guattari. Trans. Robert Hurley, Mark Seem, and Helen R. Lane. Minneapolis: U of Minnesota P, 1983. xi-xiv.

Freud, Sigmund. "Femininity." *The Standard Edition of the Complete Psychological Works of Sigmund Freud.* Ed. and trans. James Strachey. London: Hogarth, 1955. 22: 112–35.

Freud, Sigmund. *Group Psychology and the Analysis of the Ego. The Standard Edition of the Complete Psychological Works of Sigmund Freud.* Ed. and trans. James Strachey. London: Hogarth, 1955. 18: 67–143.

Freud, Sigmund. *Totem and Taboo. The Standard Edition of the Complete Psychological Works of Sigmund Freud.* Ed. and trans. James Strachey. London: Hogarth, 1955. 13: 1–162.

Freundlieb, Dieter. "The Empirical Study of Literature. How Empirical Can It Be?" *Empirical Studies of the Arts* 7.2 (1989): 115–30.

Friedan, Betty. *The Feminine Mystique.* New York: Norton, 1963.

Friedberg, Anne. "A Denial of Difference: Theories of Cinematic Identification." *Psychoanalysis and Cinema.* Ed. E. Ann Kaplan. New York: Routledge, 1990. 36–45.

Friedberg, Anne. *Window Shopping: Cinema and the Postmodern.* Berkeley: U of California P, 1993.

Fuller, Graham. "The Wuthering Heights of Jane Campion's *The Piano*." *Interview* 23.10 (November 1993): 46.

Fuss, Diana. *Essentially Speaking: Feminism, Nature and Difference*. New York: Routledge, 1989.

Fuss, Diana. *Identification Papers*. New York: Routledge, 1995.

Gagnier, Regenia. "Further Reflections on Sympathetic Identification." *Rereading Texts/Rethinking Critical Presuppositions.* Ed. Shlomith Rimmon-Kenan, Leona Toker, and Shuli Barzilai. Frankfurt: Peter Lang, 1997. 163–75.

Gaines, Jane. "White Privilege and Looking Relations: Race and Gender in Feminist Film Theory." *Feminist Film Theory.* Ed. Sue Thornham. New York: New York UP, 1999. 196–209.

Gaines, Jane. "Women and Representation: Can We Enjoy Alternative Pleasures?" *Issues in Feminist Film Criticism*. Ed. Patricia Erens. Bloomington: Indiana UP, 1990. 75–92.

Gans, Herbert. *Popular Culture and High Culture: An Analysis and Evaluation of Taste*. 1974. New York: Basic Books, 1999.

Gates, Henry Louis, Jr. "Criticism in the Jungle." *Black Literature and Literary Theory*. Ed. Henry Louis Gates, Jr. New York: Methuen, 1984. 1–24.

Gaut, Berys. "Identification and Emotion in Narrative Film." *Passionate Views: Film, Cognition, and Emotion*. Ed. Carl Plantinga and Greg M. Smith. Baltimore: Johns Hopkins UP, 1999. 200–16.

Gillett, Sue. "Lips and Fingers: Jane Campion's *The Piano*." *Screen* 36.3 (1995): 277–87.

Gledhill, Christine. "The Melodramatic Field: An Investigation." *Home Is Where the Heart Is: Studies in Melodrama and the Woman's Film.* Ed. Christine Gledhill. London: BFI Publishing, 1987. 5–39.

Gledhill, Christine. "Pleasurable Negotiations." *Female Spectators: Looking at Film and Television*. Ed. Deidre Pribram. New York: Verso, 1988. 64–89.

Goodwin, Jeff, James M. Jasper, and Francesca Polletta, eds. *Passionate Politics: Emotions and Social Movements.* Chicago: U of Chicago P, 2001.

Gordon, Suzy. "'I Clipped Your Wing, That's All:' Auto-eroticism and the Female Spectator in *The Piano* Debate." *Screen* 37.2 (1996): 193–205.

Greenberg, Clement. "Avant-Garde and Kitsch." 1939. *Art and Culture: Critical Essays.* By Clement Greenberg. Boston: Beacon P, 1961. 3–21.

Grimshaw, Roger, Dorothy Hobson, and Paul Willis. "Introduction to Ethnography at the Centre." *Culture, Media, Language: Working Papers in Cultural Studies, 1972–79.* Ed. Stuart Hall, Dorothy Hobson, Andrew Lowe, and Paul Willis. London: Hutchinson, 1980. 73–77.

Grossberg, Lawrence. "Postmodernity and Affect: All Dressed Up with No Place to Go." *Communication* 10 (1988): 271–93.

Grossberg, Lawrence. "Putting the Pop Back into Postmodernism." *Universal Abandon? The Politics of Postmodernism.* Ed. Andrew Ross. Minneapolis: U of Minnesota P, 1988. 167–90.

Grossberg, Lawrence. *We Gotta Get Out of This Place: Popular Conservatism and Postmodern Culture*. New York: Routledge, 1992.

Grossberg, Lawrence. "On Postmodernism and Articulation: An Interview with Stuart Hall." *Journal of Communication Inquiry* 10.2 (1986): 45–60.

Gubar, Susan. *Racechanges: White Skin, Black Face in American Culture*. New York: Oxford UP, 1997.

Gullette, Margaret Morganroth. "*The Piano*: Imperfect Pitch." *The Boston Globe* (3 December 1993): 51, 59.

Habermas, Jürgen. *The Philosophical Discourse of Modernity.* Trans. Frederick G. Lawrence. Cambridge: MIT P, 1987.

Hakemulder, Jèmeljan. *The Moral Laboratory: Experiments Examining the Effects of Reading Literature on Social Perception and Moral Self-Concept*. Amsterdam: John Benjamins Publishing, 2000.

Halász, Lászl6. "Self-Relevant Reading in Literary Understanding." *Reader Response to Literature: The Empirical Dimension.* Ed. Elaine Nardocchio. New York: Mouton de Gruyter, 1992. 229–45.

Hall, John R. "The Capital(s) of Cultures: A Nonholistic Approach to Status Situations, Class, Gender, and Ethnicity." *Cultivating Differences: Symbolic Boundaries and the Making of Inequality.* Ed. Michèle Lamont and Marcel Fournier. Chicago: U of Chicago P, 1992. 257–85.

Hall, Stuart. "Encoding/Decoding." *Culture, Media, Language: Working Papers in Cultural Studies, 1972–79.* Ed. Stuart Hall, Dorothy Hobson, Andrew Lowe, and Paul Willis. London: Hutchinson, 1980. 128–38.

Hall, Stuart. "Notes on Deconstructing 'The Popular.'" *People's History and Socialist Theory.* Ed. Raphael Samuel. London: Routledge and Kegan Paul, 1981. 227–40.

Halliday, Jon. *Sirk on Sirk*. London: Seckker and Warburg, 1972.

Hansen, Miriam. *Babel and Babylon: Spectatorship in American Silent Film.* Cambridge: Harvard UP, 1991.

Hansen, Miriam. "Pleasure, Ambivalence, Identification: Valentino and Female Spectatorship." *Cinema Journal* 25.4 (1986): 6–32.

Hansen, Miriam. Untitled article. *Camera Obscura* 20/21 (1990): 169–74.

Haraway, Donna J. "A Cyborg Manifesto." *Simians, Cyborgs, and Women: The Reinvention of Nature*. By Donna J. Haraway. New York: Routledge, 1991. 149–81.

Haraway, Donna J. "Situated Knowledges: The Science Question in Feminism and the Privilege of Partial Perspective." *Simians, Cyborgs, and Women: The Reinvention of Nature*. By Donna J. Haraway. New York: Routledge, 1991. 183–201.

Harris, Mark, and Kelli Pryor. "Total Exposure." *Entertainment Weekly* (25 July 1991): <http://home.comcast.net/~mcnotes/TotalExposure.html>.

Harvey, David. *The Condition of Postmodernity*. Oxford: Basil Blackwell, 1989.

Harvey, Dennis. Rev. of *Kiss of the Spider Woman. PopcornQ: The Ultimate Home for the Queer Moving Image* (1996): <http://www.planetout.com/popcornq/db/getfilm.html?1938>.

Hassan, Ihab. *The Postmodern Turn: Essays in Postmodern Theory and Culture.* Columbus: Ohio State UP, 1987.

Hebdige, Dick. *Subculture: The Meaning of Style*. New York: Routledge, 1979.

Hennessy, Rosemary. "Queer Visibility in Commodity Culture." *Cultural Critique* 29 (1994–95): 31–76.

Herget, Winfried. "Towards a Rhetoric of Sentimentality." *Sentimentality in Modern Literature and Popular Culture.* Ed. Winfried Herget. Tübingen: Narr Publishers, 1991. 1–14.

Hinton, Laura. *The Perverse Gaze of Sympathy: Sadomasochistic Sentiments from Clarissa to Rescue 911.* Albany: State U of New York P, 1999.

Hobson, Dorothy. *Crossroads: The Drama of a Soap Opera.* London: Methuen, 1982.

Hobson, Dorothy. "Housewives and the Mass Media." *Culture, Media, Language: Working Papers in Cultural Studies, 1972–79.* Ed. Stuart Hall, Dorothy Hobson, Andrew Lowe, and Paul Willis. London: Hutchinson, 1980. 105–14.

Höijer, Birgitta. "Reception of Television Narration as a Socio-Cognitive Process: A Schema-Theoretical Outline." *Poetics: Journal of Empirical Research on Literature, Media, and the Arts* 21.4 (1992): 283–304.

Holland, Norman. "Unity, Identity, Text, Self." *PMLA: Publications of the Modern Language Association of America* 90 (1975): 813–22.

Hood, Thomas. "Silence." *DayPoems* (2007): <http://www.daypoems.net/poems/600.html>.

hooks, bell. "Cool Cynicism." *Reel to Real: Race, Sex, and Class at the Movies*. By bell hooks. New York: Routledge, 1996. 47–51.

hooks, bell. "Dreams Conquest." *Sight and Sound* 5 (April 1995): 22–23.

hooks, bell. "Eating the Other." *Black Looks: Race and Representation.* By bell hooks. Boston: South End P, 1992. 1–39.

hooks, bell. "Gangsta Culture—Sexism, Misogyny: Who Will Take the Rap?" *Outlaw Culture: Resisting Representations*. By bell hooks. New York: Routledge, 1994. 115–23.

hooks, bell. "The Oppositional Gaze: Black Female Spectators." *Black Looks: Race and Representation*. By bell hooks. Boston: South End P, 1992. 115–31.

Hutcheon, Linda. *A Poetics of Postmodernism: History, Theory, Fiction*. New York: Routledge, 1988.

Hutcheon, Linda. *The Politics of Postmodernism.* New York: Routlege, 1989.

Huyssen, Andreas. *After the Great Divide: Modernism, Mass Culture, Postmodernism*. Bloomington: Indiana UP, 1986.

Huyssen, Andreas. "Memories of Utopia." *Twilight Memories: Marking Time in a Culture of Amnesia*. By Andreas Huyssen. New York: Routledge, 1995. 85–101.

Huyssen, Andreas. "The Politics of Identification: 'Holocaust' and West German Drama." *New German Critique* 19 (1980): 117–36.

Illouz, Eva. *Consuming the Romantic Utopia: Love and the Cultural Contradictions of Capitalism.* Berkeley: U of California P, 1997.

Iser, Wolfgang. *The Implied Reader: Patterns of Communication in Prose Fiction from Bunyan to Beckett*. Baltimore: Johns Hopkins UP, 1974.

Jaggar, Alison M. "Love and Knowledge: Emotion in Feminist Epistemology." *Gender/Body/Knowledge*. Ed. Susan Bordo and Alison Jaggar. New Brunswick: Rutgers UP, 1989. 145–71.

Jameson, Fredric. *Postmodernism, Or, The Cultural Logic of Late Capitalism*. Durham: Duke UP, 1991.

Jameson, Fredric. "Reification and Utopia in Mass Culture." *Signatures of the Visible*. By Fredric Jameson. New York: Routledge, 1992. 9–34.

Jay, Martin. *The Dialectical Imagination: A History of the Frankfurt School and the Institute for Social Research, 1923–1950*. Berkeley: U of California P, 1996.

Jencks, Charles. "The Postmodern Agenda." *The Postmodern Reader*. Ed. Charles Jencks. New York: St. Martin's P, 1992. 10–39.

Jencks, Charles. *What Is Post-Modernism?* New York: St. Martin's P, 1989.

Johnson, Barbara. "Muteness Envy." *The Feminist Difference: Literature, Psychoanalysis, Race, and Gender*. Cambridge: Harvard UP, 1998. 129–53.

Joyce, Joyce A. "The Black Canon: Reconstructing Black American Literary Criticism." *New Literary History* 18.1 (1987): 335–44.

Joyrich, Lynne. *Re-viewing Reception: Television, Gender, and Postmodern Culture.* Bloomington: Indiana UP, 1996.

Kaplan, Amy. "Manifest Domesticity." *American Literature* 70.3 (1998): 581–606.

Kaplan, Cora. "*The Thorn Birds*: Fiction, Fantasy, Femininity." *Sea Changes: Essays on Culture and Feminism.* By Cora Kaplan. London: Verso, 1986. 117–46.

Kaplan, E. Ann. "Mothering, Feminism, and Representation: The Maternal in Melodrama and the Woman's Film 1910–1940." *Home Is Where the Heart Is.* Ed. Christine Gledhill. London: BFI Publishing, 1987. 113–37.

Katz, Elihu. "Viewers Work." *The Audience and the Landscape*. Ed. James Hay, Lawrence Grossberg, and Ellen Wartella. Boulder: Westview P, 1996. 9–21.

Klawans, Stuart. Rev. of *The Piano*. *The Nation* (6 December 1993): 704–06.

Klinger, Barbara. "Much Ado about Excess: Genre, Mise-en-Scène, and the Woman in 'Written on the Wind'." *Wide Angle* 11.4 (1989): 5–22.

Kristeva, Julia. "Interview: Oscillation between Power and Denial." *New French Feminisms: An Anthology.* Ed. Elaine Marks and Isabelle de Courtivron. Amherst: U of Massachusetts P, 1980. 165–67.

Kristeva, Julia. *A Revolution in Poetic Language*. New York: Columbia UP, 1984.

Kroker, Arthur, and David Cook. *The Postmodern Scene: Excremental Culture and Hyper-Aesthetics.* New York: St. Martin's P, 1991.

Lacan, Jacques. *Ecrits*. Trans. Alan Sheridan. London: Tavistock, 1977.

Laclau, Ernesto. "Introduction." *The Making of Political Identities*. Ed. Ernesto Laclau. London: Verso, 1994. 1–8.

Laplanche, Jean, and Jean Bertrand Pontalis. *The Language of Psycho-Analysis*. Trans. Donald Nicholson-Smith. London: Hogarth, 1973.

László, János, and Steen Larsen. "Cultural and Text Variables in Processing Personal Experiences While Reading Literature." *Empirical Studies of the Arts* 9.1 (1991): 23–34.

Layton, Lynne. *Who's That Girl? Who's That Boy? Clinical Practice Meets Postmodern Gender Theory.* Northvale: Jason Aaronson, Inc., 1998.

Liebes, Tamar. "Notes on the Struggle to Define Involvement in Television Viewing." *The Audience and Its Landscape*. Ed. James Hay, Lawrence Grossberg, and Ellen Wartella. Boulder: Westview P, 1996. 177–86.

Liebes, Tamar, and Elihu Katz. *The Export of Meaning: Cross Cultural Readings of Dallas*. Cambridge: Polity P, 1993.

Lindstrom, Naomi. "The Problem of Pop Culture in the Novels of Manuel Puig." *The American Hispanist* 4.30–31 (1978): 28–31.

Lipsitz, George. *Dangerous Crossroads: Popular Music, Postmodernism, and the Poetics of Place.* London: Verso, 1994.

Long, Scott. "The Loneliness of Camp." *Camp Grounds: Style and Homosexuality.* Ed. David Bergman. Amherst: U of Massachusetts P, 1993. 78–91.

Longino, Helen E. *Science as Social Knowledge: Values and Objectivity in Scientific Inquiry.* Princeton: Princeton UP, 1990.

Lyotard, Jean-François. *The Postmodern Condition: A Report on Knowledge.* Trans. Geoff Bennington and Brian Massumi. Minneapolis: U of Minnesota P, 1984.

MacGregor, Jeff. "The Importance of Being Quirky (at All Costs)." *New York Times* (19 February 1995): 34+.

Machor, James L., and Philip Goldstein, eds. *Reception Study: From Literary Theory to Cultural Studies.* New York: Routledge, 2001.

MacKinnon, Catharine. *Feminism Unmodified: Discourses on Life and Law*. Cambridge: Harvard UP, 1987.

Maglin, Nan Bauer, and Donna Perry, eds. *Bad Girls /Good Girls: Women, Sex and Power in the Nineties*. New Brunswick: Rutgers UP, 1996.

Maio, Kathy. "The Key to *The Piano*." *Ms* (March-April 1994): 84.

Mann, Patricia. *Micro-Politics: Agency in a Postfeminist Era*. Minneapolis: U of Minnesota P, 1994.

Manrique, Jaime. "Manuel Puig: The Writer as Diva." *Christopher Street* (July 1993): 14–27.

Mayne, Judith. *Cinema and Spectatorship.* New York: Routledge, 1993.

McGowan, John. *Postmodernism and Its Critics*. Ithaca: Cornell UP, 1991.

McRobbie, Angela. "The Politics of Feminist Research." *Feminist Review* 12 (1982): 46–57.

McRobbie, Angela. "Post-Marxism and Cultural Studies: A Post-script." *Cultural Studies*. Ed. Cary Nelson, Paula A. Treichler, and Lawrence Grossberg. New York: Routledge, 1992. 719–30.

McRobbie, Angela. *Postmodernism and Popular Culture*. London: Routledge, 1994.

Merrim, Stephanie. "For a New (Psychological) Novel in the Works of Manuel Puig." *Novel: A Forum on Fiction* 17.2 (1984): 141–57.

Meyer, Moe. "Introduction: Reclaiming the Discourse of Camp." *The Politics and Poetics of Camp.* Ed. Moe Meyer. New York: Routledge, 1994. 1–22.

Meyrowitz, Joshua. *No Sense of Place*. Oxford: Oxford UP, 1985.

Miall, David. "Response to Poetry: Studies of Language and Structure." *Reader Response to Literature: The Empirical Dimension*. Ed. Elaine Nardocchio. Berlin: Mouton de Gruyter, 1992. 153–70.

Miall, David, and Don Kuiken. "A Feeling for Fiction: Becoming What We Behold." *Poetics: Journal of Empirical Research on Literature, Media, and the Arts* 30 (2002): 221–41.

Miller, Nancy K. "Emphasis Added: Plots and Plausibilities in Women's Fiction." *The New Feminist Criticism: Essays on Women, Literature, and Theory*. Ed. Elaine Showalter. New York: Pantheon Books, 1985. 339–60.

Miller, Stuart. "*Northern* Lights Up as Men Demos Grow." *Variety* (10 February 1992): 23.

Mills, Sara. "Reading As/Like a Feminist." *Gendering the Reader*. Ed. Sara Mills. London: Harvester Wheatsheaf, 1994. 25–46.

Mills, Sara, ed. *Gendering the Reader*. London: Harvester Wheatsheaf, 1994.

Modleski, Tania. "Femininity as Mas(s)querade: A Feminist Approach to Mass Culture." *High Theory/Low Culture: Analysing Popular Television and Film*. Ed. Colin McCabe. Manchester: Manchester UP, 1986. 37–52.

Modleski, Tania. *Feminism without Women: Culture and Criticism in a "Postfeminist" Age.* New York: Routledge, 1991.

Modleski, Tania. *Loving with a Vengeance: Mass-Produced Fantasies for Women*. Hamden Archon Books, 1982.

Morley, David. "Changing Paradigms in Audience Studies." *Remote Control: Television, Audiences, and Cultural Power.* Ed. Ellen Seiter, Hans Borchers, Gabriele Greutzner, and Eva-Marie Warth. London: Routledge, 1989. 16–43.

Morley, David. "The Geography of Television: Ethnography, Communications, and Community." *The Audience and Its Landscape*. Ed. James Hay, Lawrence Grossberg, and Ellen Wartella. Boulder: Westview P, 1996. 317–42.

Morley, David. *The "Nationwide" Audience: Structure and Decoding*. London: BFI Publishing, 1980.

Morley, David. *Television, Audiences and Cultural Studies*. New York: Routledge, 1992.

Morley, David. "Texts, Readers, Subjects." *Culture, Media, Language: Working Papers in Cultural Studies, 1972–79.* Ed. Stuart Hall, Dorothy Hobson, Andrew Lowe, and Paul Willis. London: Hutchinson, 1980. 163–73.

Morris, David B. "Postmodern Pain." *Heterotopia: Postmodern Utopia and the Body Politic*. Ann Arbor: U of Michigan P, 1994. 150–73.

Mouffe, Chantal. "Politics and Passion: Stakes of Democracy." Public lecture, U of Virginia, Charlottesville (23 February 1996).

Mouffe, Chantal. *The Return of the Political*. London and New York: Verso, 1993.

Mulvey, Laura. "Afterthoughts on 'Visual Pleasure and Narrative Cinema' Inspired by King Vidor's *Duel in the Sun*." *Visual and Other Pleasures.* By Laura Mulvey. Bloomington: Indiana UP, 1989. 29–38.

Mulvey, Laura. "Notes on Sirk and Melodrama." *Visual and Other Pleasures.* By Laura Mulvey. Bloomington: Indiana UP, 1989. 39–44.

Mulvey, Laura. "Visual Pleasure and Narrative Cinema." *Visual and Other Pleasures.* By Laura Mulvey. Bloomington: Indiana UP, 1989. 14–26.

Munt, Sallie R. *Heroic Desire: Lesbian Identity and Cultural Space*. New York: New York UP, 1998.

Nardocchio, Elaine. "Introduction." *Reader Response to Literature: The Empirical Dimension*. Ed. Elaine Nardocchio. Berlin: Mouton de Gruyter, 1992. 1–8.

Neale, Stephen. "Melo Talk: On the Meanings and Use of the Term 'Melodrama' in the American Trade Press." *The Velvet Light Trap* 32.3 (1993): 66–89.

Nelson, Cary, Paula A. Treichler, and Lawrence Grossberg. "Cultural Studies: An Introduction." *Cultural Studies.* Ed. Lawrence Grossberg, Cary Nelson, and Paula A. Treichler. New York: Routledge, 1992. 1–22.

Nelson, Dana. "Sympathy as Strategy in Sedgwick's *Hope Leslie*." *The Culture of Sentiment: Race, Gender, and Sentimentality in Nineteenth-Century America.* Ed. Shirley Samuels. New York: Oxford UP, 1992. 191–202.

Newcomb, Horace, ed. *Television: The Critical View*. New York: Oxford UP, 1994.

Newton, Esther. "Role Model." *Camp Grounds: Style and Homosexuality.* Ed. David Bergman. Amherst: U of Massachusetts P, 1993. 39–53.

Oatley, Keith. "Emotions and the Story Worlds of Fiction." *Narrative Impact: Social and Cognitive Foundations.* Ed. T.C. Brock, J.J. Strange, and M.C. Green. Mahwah: Erlbaum, 2002. 39–69.

Paglia, Camille. *Sex, Art, and American Culture: Essays.* New York: Vantage Books, 1992.

Pellón, Gustavo. "Manuel Puig's Contradictory Strategy: Kitsch Paradigms *versus* Paradigmatic Structure in *El beso de la mujer araña* and *Pubis angelical*." *Symposium: a Quarterly Journal in Modern Foreign Literatures* 37.3 (1983): 186–201.

Pells, Richard. *Not like Us: How Europeans Have Loved, Hated, and Transformed American Culture since World War II*. New York: Basic Books, 1997.

Peterson, Richard A., and Albert Simkus. "How Musical Tastes Mark Occupational Status Groups." *Cultivating Differences: Symbolic Boundaries and the Making of Inequality.* Ed. Michèle Lamont and Marcel Fournier. Chicago: U of Chicago P, 1992. 152–86.

"Piano Foreplay." *New York Magazine* (22 November 1993): 72–73.

Pihama, Leonie. "Are Films Dangerous? A Maori Woman's Perspective on *The Piano*." *Hecate* (October 1994): 239+.

Plantinga, Carl. "The Scene of Empathy and the Human Face on Film." *Passionate*

Views: Film, Cognition, and Emotion. Ed. Carl Plantinga and Greg M. Smith. Baltimore: Johns Hopkins UP, 1999. 239–55.

Pollan, Dana. "Brief Encounters: Mass Culture and the Evacuation of Sense." *Studies in Entertainment: Critical Approaches to Mass Culture*. Ed. Tania Modleski. Bloomington: Indiana UP, 1986. 167–87.

Porter, Theodore M. *Truth in Numbers: The Pursuit of Objectivity in Science and Public Life.* Princeton: Princeton UP, 1995.

Prosser, Jay. *Second Skins: The Body Narratives of Transsexuality*. New York: Columbia UP, 1998.

Puig, Manuel. *Kiss of the Spider Woman.* Trans. Thomas Colchie. New York: Vintage, 1978.

Radway, Janice. *A Feeling for Books: The Book-of-the-Month Club, Literary Taste, and Middle-Class Desire.* Chapel Hill: U of North Carolina P, 1997.

Radway, Janice. *Reading the Romance: Women, Patriarchy, and Popular Literature*. Chapel Hill: U of North Carolina P, 1991.

Reagon, Bernice Johnson. "Coalition Politics: Turning the Century." *Home Girls: A Black Feminist Anthology*. Ed. Barbara Smith. New Brunswick: Rutgers UP, 2000. 343–55.

Regard, Frédéric. "Time for Feeling: The Structure of George Orwell's Archaic Postmodernism." *Cycnos* 11.2 (1994): 3–15.

Rice-Sayre, Laura. "Domination and Desire: A Feminist-Materialist Reading of Manuel Puig's *Kiss of the Spider Woman*." *Textual Analysis: Some Readers Reading*. Ed. Mary Ann Caws. New York: Modern Language Association of America, 1986. 245–56.

Ricoeur, Paul. *Time and Narrative*. Trans. Kathleen McLaughlin and David Pellauer. Chicago: U of Chicago P, 1988.

Rodowick, David. *The Difficulty of Difference: Psychoanalysis, Sexual Difference, and Film Theory.* New York: Routledge, 1991.

Roediger, David. *The Wages of Whiteness: Race and the Making of the American Working Class*. London: Verso, 1991.

Rogin, Michael. *Blackface, White Noise: Jewish Immigrants in the Hollywood Melting Pot.* Berkeley: U of California P, 1996.

Roiphe, Katie. *The Morning After: Sex, Fear, and Feminism on Campus*. Boston: Little, Brown, 1993.

Román, David, and Alberto Sandoval. "Caught in the Web: Latinidad, AIDS, and Allegory in *Kiss of the Spider Woman, the Musical*." *American Literature* 67.3 (1995): 553–85.

Rorty, Richard. *Contingency, Irony, and Solidarity*. Cambridge: Cambridge UP, 1989.

Ross, Andrew. "Uses of Camp." *Camp Grounds: Style and Homosexuality.* Ed. David Bergman. Amherst: U of Massachussetts P, 1993. 54–77.

Rubin, Gayle. "MisGuided, Dangerous, and Wrong: An Analysis of Anti-pornography Politics." *Bad Girls and Dirty Pictures: The Challenge to Reclaim Feminism*. Ed. Alison Assiter and Avedon Carol. Boulder: Pluto P, 1993. 18–40.

Sanchez-Eppler, Karen. *Touching Liberty: Abolition, Feminism, and the Politics of the Body.* Berkeley: U of California P, 1993.

Sartre, Jean-Paul. *"What Is Literature?" and Other Essays*. Trans. Bernard Frechtman. Cambridge: Harvard UP, 1988.

Savage, Michael, James Barlow, Peter Dickens, and A.J. Fielding. *Property, Bureaucracy, and Culture: Middle Class Formation in Contemporary Britain*. London: Routledge, 1992.

Savile, Anthony. "Sentimentality." *Arguing about Art*. Ed. Alex Neill and Aaron Ridley. New York: McGraw Hill, 1995. 223–27.

Schmidt, Siegfried J. "The Empirical Study of Literature: Why and Why Not?" *The Systemic and Empirical Approach to Literature as Theory and Application*. Ed. Steven Tötösy de Zepetnek and Irene Sywenky. Edmonton: U of Alberta; Siegen: Siegen U, 1997. 137–53.

Sedgwick, Eve Kosofsky. *Tendencies.* Durham: Duke UP, 1993.

Seidman, Steven. "Identity and Politics in a 'Postmodern' Gay Culture: Some Historical and Conceptual Notes." *Fear of a Queer Planet: Queer Politics and Social Theory*. Ed. Michael Warner. Minneapolis: U of Minnesota P, 1993. 105–42.

Seiter, Ellen. "Making Distinctions in TV Audience Research: Case Study of a Troubling Interview." *Television: The Critical View*. Ed. Horace Newcomb. New York: Oxford UP, 1994. 387–410.

Seiter, Ellen, Hans Borchers, Gabriele Kreutzner, and Eva-Marie Warth. "Introduction." *Remote Control: Television, Audiences, and Cultural Power.* Ed. Ellen Seiter, Hans Borchers, Gabriele Kreutzner, and Eva-Marie Warth. London: Routledge, 1989. 1–15.

Sharpe, Patricia, and Frances Mascia-Lees. "Piano Lessons." *American Anthropologist* 97.4 (1995): 763–73.

Sharrett, Christopher. "Introduction: Crisis Cinema." *Crisis Cinema: The Apocalyptic Idea in Postmodern Narrative Film*. Ed. Christopher Sharrett. Washington: Maisonneuve P, 1993. 1–9.

Sharrett, Christopher, ed. *Crisis Cinema: The Apocalyptic Idea in Postmodern Narrative Film*. Washington: Maisonneuve P, 1993.

Shattuc, Jane M. "Postmodern Misogyny in *Blue Velvet*." *Genders* 13 (1992): 73–89.

Sherman, Scott. "Glaad Tidings: CBS' *Northern Exposure*." *Outweek* (26 June 1991): 22.

Siebers, Tobin. "Introduction." *Heterotopia: Postmodern Utopia and the Body Politic*. Ed. Tobin Siebers. Ann Arbor: U of Michigan P, 1994. 1–38.

Silverman, Kaja. "Fragments of a Fashionable Discourse." *Studies in Entertainment: Critical Approaches to Mass Culture*. Ed. Tania Modleski. Bloomington: Indiana UP, 1986. 139–52.

Silverman, Kaja. *Male Subjectivity at the Margins*. New York: Routledge, 1992.

Silverman, Kaja. *The Subject of Semiotics*. New York: Oxford UP, 1983.

Silverman, Kaja. *The Threshold of the Visible World*. New York: Routledge, 1996.

Smith, Mark C. *Social Science in the Crucible: The American Debate over Objectivity and Purpose, 1918–1941*. Durham: Duke UP, 1994.

Smith, Murray. *Engaging Characters: Fiction, Emotion, and the Cinema*. Oxford: Clarendon P, 1995.

Sommer, Doris. *Proceed with Caution: When Engaged by Minority Writing in the Americas*. Cambridge: Harvard UP, 1999.

Sommer, Doris. "Resistant Texts and Incompetent Readers." *Poetics Today* 15.4 (1994): 523–51.

Sontag, Susan. "Notes on Camp." *A Susan Sontag Reader*. By Susan Sontag. New York: Vintage Books, 1983. 105–19.

Spivak, Gayatri Chakravorty. "Subaltern Studies: Deconstructing Historiography." *In Other Worlds: Essays in Cultural Politics*. By Gayatri Spivak. New York: Methuen, 1987. 197–221.

Stacey, Jackie. "Feminine Fascinations: Forms of Identification in Star-Audience Relations." *Feminist Film Theory*. Ed. Sue Thornham. New York: New York UP, 1999. 196–209.

Stacey, Jackie. *Star Gazing: Hollywood Cinema and Female Spectatorship*. London: Routledge, 1994.

Studlar, Gaylyn. "Masochism and the Perverse Pleasures of Cinema." *Quarterly Review of Film Studies* 9.4 (1984): 267–82.

Swanson, Philip. "Sailing Away on a Boat to Nowhere: *El beso de la mujer araña* and *Kiss of the Spider Woman*, from Novel to Film." *Essays on Hispanic Themes: In Honour of Edward C. Riley*. Ed. Jennifer Lowe and Philip Swanson. Edinburgh: U of Edinburgh P, 1989. 331–59.

Tan, Ed. *Emotion and the Structure of Narrative Film: Film as an Emotion Machine*. Trans. Barbara Fasting. Mahwah: Erlbaum, 1996.

Tan, Ed, and Inge J.M. van den Boom, "Explorations in the Psychological Affect Structure of Narrative Film." *Reader Response to Literature: The Empirical Dimension*. Ed. Elaine Nardocchio. Berlin: Mouton de Gruyter, 1992. 57–94.

Taylor, Annette M. "Landscape of the West in *Northern Exposure*." *The Mid-Atlantic Almanack* 3 (1994): 23–33.

Taylor, Annette M., and David Upchurch. "*Northern Exposure* and Mythology of the Global Community." *Journal of Popular Culture* 30.2 (1996): 75–85.

Thomas, Calvin. "Straight with a Twist: Queer Theory and the Subject of Heterosexuality." *The Gay '90s: Disciplinary and Interdisciplinary Formations in Queer Studies*. Ed. Thomas C. Foster, Carol Siegel, and Ellen E. Berry. New York: New York UP, 1997. 83–115.

Thompson, Robert J. *Television's Second Golden Age: From* Hill Street Blues *to* ER. New York: Continuum, 1996.

Thurston, Carol. *The Romance Revolution: Erotic Novels for Women and the Quest for a New Sexual Identity.* Urbana: U of Illinois P, 1987.

Tittler, Jonathan. *Manuel Puig*. New York: Twayne Publishers, 1993.

Tompkins, Jane. *Sensational Designs: The Cultural Work of American Fiction, 1790–1860.* New York: Oxford UP, 1985.

Tompkins, Jane, ed. *Reader-Response Criticism: From Formalism to Post-Structuralism.* Baltimore: Johns Hopkins UP, 1980.

Torres, Sasha. "Melodrama, Masculinity and the Family: *thirtysomething* as Therapy." *Male Trouble*. Ed. Constance Penley and Sharon Willis. Minneapolis: U of Minnesota P, 1993. 283–302.

Tötösy de Zepetnek, Steven. "From Comparative Literature Today toward Comparative Cultural Studies." *Comparative Literature and Comparative Cultural Studies*. Ed. Steven Tötösy de Zepetnek. West Lafayette: Purdue UP, 2003. 235–67.

Tötösy de Zepetnek, Steven. *Comparative Literature: Theory, Method, Application.* Amsterdam: Rodopi, 1998.

Tötösy de Zepetnek, Steven. "The Empirical Science of Literature/Constructivist Theory of Literature." *Encyclopedia of Contemporary Literary Theory: Approaches, Scholars, Terms*. Ed. Irene R. Makaryk. Toronto: U of Toronto P, 1993. 36–39.

Vattimo, Gianni. *The Transparent Society*. Trans. David Webb. Baltimore: Johns Hopkins UP, 1992.

Viehoff, Reinhold. "Literary Understanding and Emotion." *Emotion and Art: Problems, Approaches, Explorations.* Ed. L.Ya. Dorfman, D.A. Leontiev, V.M. Petrov, V.A. Sozinov. Perm: Perm Institute for Art and Culture, 1992. 23–43.

Wald, Gayle. *Crossing the Line: Racial Passing in Twentieth-Century U.S. Literature and Culture*. Durham: Duke UP, 2000.

Wald, Gayle, and You-me Park. "Native Daughters in the Promised Land: Gender, Race, and the Question of Separate Spheres." *American Literature* 70.3 (1998): 607–33.

Walkerdine, Valerie. *Daddy's Girl: Young Girls and Popular Culture*. Cambridge: Harvard UP, 1997.

Walkerdine, Valerie. "Video Replay: Families, Films, and Fantasy." *Feminist Film Theory: A Reader*. Ed. Sue Thornham. New York: New York UP, 1999. 180–95.

Wiegman, Robyn. *American Anatomies: Theorizing Race and Gender*. Durham: Duke UP, 1995.

Wilde, Alan. *Horizons of Assent: Modernism, Postmodernism, and the Ironic Imagination*. Baltimore: Johns Hopkins UP, 1981.

Willemen, Paul. "Towards an Analysis of the Sirkian System." *Screen* 13.4 (1972–73): 128–34.

Williams, Betsy. "'North to the Future': *Northern Exposure* and Quality Television." *Television: The Critical View*. Ed. Horace Newcomb. New York: Oxford UP, 1994. 141–54.

Williams, Linda. *Hard Core: Power, Pleasure, and the "Frenzy of the Visible."* Berkeley: U of California P, 1989.

Wilkinson, James D. *The Intellectual Resistance in Europe*. Cambridge: Harvard UP, 1981.

Wolf, Naomi. *Fire with Fire: The New Female Power and How It Will Change the 21st Century.* New York: Random House, 1993.

Wood, Michael. "Where the Wolf Howls." *New York Review of Books* (13 December 1973): 19–23.

Zillmann, Dolf. "Mechanisms of Emotional Involvement with Drama." *Poetics: Journal of Empirical Research on Literature, Media, and the Arts* 23.1 (1994): 33–51.

Zinman, Toby Silverman. "The Muses of Terrence McNally." *American Theatre* 12.3 (1995): 12–17.

Index